Rereading Heterosexuality

Rereading Heterosexuality

Feminism, Queer Theory and Contemporary Fiction

Rachel Carroll

EDINBURGH
University Press

© Rachel Carroll, 2012

Edinburgh University Press Ltd
22 George Square, Edinburgh EH8 9LF

www.euppublishing.com

Typeset in 10.5/13 pt Sabon
by Servis Filmsetting Ltd, Stockport, Cheshire, and
printed and bound in Great Britain by
CPI Group (UK) Ltd, Croydon, CR0 4YY

A CIP record for this book is available from the British Library

ISBN 978 0 7486 3955 7 (hardback)
ISBN 978 0 7486 4908 2 (webready PDF)
ISBN 978 0 7486 4928 0 (epub)
ISBN 978 0 7486 4927 3 (Amazon)

The right of Rachel Carroll
to be identified as author of this work
has been asserted in accordance with
the Copyright, Designs and Patents Act 1988.

Contents

Acknowledgements	vii
Introduction: feminism, queer theory and heterosexuality	1

Part One: Revisiting the spinster

1. 'Becoming my own ghost': spinsterhood and the 'invisibility' of heterosexuality in Sarah Waters' *Affinity* — 25
2. Telling tales out of school: spinsters, scandals and intergenerational heterosexuality in Zoë Heller's *Notes on a Scandal* — 45

Part Two: Transgressive female heterosexuality

3. Queering Alice, killing Lolita: feminism, queer theory and the politics of child sexuality in A. M. Homes's *The End of Alice* — 67
4. Unauthorised reproduction: class, pregnancy and transgressive female heterosexuality in Alan Warner's *Morvern Callar* — 91

Part Three: Reproducing heterosexuality

5. 'First one thing and then the other': rewriting the intersexed body in Jeffrey Eugenides' *Middlesex* — 111
6. Imitations of life: cloning, heterosexuality and the human in Kazuo Ishiguro's *Never Let Me Go* — 131

Bibliography	149
Index	157

Acknowledgements

Some of the material contained in this book has been published previously; I would like to thank the publishers for permission to reproduce work from the following publications:

- '"Becoming my own ghost": spinsterhood, heterosexuality and Sarah Waters's *Affinity*', *Genders* (Spring 2007), n.p.
- 'Imitations of life: cloning, heterosexuality and the human in Ishiguro's *Never Let Me Go*', *Journal of Gender Studies*, 19: 1 (2010), pp. 59–71.
- 'Retrospective sex: rewriting intersexuality in Jeffrey Eugenides's *Middlesex*', *Journal of American Studies*, 44: 1 (2010), pp. 187–201.

I am very grateful to my friends Heike Salzer and Ingi Jensson for allowing me to use a still image from their work for the cover of this book.

Introduction: feminism, queer theory and heterosexuality

The 'invisibility' of heterosexuality as a normative category of identity is a recurring motif in recent work on heterosexuality; its '"unmarked" and "naturalised"'[1] status is understood as serving to perpetuate its power as an identity which tends to be taken for granted and to pass unquestioned. Indeed, as Linda Schlossberg puts it, 'heterosexual culture continually *passes itself off* as being merely natural, the undisputed and unmarked norm [emphasis added].'[2] *Rereading Heterosexuality: Feminism, Queer Theory and Contemporary Fiction* aims to contribute to what Richard Johnson has described as the 'impetus to render heterosexuality visible to critical scrutiny'.[3] Heterosexuality as an institution continues to have immense normative power; while this power impacts most explicitly on non-heterosexual identities it also extends to heterosexual identities which do not conform to familial, marital or reproductive norms – norms which have a particular impact on female identities, the principal concern of this book. Drawing on feminist and queer theories of sex, gender and sexuality, *Rereading Heterosexuality* takes as its distinctive focus the representation of female identities at odds with heterosexual norms; more specifically, it explores representations which serve to question the conventional equation between heterosexuality, reproductive sexuality and female identity. In this context, it will offer close readings of six novels published by British and American authors between 1995 and 2005: *Morvern Callar* by Alan Warner (1995), *The End of Alice* by A. M. Homes (1996), *Affinity* by Sarah Waters (1999), *Middlesex* by Jeffrey Eugenides (2002), *Notes on a Scandal* by Zoë Heller (2003) and *Never Let Me Go* by Kazuo Ishiguro (2005). The diverse subject matter of these novels reflects contemporary concerns and anxieties about the future of sex, gender and sexuality; some address topics which have been the focus of media attention and social policy debate, including child sexual abuse, human cloning and transgender identity, while others turn to historical periods which have played a pivotal role in the development of modern discourses of sexuality, including the late Victorian era and the 'sexual revolution' of the late 1960s and early 1970s. I have selected these texts for the unique opportunities they provide to reflect on the dynamic and often contested relationship between feminism and queer theory in relation to the analysis of heterosexuality.

This introduction offers a selective overview and evaluation of relevant work on heterosexuality in the context of contemporary gender and sexuality studies. Its focus is on the formative contribution of two key theoretical frameworks: feminism and queer theory. Feminist and lesbian feminist theorists have offered an ideological critique of heterosexuality in relation to the gendered and sexual oppression of women; in this way, heterosexuality has been analysed as a patriarchal institution which perpetuates gendered power relations through sexuality. More recently, queer theory has extended the terms by which heterosexuality can be understood through its discursive analysis of heterosexuality as an effect of historical and cultural construction. Queer theory approaches heterosexuality as a normative category of sexed, gendered and sexual identity which serves both to support the binary logic by which 'hetero-' and 'homosexual' identities are produced and to perpetuate the construction of homosexual identities as deviant and abnormal. The work of leading Second Wave feminists has had a lasting impact on feminist critiques of heterosexuality; however, tensions emerging from the legacy of this movement have also contributed to what has been described as an ideological impasse where female heterosexuality is concerned. Queer theoretical frameworks offer to reconfigure critical perspectives on heterosexuality but also present challenges for feminist frameworks and have provoked often polarised responses. In what follows, feminist and queer contributions to the analysis of heterosexuality will be considered, as will affinities and tensions between the two frameworks.

Compulsory heterosexuality: feminism and heterosexuality

Lesbian feminist theorists have been instrumental in establishing heterosexuality as an object of feminist critique and in setting the terms by which it is approached. Adrienne Rich's ground-breaking essay, 'Compulsory Heterosexuality and Lesbian Existence' (first published in 1980) documents the ways in which heterosexuality is constructed as the 'natural' destination for all women, in patriarchal and feminist discourses alike, and the coercive means by which this presumption is imposed, both discursively and materially. Her assertion that 'heterosexuality, like motherhood, needs to be recognized and studied as a *political institution* [emphasis in original]'[4] retains its counter-intuitive power, challenging as it does persistent assumptions about heterosexuality as rooted in the natural and instinctual (especially where reproductive sexuality is concerned), rather than the ideological. Rich asks why 'such violent strictures should be found necessary to enforce women's total emotional, erotic loyalty and subservience to men'[5] and in doing so establishes heterosexuality not simply as a sexual relation but also as a power relation. According to this thesis, 'compulsory heterosexuality' divides women from each other by its 'othering' of lesbians as 'deviant, as pathological, or as emotionally and sensually deprived'.[6] Rich offers the 'lesbian continuum' not only as an antidote to compulsory heterosexuality but also as a form of collective resistance to patriarchy; the lesbian continuum places same-sex desire between women within a spectrum of female attachment and solidarity and in doing so repairs the division between 'women' and 'lesbians' imposed by compulsory heterosexuality. As Rich writes:

> Woman-identification is a source of energy, a potential springhead of female power, violently curtailed and wasted under the institution of heterosexuality. The denial of the reality and visibility of women's passion for women, women's choice of women as allies, life companions, and community; the forcing of such relationships into dissimulation and their disintegration under intense pressure have meant an incalculable loss to the power of all women *to change the social relations of the sexes, to liberate ourselves and each other* [emphasis in original].[7]

The category of 'women' is self-evidently central to Rich's analysis. She rejects the possibility of alliance between lesbians and gay men as serving to 'deny and erase female reality once again',[8] arguing that 'to separate those women stigmatised as "homosexual" or "gay" from the complex continuum of female resistance to enslavement, and attach them to a male pattern, is to falsify our history.'[9] Significantly, sexed identity is privileged as the source of female solidarity; when Rich states that 'lesbian experience [is] like motherhood, a profoundly female experience'[10] she is contesting the accusation that lesbians are not 'real' women but at the same time seems to posit reproductive sexuality, premised on sexed identity, as integral to feminist definitions of women.

Where Rich subverts the category of women by universalising 'woman-identification'[11] as a female and feminist, rather than exclusively lesbian, experience, Monique Wittig abandons 'women' as an irrecoverably ideological concept, arguing in her important essay 'One Is Not Born a Woman' (first published in 1981) that 'the refusal to become (or to remain) heterosexual always meant to refuse to become a man or a woman, consciously or not.'[12] Here heterosexuality is integral to the patriarchal construction of gender; the lesbian is celebrated as a subversive outlaw whose very identity is understood as a form of resistance and refusal:

> Lesbian is the only concept I know of which is beyond the categories of sex (woman and man), because the designated subject (lesbian) is not a woman, either economically, or politically, or ideologically. For what makes a woman is a specific social relation to a man, a relation that we have previously called servitude, a relation which implies personal and physical obligation as well as economic obligation ... a relation which lesbians escape by refusing to become or stay heterosexual.[13]

Where Rich extends the category of 'women' by means of the 'lesbian continuum', Wittig abandons 'women' as an inherently compromised subject position. Rich and Wittig interrogate heterosexuality as an agent of patriarchy, challenging both the unacknowledged and overt homophobia at work in the women's movement by offering the lesbian as the (feminist) woman par excellence, both in her subjection and her defiance. To some degree 'lesbian' seems to stand for 'woman' and 'heterosexual' for 'patriarchal'; this rhetorical strategy has the advantage of thoroughly politicising heterosexuality but arguably does so by conflating it with patriarchy in ways which may overlook their operative differences.

Crucially, Rich and Wittig understand heterosexuality as an institution rather than simply a sexual identity; heterosexual *sexuality*, however, is foregrounded in the influential work of radical feminist theorists such as Andrea Dworkin and Sheila Jeffreys, where it is posited as intimately complicit in the perpetuation of hierarchical power relations. The assumptions underlying this position are exemplified in the following assertion by Jeffreys:

> Masculinity and femininity, the genders of dominance and submission, are eroticised to create the sexuality of male supremacy which I call heterosexual desire. By the term 'heterosexual desire' I do not mean desire for the opposite sex, but a desire that is organised around eroticised dominance and submission.[14]

The presumption of heterosexual women's complicity in patriarchy is also advanced by Andrea Dworkin, whose analysis of penetration as a form of 'occupation and/or colonisation'[15] makes it analogous to rape even when consensual. In works like *Intercourse*, published by Dworkin in 1987, and *Anticlimax*, published by Jeffreys in 1990, heterosexuality is understood principally in terms of sexual relationships between men and women, heterosexual sexual practice equated with penetration and penetration equated with oppression; these analyses have proved controversial in that they proceed from provocative and problematic assumptions. The thesis that forms of heterosexuality eroticise power difference and that sexuality can be a powerful way in which ideology is internalised continues to have currency; however, the denunciation of all heterosexual encounters – and all female heterosexuals – as ideologically compromised constructs heterosexuality as a monolithic, unified and omnipotent force, thereby underestimating its complexities and contradictions. Carol Smart observes that such polarised positions have had the effect of transforming feminist identity politics into a battlefield in which a 'rhetoric of war, treachery and violence'[16] prevails. Smart captures the impasse at which some feminist debates on heterosexuality had arrived when, in a discussion of Sue Wilkinson and Celia Kitzinger's 1993 collection *Heterosexuality: A Feminism and Psychology Reader*, she states: 'It was as if there were really only two available positions; one which seemed to gloat over the mistakes of heterosexual women and one which seemed to apologise for being heterosexual.'[17] Within this context heterosexuality is constructed as an oppressive norm but the construction of its normative power, and the implications of this power for diverse heterosexual identities, are not examined. The oppositional politics in which this ideological critique is grounded seemed to have reached deadlock by the late 1980s and early 1990s. By contrast, new work on sexuality emerging in the 1990s, and influenced by the work of poststructuralist historian and philosopher Michel Foucault, was informed by an understanding of power as both repressive *and* productive.

Heteronormativity: queer theory and heterosexuality

Michel Foucault's assertion that the very concept of sexual identity is historically and discursively produced has played a formative role in the development of queer theory. In a now celebrated passage from the first volume of his *History of Sexuality*, Foucault writes that:

> The nineteenth-century homosexual became a personage, a past, a case history, and a childhood ... Nothing that went into his total composition was unaffected by his sexuality. It was everywhere present in him ... The sodomite had been a temporary aberration; the homosexual was now a species.[18]

This insight into the 'invention' of homosexuality is central to queer theory's interrogation of how sexual identities are produced and policed and pivotal for its critique of identity politics. However, it is not only homosexuality which emerges as a modern category of identity. The influence of Foucault is reflected in a book which has come to be seen as a landmark text for queer theory, Eve Kosofsky Sedgwick's *Epistemology of the Closet*, in which she wryly observes that

> the period stretching roughly between Wilde and Proust was prodigally productive of attempts to name, explain, and define this new kind of creature, the homosexual person – a project so urgent that it spawned in its rage of distinction an even newer category, that of the heterosexual person.[19]

The oppressive power attributed to a universalised heterosexuality by some feminist ideological critiques is here complicated by the 'discovery' of its invention and, moreover, the revelation of the provisional nature of its power. Queer theory is concerned with questioning the binary structures by which sex, gender and sexuality are conventionally understood, whereby all human persons are required to identify/be identified as either male or female, either masculine or feminine and either heterosexual or homosexual. The causal logic by which sex is assumed to determine gender and both to determine sexuality, and the 'spectres of discontinuity and incoherence'[20] which result from the failure of this logic to fulfil its own requirements, have been the particular focus of Judith Butler's critique. In *Gender Trouble* (first published in 1990), Butler writes:

> The cultural matrix through which gender identity has become intelligible requires that certain kinds of 'identities' cannot 'exist' – that is, those in which gender does not follow from sex and those in which the practices of desire do not 'follow' from either sex or gender.[21]

Queer theory has been principally concerned with the hierarchical nature of the heterosexual/homosexual binary, but this binary is understood as not so much expressive as *constitutive* of heterosexual power. Butler argues that 'for heterosexuality to remain intact as a distinct social form, it *requires* an intelligible concept of homosexuality and also requires the prohibition of that conception in rendering it culturally unintelligible [emphasis in original].'[22] In this way, 'heterosexuality' depends on 'homosexuality' in order to sustain its own identity – or rather the fiction of its own identity. While heterosexuality denies its reliance on homosexuality by seeking to repress or erase the latter's existence, it is nevertheless subject to the same kinds of discursive complications and contradictions. A recognition of the 'incoherence' of heterosexuality significantly qualifies any assumptions about its power; Sedgwick refers to 'the plurality and the cumulative incoherence of modern ways of conceptualising same-sex desire and, hence, gay identity, an incoherence that answers, too, to the incoherence with which *hetero*sexual desire and identity are conceptualized [emphasis in original].'²³ With its emphasis on the discursive *production* of sexed, gendered and sexual identities, the object of queer theoretical concern is not principally heterosexuality as a sexual identity; as a normalising category of sexual identity, heterosexuality is problematised in the same way as homosexuality. Queer theory distinguishes between heterosexuality and the discourses, practices and institutions which serve to construct and universalise it through its conceptualisation and critique of 'heteronormativity'. Foucauldian frameworks prevail in queer theorising of heteronormativity which emerges as a discursive field implicated in disciplinary power; hence, Cathy J. Cohen defines 'heteronormativity' as follows: 'both those localised practices and those centralised institutions which legitimise and privilege heterosexuality and heterosexual relationships as fundamental and "natural" within society'.²⁴ Lauren Berlant and Michael Warner emphasise that while heteronormativity serves to privilege heterosexuality this privilege remains contingent and unevenly enjoyed; they define heteronormativity as 'the institutions, structures of understanding, and practical orientations that make heterosexuality seem not only coherent – that is, organised as a sexuality – but also privileged', but add that its 'coherence is always provisional, and its privilege can take several (sometimes contradictory) forms'.²⁵ Contingent and contradictory, heterosexuality does not possess a power that is unequivocal, nor does the functioning of heteronormativity announce itself through conventional modes of oppressive power. Berlant and Warner stress its pervasive and endemic nature which assumes a kind of invisibility:

> Heteronormativity is more than ideology, or prejudice, or phobia against gays and lesbians; it is produced in almost every aspect of the forms and arrangements of social life: nationality, the state, and the law; commerce; medicine; and education; as well as in the conventions and affects of narrativity, romance, and other protected spaces of culture.²⁶

Crucially, then, the meaning of heterosexuality within heteronormativity is not limited to heterosexual sexuality; as Annamarie Jagose puts it: 'it is not simply that heterosexuality seems irreducible to the sex acts that it nevertheless privileges, but also that heterosexuality is naturalized through a range of practices and institutions that don't seem to be about sexuality at all.'²⁷ Indeed, Berlant and Warner observe that 'contexts that have little visible relation to sex practice, such as life narrative and generational identity, can be heteronormative in this sense, while in other contexts forms of sex between men and women might not be heteronormative.'[28] The recognition that forms of heterosexual desire and practice might be at odds with heteronormativity starts to tease apart the potentially reductive conflation of heterosexual identity with heterosexual power. Such a distinction suggests that not all heterosexuals are complicit in heteronormative regimes and, moreover, that some heterosexuals may be subject to its penalties. Indeed, queer theorists have stressed the need to interrogate any presumptions about the uniformity of heterosexuality; Cohen makes such a project central to queer enquiry: 'fundamental to my concern about the current structure and future agenda of queer politics is the unchallenged assumption of a uniform heteronormativity from which all heterosexuals benefit.'[29]

If heterosexuality was once, somewhat paradoxically, the 'proper object' of lesbian feminist theory within feminist contexts, queer theory has made interventions into its analysis which offer to transform the very object under consideration. If this intervention has not been welcomed by all feminist theorists as a way out of the 'sleeping with the enemy' impasse this is perhaps because queer theory also questions some of the founding principles of Second Wave feminist politics: principally, its investment in identity politics.

Between feminism and queer theory

Judith Butler's '*heterosexual matrix* [emphasis in original]'[30] – 'that grid of cultural intelligibility through which bodies, genders, and desires are naturalized'[31] – has played a key role in the conceptualisation of heteronormativity in queer theory. Butler defines it as a

> model of gender intelligibility that assumes that for bodies to cohere and make sense there must be a stable sex expressed through a stable gender (masculine expresses male, feminine expresses female) that is oppositionally and hierarchically defined through the compulsory practice of heterosexuality.[32]

In *Gender Trouble*, Butler acknowledges the contribution of Wittig's 'heterosexual contract' and Rich's 'compulsory heterosexuality' to her theorising of the 'heterosexual matrix'; a degree of continuity between lesbian feminist theory and queer theory can be deduced from this gesture. This is striking since the relationship between lesbian feminist and feminist theory and queer theory is often depicted as one of discontinuity. Where Rich and Butler's work is grounded in feminist politics, queer theories of heteronormativity are not necessarily concerned with patriarchal definitions of power. Indeed, where queer theory has been seen as 'coming out' of feminism this relationship has been seen by some of queer theory's feminist critics as one of departure tantamount to a betrayal.[33] Two competing ways in which the emergence of queer theory, and its relationship to feminism, has been received by feminists is encapsulated by Sharon Marcus in her 2005 essay 'Queer Theory for Everyone'. Marcus observes that 'If sexuality is one of the elements making up the sign woman, and if the goal of feminist theory is to challenge what we mean by woman, then queer studies is a crucial tool for feminist theory';[34] this account reflects the perception that queer theory offers a new critical emphasis – on 'sexuality' – which can be added to the feminist focus on gender and deployed in support of the feminist project of critiquing the ideological construction of woman. The tendency to see queer theory as an extension of feminist theory can be problematic, however; efforts to incorporate queer insights into existing feminist practice, sometimes with the effect that feminist analysis is found to be queer *avant la lettre*, can have the effect of defusing the questions queer theory asks of feminism. However, Marcus qualifies her observation in a footnote in which she adds: 'It could be argued that by undermining gender as a stable category, queer theory undermines feminism, which depends on the concept of woman.'[35] Indeed, queer theory has been dismissed or denounced by some feminist theorists as antithetical to feminist politics; the expansion of queer theory is here seen as posing a threat to feminism and its future.[36] Conversely, concerns about the appropriation of queer theory and the dilution of its radical politics have also been given expression.[37] Evidently, queer theory is no less diverse and dynamic than feminism; however, where tensions between specific iterations of queer and feminist politics become entrenched the richly complex relationship between queer theories and feminisms can be reduced to a struggle between apparently monolithic and mutually exclusive entities. In a revised version of her essay 'Against Proper Objects', Butler reflects: 'It seemed that an exploration of the "encounter" between feminist and queer theory was timely and potentially productive, but I forgot how quickly a critical encounter becomes misconstrued as a war.'[38] However, while queer interventions have been met with resistance and even hostility by some schools of feminist thought, others have made considered and concerted attempts to synthesise feminist and queer frameworks for the analysis of heterosexuality; the tensions that persist even in these efforts illustrate, in less inflammatory fashion, what is at stake in the engagement between feminism and queer theory.

Feminist theorist Stevi Jackson has written extensively on the subject of heterosexuality and feminism; in the course of her reflections, collated in her collection entitled *Heterosexuality in Question*, she articulates in exemplary fashion a key challenge encountered by feminist efforts to conceptualise and critique heterosexuality:

> An effective critique of heterosexuality – at the levels of social structure, meaning, social practice and subjectivity – must contain two key elements. The first of these is a critique of heteronormativity, of the normative status of heterosexuality which renders any alternative sexualities 'other' and marginal. The second is a critique of what some have called 'hetero-patriarchy' or 'hetero-oppression' ... in other words heterosexuality as systematically male-dominated.[39]

When Jackson refers to '"hetero-patriarchy" or "hetero-oppression"'[40] she evokes the dominant way in which heterosexuality has been considered within Second Wave feminist frameworks; understood as being 'implicated in the subordination of women'[41] it is a supplementary category of analysis, symptomatic of the primary category: patriarchy. While 'heterosexuality' is foregrounded in the work of key lesbian feminist theorists such as Rich and Wittig, their works are less concerned with defining what heterosexuality is than with exploring the implications of its normative power for non-heterosexual females. However, Jackson's reference to 'heteronormativity' indicates the impact of queer theory on the field of feminist enquiry; an understanding of heterosexuality as an institution which oppresses and marginalises non-heterosexual identities is clearly not new for feminism but queer theory brings new conceptual frameworks for the analysis of gender and sexuality, frameworks not exclusively concerned with the lived experiences of women. Jackson's 'effective critique' implies the need for a synthesis of two imperatives; however, such an endeavour entails reconciling mandates which are not identical and even potentially in tension with each other. This tension is made explicit when Jackson asserts that 'queer ... is centrally concerned with destabilising the heterosexual norm, but not with heterosexuality as patriarchal. Where queer takes gender seriously, it is usually as division without hierarchy.'[42] While the contribution of queer theory to the interrogation of heterosexuality is acknowledged, reservations about its usefulness for the feminist agenda are disclosed here; more than that, there is a sense that, in its purported failure to acknowledge what Jackson calls the 'hierarchical relation between (social) men and (social) women'[43] integral to heterosexuality, queer theory (and its popularity) may serve to undermine the goals of feminism. Jackson's two key elements – 'heteronormativity' and 'hetero-patriarchy' – perhaps suggest that the 'heterosexuality in question' is differently constituted in each case; the 'alternative sexualities' subject to marginalisation by the former are implicitly non-heterosexual and the 'male-domination' integral to the latter is a category of oppression which constructs its victims as female.

If the 'proper object' of feminist perspectives on heterosexuality has implicitly been the lesbian and the 'proper object' of queer perspectives on heterosexuality has implicitly been the homosexual (with male homosexuality foregrounded in Foucault's formative work), this book seeks to investigate the potential blindspots in such frameworks through a focus on representations of female heterosexuality. Recent work both within and between feminist and queer theory has suggested that the 'homosexual' is not the only identity formation subject to heteronormative forces; efforts to disentangle heterosexuality as an institution from the diversity of heterosexual desires, identities and practices make it possible to explore the ways in which non-normative *heterosexual* identities are constructed. Moreover, the conventional conflation of heterosexuality with reproductive sexuality, and the close implication of reproductive sexuality in the construction of sexed, gendered and sexual identity for women, ensures that the figure of the non-normative *female* heterosexual occupies an especially complex and fraught position in relation to heteronormativity.

(Im)proper objects: female heterosexuality in contemporary fiction

> To the extent that we are not normatively female or normatively women, we are not considered the proper subjects of feminist concern.[44]

In *Gender Trouble* Judith Butler provocatively asks whether 'the construction of the category women as a coherent and stable subject' might be 'contrary to feminist aims'.[45] She goes on to articulate a question which is central to this book: 'To what extent does the category of women achieve stability and coherence *only* in the context of the heterosexual matrix? [emphasis added].'[46] If feminist analyses of heterosexuality as a patriarchal institution cannot fully account for the ways in which female heterosexuals are subject to the forces of heteronormativity, then the questions which queer theory asks of feminism may prove enabling: this is the premise of this book. Queer theory reframes debates about sex, gender and sexuality in ways which are productive for a reflexive feminism invested in perpetually renewing its own methods. My focus on specific configurations, and discontinuities, of female identity, reproductive sexuality and heterosexuality makes a feminist framework of analysis invaluable. However, to the extent that I wish to simultaneously question the construction of 'women' formed by this configuration, the 'subjectless'[47] critique of queer theory and its interrogation of identity categories is also indispensable.

Women's writing and women's representations of women's experience continue to constitute a 'proper object' for feminist analysis within the field of contemporary fiction; this imperative is the legacy of the pioneering works of feminist literary scholarship of the Second Wave and continues to animate contemporary feminist scholarship. All but one of the novels explored in this collection of essays features a female protagonist-narrator; as narratives about 'women' they might seem the 'proper object' of feminist analysis, and indeed feminist frameworks are essential to what follows. However, the chapters which follow are not concerned principally with representations of femininity, nor with representations of girls and women in relation to men, nor with representations of male domination, although inequalities of gendered power are evident throughout. Moreover, in other regards these texts might be considered as 'improper objects' of analysis where feminist literary criticism is concerned. Waters' *Affinity* is a neo-Victorian fiction which arguably resists the revisionary lesbian feminist imperative to identify the repressed sexuality of an upper-class spinster as 'lesbian'. Heller's *Notes on a Scandal* activates (however satirically) demeaning stereotypes of spinsterhood and offers a portrait of 'liberated' female heterosexuality difficult to reconcile with feminist constructions of sexuality as empowering, since its object is a minor. Homes's *The End of Alice* confounds readerly feminist identification since it is narrated by a man convicted of the sexual abuse and murder of a young girl and depicts the apparent apprenticeship of a young woman in the sexual abuse of a boy. *Morvern Callar*, *Middlesex* and *Never Let Me Go* are all male-authored narratives employing female first-person narrators; sensitivities about authorial prerogative where gendered identity is concerned have led to Warner, for one, being charged with writing as a 'colonist of female experience'.[48] Eugenides' narrative is female narrated to the extent that its narrator is raised as a girl but she renounces her gender when diagnosed as intersexed, refusing to 'become' both a woman and, by implication, a lesbian (given her attraction to other girls). While Ishiguro's narrator is female her account of her girlhood is curiously ungendered, as if her genetically engineered inability to reproduce has divested her of her status as a woman. What, then, do these diverse texts have in common and why do they invite a critical framework informed by both feminism and queer theory? All are suggestive of a complex relationship between female identity, reproductive sexuality and heterosexuality. Feminist theory has offered critiques of the ways in which reproductive sexuality is governed by patriarchal institutions, discourses and practices, from the family and marriage to the development of reproductive technologies. However, a feminist insistence on female experience has sometimes served to reinforce the conflation of female identity, reproductive sexuality and heterosexuality. Moreover, reproductive sexuality has become increasingly detached from heterosexual sexuality in contemporary culture through both new reproductive technologies and new social arrangements where family and marriage are concerned. Technologies developed to enable women to fulfil their 'natural' destinies as women have had the inadvertent effect of removing reproduction from the realm of heterosexuality. The increased incidence and social acceptance of same-sex parenting in Western cultures further questions the status of reproduction as an exclusively heterosexual prerogative and reproductive sexuality as the norm against which homosexual identities are defined.[49] The narratives explored in this book all depict (nominally) female figures who 'fail', refuse or are not permitted to 'become women' in the ideological sense; despite being nominally heterosexual they do not benefit from the privileges which heteronormativity is supposed to grant but rather are subject to its penalties. While some undertake acts which defy social convention it could be argued that none are offered as affirming figures of volitional transgression; if they find themselves at odds with heterosexual norms it is because the combined forces of patriarchy and heteronormativity have placed them as such.

This book does not claim to provide a 'new' theory of heterosexuality; such a totalising project would arguably compound rather than complicate its universalising power. Nor does it seek to seamlessly synthesise the insights of feminism and queer theory; it is as much interested in differences as affinities between the two frameworks. It is not the intention of this book to provide a comprehensive overview of motifs to do with female heterosexuality in contemporary fiction; the texts selected for analysis are approached as providing unique insights into the complex ways in which female heterosexuality is produced and policed, rather than offered as representative case studies. Adapting Judith Butler, I would propose that they can be considered as giving representation to 'spectres of [heterosexual] discontinuity and incoherence';[50] as such, these texts can be interpreted as making visible, however inadvertently, the discontinuities and incoherence of normative female heterosexuality.

Rereading Heterosexuality is structured into three thematic parts: Sarah Waters' *Affinity* (1999) and Zoë Heller's *Notes on a Scandal* (2003) are discussed in Part One: Revisiting the Spinster, A. M. Homes's *The End of Alice* (1996) and Alan Warner's *Morvern Callar* are discussed in Part Two: Transgressive Female Heterosexuality, and finally

Jeffrey Eugenides' *Middlesex* (2002) and Kazuo Ishiguro's *Never Let Me Go* by (2005) are discussed in Part Three: Reproducing Heterosexuality. While a progressive exploration of gendered, sexual and sexed identity informs this structure, any single chapter can be read independently as offering an interpretation sufficient to itself. A rationale for each thematic section and summaries of each individual chapter are provided below.

Revisiting the spinster

The figure of the spinster has been the object of considerable interest within the traditions of feminist literary criticism and history; feminist scholars have sought to emphasise the autonomy and agency exercised by women who remained unmarried whether by circumstance or choice, while lesbian feminist scholars in particular have recovered hidden histories of same-sex desire and lesbian identity. In contemporary culture, the figure of the 'spinster' has been superseded by the postfeminist 'singleton', the latter being defined largely in terms of sexual agency in a Western, post-1960s context in which notions of women's personal liberty are closely associated with expressions of sexual identity. Part One revisits the figure of the spinster; nominally heterosexual, but outside the structure of family and marriage, she reveals the contradictions at work in the construction of normative heterosexuality – and hence constitutes a 'blindspot' whose invisibility the following chapters seek to explore.

The late Victorian period has been the object of considerable interest both to historians of sexuality and to contemporary writers. Following the work of Michel Foucault in his *History of Sexuality*, queer theorists have suggested that the emergence of discourses of sexology in this era saw the 'invention' of homosexuality as a category of identity; it can be added that this era also saw the emergence, by default, of heterosexuality as a normative identity. '"Becoming My Own Ghost": Spinsterhood and the "Invisibility" of Heterosexuality in Sarah Waters' *Affinity*' explores the historical and cultural construction of heterosexuality in relation to a contemporary neo-Victorian novel. The prominence of the 'ghostly' in *Affinity*, Waters' 1999 historical fiction of female same-sex desire, might be read as a fantastic fictional evocation of a recurring trope in lesbian feminist literary history and historiography: the historical 'invisibility' of lesbian identity. However, this chapter will explore the ways in which the narrative of *Affinity* confounds the very desires which it seems to evoke: that is, the way in which it refuses to satisfy the desire of the contemporary reader for the retrospective materialisation into existence of lesbian identity. The protagonist of *Affinity*, Margaret Prior, discloses an apprehension that she is 'becoming [her] own ghost';[51] rather than recuperate the apparitional as the spectral trace of a suppressed identity awaiting restoration to visibility, this chapter will suggest that it reveals the implication of categories of sexual identity in heteronormative regimes of visibility. Moreover, Margaret's apparitional indeterminacy as a 'spinster' will be interpreted as revealing the contradictions inherent in a very differently constituted invisibility: the normative 'invisibility' of heterosexuality.

In an analysis of representations of female sexual agency in contemporary culture, Rosalind Gill has argued that '*compulsory (sexual) agency* [emphasis in original]' is becoming 'a required feature of contemporary postfeminist neoliberal subjectivity'.[52] In a familiar appropriation of feminist discourses of female empowerment, the exercise of sexual agency is conflated with the enjoyment of personal power; sexual agency is assumed to be innately empowering, so long as it is aligned with heteronormative imperatives. Zoë Heller's 2003 novel *Notes on a Scandal* depicts the exposure of a sexual affair between a mature female teacher, Sheba Hart, and her fifteen-year-old male pupil, resulting in her prosecution for indecent assault and her separation from her husband and two children; in its representation of an 'intergenerational' sexual relationship this novel offers an expression of female heterosexual agency which is not easily recuperated either by feminist or postfeminist discourses of sexuality. However, *Notes on a Scandal* is a narrative of female heterosexual transgression which is 'translated' by a narrator – Barbara Covett, Sheba's mature and unmarried colleague – whose reliability is quickly cast into doubt by her vicarious investment in the narrative she recounts. 'Telling Tales Out of School: Spinsters, Scandals and Intergenerational Heterosexuality in Zoë Heller's *Notes on a Scandal*' will argue that in this novel troubling questions about female heterosexual agency are displaced through the production of a more familiar and less threatening stereotype of non-normative female heterosexuality: the spinster as socially marginal, emotionally suspect and sexually repressed. In other words, in *Notes on a Scandal*, the satirical momentum of a narrative ostensibly investigating deviant female heterosexuality finds its displaced target in a figure who has long functioned as a coded repository for homophobic ridicule.

Transgressive female heterosexuality

Part Two will focus on representations of the single woman as deviant or transgressive in relation to heterosexual norms. Heteronormativity is a key term in gender and sexuality studies which refers to institutions and practices which serve to privilege the heterosexual over the homosexual; however, while heteronormativity legitimises specific manifestations of heterosexual identity it also works to marginalise others. These distinctions are especially at work in relation to female sexuality, reproductive sexuality and heterosexuality. Part Two will explore representations of 'single' women as socially subversive agents who reveal the contradictions and asymmetries of power at work within heteronormativity.

A. M. Homes's controversial 1996 novel *The End of Alice* is disturbing in its apparent depiction of an unnamed female college student intent on the seduction of a twelve-year-old boy. Vikki Bell has referred to the '"perpetual asymmetry"'[53] of child sexual abuse – namely the massive statistical predominance of male offenders. Indeed, founding feminist critiques of child sexual abuse seem to proceed from the assumption that it is a male crime against female victims. By suggesting the possibility of the female sexual exploitation of boys, and by focusing on the perspective of the nominal perpetrator rather than the testimony of the victim, this novel occupies provocative territory where feminist thinking about sexuality is concerned. More specifically, it troubles the binary theorised in Carole Vance's classic 1984 essay, 'Pleasure and Danger: Toward a Politics of Sexuality',[54] in which expressions of female sexual agency are posited as empowering and subversive in opposition to the kinds of exploitative, abusive and oppressive sexuality inflicted by men on women. Hence this novel raises uncomfortable questions for feminist constructions of sexuality and power, especially with regard to efforts to reclaim and empower female (hetero)sexual agency; these questions will be explored in 'Queering Alice, Killing Lolita: Feminism, Queer Theory and the Politics of Child Sexuality in A. M. Homes *The End of Alice*'. The tensions within feminist and gender studies with regard to how 'intergenerational' sexual experiences are understood and represented are mobilised in provocative and productive ways in Homes's novel, where questions of power and agency in relation to sexuality remain deeply ambiguous. The intertextual relationship between Homes's *The End of Alice* and both Vladimir Nabokov's *Lolita* and Lewis Carroll's Alice stories will provide a focal point for reflection on significant tensions between specific iterations of feminist and queer politics where questions of consent and abuse are concerned: namely, feminist suspicion of a queer advocacy of sexual libertarianism at the expense of the rights of the children, and queer suspicion of feminist complicity with agencies of sexual regulation.

The conflation of reproductive sexuality with heterosexuality is central both to the construction of the homo/heterosexual binary and the patriarchal construction of woman as defined by a reproductive destiny. However, not all forms of reproductive sexuality benefit from the privileges which heterosexuality purports to award. Janet Fink and Katherine Holden write that 'the figure of the spinster and the unmarried mother have been positioned at opposite ends of a spectrum of female deviancy and have frequently been drawn upon as warnings to women who might be tempted to challenge social norms.'[55] 'Unauthorised Reproduction: Class, Pregnancy and Transgressive Female Heterosexuality in Alan Warner's *Morvern Callar*' takes as its starting point the illegitimate pregnancy with which Alan Warner's 1995 novel concludes; the latter is examined as one of two acts of 'unauthorised' reproduction which bookend the novel, the first being the eponymous narrator's appropriation of her dead boyfriend's unpublished manuscript. This chapter will focus on the role of class in the construction of Morvern as a figure of transgressive heterosexuality; by violating principles of patrilineal law, property and inheritance, Morvern's reproductive labour serves not to increase but to disperse the gendered and class power inherent in economic and cultural capital.

Reproducing heterosexuality

Part Three seeks to extend the scope of this study by examining texts in which the very origins of sexed identity – often taken as the fixed foundation from which gendered and sexual identity is constructed – are questioned. Normative discourses of heterosexuality rely on the binary logic of 'sex' (male or female) and 'gender' (masculine or feminine) and also conventionally equate heterosexual sexuality with reproductive sexuality. Intersexed identity, the topic of Jeffrey Eugenides' novel *Middlesex*, confounds an assumption that binary sex categories are fixed unequivocally by biology. New reproductive technologies, whose implications are imagined in Kazuo Ishiguro's speculative fiction *Never Let Me Go*, separate reproduction from reproductive sexuality. Indeed, both texts are suggestive of the normative effects of medical technologies: technologies which make 'real' the cultural construction of sex and reproduction.

The narrative of Jeffrey Eugenides' 2002 comic epic of Greek American identity, *Middlesex*, journeys through time and space from Greco-Turkish hostilities in Smyrna in 1912 to the 1967 'race riots' in Detroit through to post-unification Berlin in 2001. However, this reconstructed family history is also mapped against the narrator's retrospective account of an ambiguously sexed identity. Calliope

Stephanides, the first-person narrator of this novel, tells of a childhood lived as a girl but from an adult vantage point in which he identifies as a man. Indeed, intersexed identities demonstrate both the indeterminacy of 'sex' as a category by which to define bodies and identities and the normative violence to which 'deviant' bodies are subject. Queer theorists have suggested that the medical and surgical management of intersexed bodies can be considered symptomatic of a heteronormative imperative; however, Cal's refusal of 'corrective' surgery in *Middlesex* arguably serves less to contest the binary logic of sexed, gendered and sexual identities than to preserve a normative sexual identity as heterosexual. '"First One Thing and Then the Other": Rewriting the Intersexed Body in Jeffrey Eugenides' *Middlesex*' will focus on Eugenides' depiction of teenage girlhood in relation to motifs of same-sex desire and female masculinity. It will explore the ways in which the retrospective narration recuperates the contingencies of adolescent female sexuality and identity as signifiers of an incipient heterosexuality, which is then mobilised to authorise a sexed identity which *follows* rather than *precedes* Cal's desires. Through a focus on the process by which Cal 'becomes' intersexed, this chapter will suggest that the retrospective logic at work in this narrative is complicit in a heteronormative temporality.

Feminist theory has interrogated the relationship between new reproductive technologies and patriarchal power; 'Imitations of Life: Cloning, Heterosexuality and the Human in Ishiguro's *Never Let Me Go*' will examine the relationship between cloning, as a reproductive technology, and normative heterosexuality. The protagonists of Ishiguro's 2005 novel live outside of conventional family and kinship structures and express a sense of collective identity which they define against that of the '"normals"'.[56] While the narrator of *Never Let Me Go*, Kathy H., is nominally heterosexual she is nevertheless at odds with normative reproductive sexuality; this chapter will explore the 'queerness' of Ishiguro's protagonists and the ways in which it can be attributed to their unconventional relationship to reproductive origin, a situation only compounded by their genetically engineered inability to reproduce. In this way, Kathy can be interpreted as embodying a heterosexual identity which is disempowered and marginalised by normative heterosexuality; as such she reveals the tensions and contradictions at work within heterosexuality as an institution and an identity. This chapter will consider the contested status of Ishiguro's protagonists as human in relation to their alienation from the familial culture of heterosexual reproduction. It will suggest that the discursive construction of the human clone as 'unnatural' and 'inhuman' is compelled by the imperatives of heteronormativity – and hence that our very understanding of what it is to be human is implicated in normative constructions of heterosexuality.

Notes

1. Mason Stokes, 'White Heterosexuality: A Romance of the Straight Man's Burden', in Chrys Ingraham (ed.), *Thinking Straight: The Power, the Promise and the Paradox of Heterosexuality* (New York and London: Routledge, 2005), p. 131.
2. Linda Schlossberg, 'Introduction: Rites of Passing', in María Carla Sánchez and Linda Schlossberg (eds), *Passing: Identity and Interpretation in Sexuality, Race and Religion* (New York: New York University Press, 2001), p. 5.
3. Richard Johnson, 'Contested Borders, Contingent Lives: An Introduction', in Deborah Lynn Steinberg, Debbie Epstein and Richard Johnson (eds), *Border Patrols: Policing the Boundaries of Heterosexuality* (London: Cassell, 1997), p. 5.
4. Adrienne Rich, 'Compulsory Heterosexuality and Lesbian Existence', *Signs*, 5 (1980), p. 637.
5. Ibid.
6. Ibid., p. 652.
7. Ibid., p. 657.
8. Ibid., p. 649.
9. Ibid.
10. Ibid., p. 650.
11. Ibid., p. 657.
12. Monique Wittig, 'One Is Not Born a Woman' [1981], in *The Straight Mind and Other Essays* (Boston: Beacon Press, 1992), p. 13.
13. Ibid., p. 20.
14. Sheila Jeffreys, 'Heterosexuality and the Desire for Gender', in Diane Richardson (ed.), *Theorising Heterosexuality: Telling It Straight* (Buckingham and Philadelphia: Open University Press, 1996), p. 76.
15. Carol Smart, 'Collusion, Collaboration and Confession: On Moving Beyond the Heterosexuality Debate', in Diane Richardson (ed.), *Theorising Heterosexuality: Telling It Straight* (Buckingham and Philadelphia: Open University Press, 1996), p. 167.
16. Ibid., p. 169.
17. Ibid., p. 168.
18. Michel Foucault, *The Will to Knowledge: The History of Sexuality: Volume One* [1976], trans. Robert Hurley (1978) (London: Penguin, 1978), p. 43.
19. Eve Kosofsky Sedgwick, *Epistemology of the Closet* (Berkeley and Los Angeles: University of California Press, 1990), p. 83.
20. Judith Butler, *Gender Trouble: Feminism and the Subversion of Identity* (New York and London: Routledge, 1999), p. 3.
21. Ibid., pp. 23–4.
22. Ibid., p. 98.

23. Sedgwick, op. cit., p. 82.
24. Cathy J. Cohen, 'Punks, Bulldaggers, and Welfare Queens: The Radical Potential of Queer Politics?', *GLQ: Journal of Lesbian and Gay Studies*, 3 (1997), p. 440.
25. Lauren Berlant and Michael Warner, 'Sex in Public', *Critical Inquiry*, 24: 2 (1998), p. 548.
26. Ibid., pp. 554–5.
27. Annamarie Jagose, *Inconsequence: Lesbian Representation and the Logic of Sexual Sequence* (Ithaca, NY and London: Cornell University Press, 2002), pp. 4–5.
28. Berlant and Warner, op. cit., p. 548.
29. Cohen, op. cit., p. 452. Cohen emphasises the need to address 'the ways in which heteronormativity works to support and reinforce institutional racism, patriarchy, and class exploitation' (p. 455). For the most part this book is concerned with formations of female identity which are otherwise privileged by race and class; however, the contested nature of 'whiteness' is briefly addressed in my discussion of Eugenides' *Middlesex* and the role of class in the construction of normative reproductive sexuality is foregrounded in my analysis of Warner's *Morvern Callar*.
30. Butler, *Gender Trouble*, op. cit., p. 194.
31. Ibid.
32. Ibid.
33. The relationship between feminism and queer theory is explored in the essays collected in Mandy Merck, Naomi Segal and Elizabeth Wright's *Coming Out of Feminism?* (London: Blackwell, 1998).
34. Sharon Marcus, 'Queer Theory for Everyone', *Signs*, 31: 1(2005), p. 200.
35. Ibid.
36. See, for example, Sheila Jeffreys, 'Heterosexuality and the Desire for Gender', in Diane Richardson (ed.), *Theorising Heterosexuality: Telling It Straight* (Buckingham and Philadelphia: Open University Press, 1996), pp. 75–90.
37. For example, Annette Schlichter critiques forms of 'queer heterosexuality' which rely on 'the straight authors' aspiration to identify as queer'. 'Queer at Last? Straight Intellectuals and the Desire for Transgression', *GLQ: Journal of Lesbian and Gay Studies*, 10: 4 (2004), p. 545.
38. Judith Butler, 'Against Proper Objects', in Elizabeth Weed and Naomi Schor (eds), *Feminism Meets Queer Theory* (Bloomington: Indiana University Press, 1997), p. 1.
39. Stevi Jackson, 'Heterosexuality, Heteronormativity and Gender Hierarchy', in *Heterosexuality in Question* (London: Sage, 1991), p. 163.
40. Ibid., p. 163.
41. Stevi Jackson, 'Gender and Heterosexuality: A Materialist Feminist Analysis', in *Heterosexuality in Question* (London: Sage, 1991), p. 123.
42. Jackson, 'Heterosexuality, Heteronormativity and Gender Hierarchy', op. cit., p. 164.
43. Jackson, 'Gender and Heterosexuality', op. cit., p. 131.
44. Cheryl Chase, 'Hermaphrodites with Attitude: Mapping the Emergence of Intersex Political Activism', *GLQ: Journal of Lesbian and Gay Studies*, 4:

2 (1998), p. 208. For a critical examination of feminist perspectives on transgender see Rachel Carroll, '"Violent Operations": Revisiting the Transgendered Body in Angela Carter's *The Passion of New Eve*', *Women: A Cultural Review*, 22: 2/3 (September 2011), pp. 241–55.
45. Butler, *Gender Trouble*, op. cit., p. 9.
46. Ibid.
47. David L. Eng, Judith Halberstam and José Esteban Muñoz write that 'the "subjectless" critique of queer studies disallows any posting of a proper subject *of* or object *for* the field by insisting that queer has no fixed political referent [emphasis in original]'. 'Introduction: What's Queer About Queer Studies Now?', *Social Text*, 23: 3–4 84–5 (2005), p. 3.
48. Carole Jones, 'The "Becoming Woman": Femininity and the Rave Generation in Alan Warner's *Morvern Callar*', *Scottish Studies Review*, 5: 2 (2004), p. 56.
49. For a critique of what she terms the 'new homonormativity' see Lisa Duggan, 'The New Homonormativity: The Sexual Politics of Neoliberalism', in Dana D. Nelson (ed.), *Materializing Democracy: Toward a Revitalized Cultural Politics* (Durham, NC and London: Duke University Press, 2002), pp. 175–94.
50. Butler writes that the 'spectres of discontinuity and incoherence, themselves thinkable only in relation to existing norms of continuity and coherence, are constantly prohibited and produced by the very laws that seek to establish causal or expressive lines of connection among biological sex, culturally constituted genders, and the "expression" or "effect" of both in the manifestation of sexual desire through sexual practice' (*Gender Trouble*, op. cit., p. 23).
51. Sarah Waters, *Affinity* (London: Virago, 1999), p. 289.
52. Rosalind Gill, 'Empowerment/Sexism: Figuring Female Sexual Agency in Contemporary Advertising', *Feminism and Psychology*, 18: 1 (2008), p. 40.
53. Vicki Bell, *Interrogating Incest: Feminism, Foucault and the Law* (London: Routledge, 1993), p. 71.
54. Carole Vance, 'Pleasure and Danger: Toward a Politics of Sexuality', in Sandra Kemp and Judith Squires (eds), *Feminisms* (Oxford: Oxford University Press, 1997), pp. 327–34.
55. Janet Fink and Katherine Holden, 'Pictures from the Margins of Marriage: Representations of Spinsters and Single Mothers in the Mid-Victorian Novel, Inter-War Hollywood Melodrama and the British Film of the 1950s and 1960s', *Gender and History*, 11: 2 (1999), p. 233.
56. Kazuo Ishiguro, *Never Let Me Go* (London: Faber & Faber, 2005), p. 94.

Part One: Revisiting the spinster

Chapter 1

'Becoming my own ghost': spinsterhood and the 'invisibility' of heterosexuality in Sarah Waters' *Affinity*

The prominence of the 'ghostly' in *Affinity*, Sarah Waters' 1991 neo-Victorian gothic fiction of female same-sex desire, might be read as a fantastic fictional evocation of a recurring trope in lesbian feminist literary history and historiography: the historical 'invisibility' of lesbian identity. However, I wish to explore the ways in which the narrative of *Affinity* confounds the very desires which it seems to evoke: that is, the way in which it refuses to satisfy the desire of the contemporary reader for the retrospective materialisation into late Victorian existence of lesbian identity.[1] The protagonist of *Affinity*, Margaret Prior, discloses an apprehension that she is 'becoming [her] own ghost';[2] rather than recuperate the apparitional as the spectral trace of a suppressed identity awaiting restoration to visibility, I will argue that it reveals the implication of categories of sexual identity in heteronormative regimes of visibility. Moreover, Margaret's apparitional indeterminacy as a 'spinster' can be interpreted as revealing the contradictions inherent in a very differently constituted invisibility: the normative 'invisibility' of heterosexuality.

Recovering from a suicide attempt following the marriage of her former female lover, Margaret seeks to lose herself in charitable work as a prison visitor; however, she finds in Selina Dawes, an imprisoned spiritualist medium, not only the rekindled possibility of reciprocated desire but also a language through which to express it. Margaret's journals record her growing conviction in the spiritualist doctrine of 'affinity' and in the possibility of the supernatural materialisation of Selina's body out of the confines of Millbank prison. However, the ultimate failure of Margaret's desires to materialise, and the revelation that she has been the unwitting victim of a plot on the part of Selina and her own maid, constitute a devastating culmination to the narrative both for Margaret and the reader who has become affectively identified with her: 'There never was a cord of darkness, never a space in which our spirits touched. There was only my longing – and hers, which so resembled it, it seemed my own.'³ I would suggest that Margaret's longing can be understood as expressive of a 'desire to live' in the face of 'normative violence';⁴ this violence takes the form of disciplinary discourses, including the medical and the criminal, which deny a reality to her experience of her own desires and which prompt her to attribute her 'faults' to 'me and my queer nature, that set me so at odds with the world and all its ordinary rules, I could not find a place in it to live and be content.'⁵ Margaret acknowledges both a sense of her difference and of its implications: '"Women are *bred* to do more of the same – that is their function. It is only ladies like me that throw the system out, make it stagger" [emphasis in original].'⁶ She is a woman who makes the system stagger by her inability to comply with its self-perpetuating reproductive logic; her refusal to 'do more of the same' is a refusal of the marital/maternal role integral to compulsory heterosexuality and a refusal to reproduce that role ideologically. Margaret's intuition that there is a 'system' and that such a system can be made to stagger is accompanied by the insight that there are 'ladies like me'; this insight prompts the question of what constitutes the 'likeness' which these ladies share. The late Victorian society depicted in *Affinity* is able to account for this likeness in only two ways; Margaret is constructed by gendered heterosexual discourses as a 'spinster' and by pathologising and criminalising discourses as a 'suicide'. However, a further likeness is inferred by Margaret's affinity with Selina. Margaret's desire to live – the 'little *quickening* within me [emphasis in original]'⁷ – finds expression through the unorthodox discourse of spiritualism and its doctrine of affinity; it is only in this context that the possibility of the materialisation of non-normative desires is entertained: '"Did you think there is only the kind of love your sister knows for her husband?"'⁸ Through a close examination of the discourses, both normative and marginal, by which Margaret's 'likeness' to others of her kind is understood, I wish to explore how she becomes 'ghostly' to herself as a woman outside of the institution of heterosexuality.

'The mark of the shelf': becoming a spinster

> They found me with my hand upon the chair-back, trembling with fear and shame, the mark of the shelf I suppose at my cheek.⁹

Yopie Prins importantly acknowledges the historical agency of elective spinsters when she suggests that 'the generation of unmarried middle-class women that came of age in the 1870s and 1880s played an important role in the transition from mid-Victorian Old Maid to fin-de-siècle New Woman; during the last three decades of the century, single women were beginning to redefine familial relations and conventional female domesticity.'[10] However, the reproductive and teleological logic implicit in this generational narrative retrospectively posits women as 'coming of age' into identities which are already inscribed by feminist historiography; in *Affinity*, by contrast, the normative violence experienced by unmarried women creates a more problematic relation to linear temporality. In a narrative in which the crossing of thresholds between worlds is theatrically enacted through the practices of spiritualism, another 'passing over' is less dramatically realised but is just as transformative; in passing over into the world of spinsterhood, Margaret has departed a world in which social and familial futures can be anticipated for an existence which is characterised by a suspension of time and being. As Margaret comments somewhat ironically of her newly married sister Priscilla: '"She has *evolved*, like one of your spirits. She has moved on. And I am left, more firmly *un*evolved than ever" [emphasis in original].'[11]

Given the centrality of marriage and motherhood to the normative gendered identity of adult women in late Victorian England, to fail to proceed to these conditions is in some way to forfeit the identity of 'woman', a failure signified by the construction of a gendered category of identity other than woman: the spinster. Where femininity is equated with reproductive sexuality, reproduction is deemed the natural destiny of all women and marriage the only legitimate means for its fulfilment; women whose desires or social roles escape this function confound the ideological construction of biological females as women. As Janet Fink and Katherine Holden write, the figure of the spinster 'challenge[s] the institution of marriage and the emotional, sexual and financial dependency assigned to the roles of wife and mother by the marriage contract.'[12] Spinsterhood, whether elective or unsought, calls into question the heterosexual construction of gender. To paraphrase Monique Wittig: a spinster is not a woman.[13] However, spinsterhood constructs Margaret's difference as heterosexual failure; the agency potentially at work in a refusal of gendered heterosexuality is rewritten as an inability to accept a natural destiny. The spinster is transformed from a woman whose wants are other than those permitted by normative gendered identity into a woman who is found wanting and not wanted.

Spinsterhood denotes an identity which is fixed and irrevocable in time; it is a default identity, defined by what has not happened and confirmed by the temporal certainty that it will not happen. However, there is a strong sense in which Margaret's spinsterhood is constructed for her well in advance of the temporal moment in which it might be said to have arrived; Margaret's rather uncanny sense of 'becoming a spinster' suggests a process which has had a trajectory rather than a retrospective logic. Returning to the British Library Reading Room after an absence of two years since her father's death, Margaret finds that she has changed: 'The others, who do not know me, call me "madam" now, I noticed, instead of "miss". I have turned, in two years, from a girl into a spinster.'[14] As a visitor to the Library in the company of her father, Margaret's scholarly interests are seen as in keeping with the attentions of a dutiful daughter. It is perhaps not simply the passage of time that has transformed Margaret from 'miss' to 'madam' so much as the fact of her returning independently and alone; her pursuit of her intellectual interests suggest an autonomy at odds with a femininity defined in relation to the service of masculine needs. Without the legitimising paternal presence, Margaret's desire for knowledge becomes transgressive.

Margaret's spinsterhood is further confirmed publicly by her sister's 'passing'; in marrying before her older sister, Priscilla has surpassed her and Margaret's marital belatedness has been exposed. When Margaret witnesses her sister 'pass me in the church'[15] her identity undergoes a transformative shift: 'I thought that there were one or two curious or pitying glances cast my way – but not so many, I am sure, as there were at Stephen's wedding. Then, I suppose, I was my mother's burden. Now I am become her *consolation* [emphasis in original].'[16] The spinsterhood which might have designated a freedom from the obligations of unwanted marriage and motherhood here signifies an ongoing subjection to a patriarchal mother. The widowed mother appropriates the emotional labour of her unmarried daughter as compensation for the loss both of her husband and of the daughter with whom she identifies as reproducing her own role. Margaret's identity as spinster is its own punishment as it exposes her to her mother's contempt: '"You are not Mrs Browning, Margaret – as much as you would like to be. You are not, in fact, Mrs Anybody. You are only *Miss Prior*. And your place – how often must I say it? – your place is here, at your mother's side" [emphasis in original].'[17] Indeed, spinsters are elsewhere incarcerated in the guise of useful occupation: 'none of the wardresses there have husbands, but are all spinsters, or else widows . . . "You must not be a matron," she [Mrs Jelf] said, "and also married."'[18] The spinster and prison inmate, whether warder or convict, are institutionalised alike through patriarchal confinement. A further analogy between the spinster and the female convict, as problems requiring a solution, is confirmed in *Affinity* when Miss Haxby recounts the kinds of assistance which lady visitors have brought to their charges: 'She said that ladies had helped many of her girls – had helped them at last to places suited to their station, had led them to new lives, away from their shame, away from their old influences, away from England itself sometimes, to marriage, in the Colonies.'[19] As the object of public anxieties about 'surplus', 'superfluous' and 'redundant' women, and despite the significant contributions, often voluntary and unpaid, made by unmarried women to the social sphere,[20] the spinster is perceived as problematically non-(re)productive. Hence, the female convict and spinster alike must be 'placed' within the legitimate and (re)productive sphere of marriage.

Priscilla's marriage is one manifestation of a sequence of 'difficult times' which, within the logic of the family script, anticipate Margaret's 'passing over' into spinsterhood:

> Oh, I said, I had heard words like that, so many times! When Stephen went to school when I was ten: they said that that would be 'a difficult time', because of course I was so clever, and would not understand why I must keep my governess. When he went to Cambridge it was the same; and then, when he came home and was called to the bar. When Pris turned out so handsome they said that would be difficult, we must expect it to be difficult, because of course I was so plain. And then, when Stephen was married, when Pa died, when Georgy was born – it had been one thing leading to another, and they had said only, always, that it was natural, it was to be expected that I should feel the sting of things like that; that older, unmarried sisters always did.[21]

The difficulty of these times is attributed 'only' and 'always' to Margaret's inability to accept as natural the 'sting' of inequality embedded in normative gender roles, both in terms of the differences of opportunity available to men and women and the differences in status allotted to women on the basis of their feminine desirability. Feelings which might be deemed unnatural within the terms of the dominant discourses of gender – Margaret's desire for intellectual development, her disinterest in competing in the marriage market – are naturalised when placed within a narrative which prepares for her in advance the role of spinster. Each 'time' constitutes a threshold from one stage of identity to another; as a spinster Margaret suffers a difficulty *with* time in her refusal to comply with its linear and reproductive logic.

The pathologising of the spinster as a woman whose femininity has deviated from the norm is evident in Margaret's mother's equation of her 'illness' with her unmarried status: '"You wouldn't be ill like this ... if you were married."'[22] The spinster is ridiculed as a figure whose emotions have found improper, or perhaps inappropriately gendered, objects. An 'unmarried cousin of the family's'[23] at Marishes is implicitly proposed as a fitting companion for Margaret: 'a very clever lady – she collects moths and beetles, and has exhibited to entomological societies, "alongside gentlemen".'[24] The inference is that the lady is herself the 'exhibit', kept behind glass, like her insect specimens, within the family home for the amusement of visitors. While Margaret recoils from this likeness she emphatically identifies herself as a spinster in the eyes of others in her passionate attachment to Selina: 'It was myself, a spinster, pale and plain and sweating and wild, and groping from a swaying prison ladder after the severed yellow tresses of a handsome girl . . .'[25] Haunted by 'that gross vision, of the spinster, grasping after the switch of hair . . .',[26] it is evident that Margaret has internalised a conviction that, as a spinster, any display of passion will be read as evidence of incipient deviancy; the fact that her passion is for a woman also hints at the possibility that the identity of spinster is one which potentially contains desires not granted a legitimate existence.

In becoming a spinster, Margaret forfeits her gendered identity; if a spinster is one who has not fully acceded to her place within the order of reproductive sexuality, then she is something other than a woman. Significantly, Margaret's recognition of her likeness with others of her kind is expressed in apparitional terms: 'There were many spinsters there to-day, I think – more, certainly, than I remember. Perhaps, however, it is the same with spinsters as with ghosts; and one has to be of their ranks in order to see them at all.'[27] The ghostliness of the spinster is less to do with her visibility than with her legibility within heteronormative terms; she is not invisible so much as unseen by those for whom her meaning has no significance.

'Breaking out': being a suicide

'Will you go on being a prisoner, in your own dark cell, forever?'[28]

The marginalised identity constituted by spinsterhood is nevertheless socially sanctioned; in Millbank prison, however, Margaret encounters her likeness in illicit form. The disciplinary power exercised by the prison as an institution is not confined to the incarceration of bodies; it also extends to the reinscription of identities in that its inmates are interpellated into criminal categories. Mrs Pretty's roll call of the 'troublesome . . . or incorrigible'[29] residents of Wards D and E gives rise to a deeply uncanny moment:

'Jane Hoy, ma'am: child murderer. Vicious as a needle.
'Phœbe Jacobs: thief. Set fire to her cell.

'Deborah Griffiths: pickpocket. Here for spitting at the chaplain.
'Jane Samson: suicide –'[30]

Samson is imprisoned for her repeated suicide attempts, or, more properly, she is punished for the repeated 'failure' of her efforts to take her own life, for surviving her efforts to erase her own existence. Moreover, her punishment is the social death of imprisonment as a criminal. Samson's sentence can be seen as evidence of the criminalising of 'madness', if attempted suicide is taken as an expression of profound psychological distress. Conversely, the penitential cure to which convicts are subject is perceived by Margaret as inducing madness: 'It was as if the prison had been designed by a man in the grip of a nightmare or a madness – or had been made expressly to *drive* its inmates mad [emphasis in original].'[31] Millbank, then, is a space to which madness is committed, a place within which it is produced in order to be regulated; it is a form of confinement designed to withdraw the criminal and mad alike from view and to subject them to a punitive surveillance.[32] However, the unspoken affinity between Margaret and Jane Samson – as 'suicides' – exposes this boundary as fragile and contingent.

Margaret crosses this boundary when, empowered by the chloral which has been prescribed as the cure for her illness, she manifests her 'madness' by speaking with a 'fearful kind of clarity':[33] '"Don't you think that queer ? That a common coarse-featured woman might drink morphia and be sent to gaol for it, while I am saved and sent to visit her – and all because I am a *lady*?" [emphasis in original].'[34] Margaret transgresses the spatial boundary between home and prison when, in her delirium, her gown transforms itself into the straitjacket used as a restraint at Millbank: 'Now my gown had me gripped like a fist, so that the more I wriggled to undo it, the tighter it grew – at last, *There is a screw at my back*, I thought, *& they are tightening it*! [emphasis in original].'[35] This delusion might seem to indicate the return of Margaret's madness but it also signifies a meaningful recognition: that of the domestic space of her familial room as itself a form of 'dark cell'. Millbank represents the violence held in reserve for those who do not conform: '[The walls were] densely hung with iron – with rings and chains and fetters, and with other, nameless, complicated instruments whose purposes I could only, shuddering, guess at.'[36] However, it is a violence which is not unknown to Margaret's memory as she recalls the events following the discovery of her suicide attempt: 'the weeping and the shrieking, and Dr Ashe and Mother, the bitter reek of morphia, and my tongue swollen from the pressing of the tube.'[37]

However, Millbank offers models not only of repressive violence but also of transgressive violence. The '*breaking out* [emphasis in original]' which is '"peculiar to female gaols"'[38] is contained to the space of the cell and the body of the prisoner; as a form of destruction it has an internalising quality which renders it peculiarly feminine: '"The blankets not just ripped but *shredded*. They do that with their mouths. We have found teeth, in the past, that they have lost in their great fury..." [emphasis in original]'[39] This 'breaking out' is re-enacted by Margaret on discovering her betrayal by Selina:

> I seized the mattress and then the bed; the sheets I ripped. The tearing cotton – how can I write it? – it was like a drug upon me. I tore and tore, until the sheets were rags, until my hands were sore; and then I put the seams to my own mouth and tore with my teeth.[40]

Margaret's attempted suicide is taken as evidence of her illness; her cure requires her to assume the status of a patient subject to medical intervention and hence confirms the pathologising of her identity. The identity of the illness which prompted Margaret's attempt to take her own life, however, remains unspecified. The cause of Margaret's suicide is held to be grief for the loss of her father yet the '"old griefs"'[41] to which Helen refers suggest causes less singular and more long-standing. The locket worn by Margaret, given to her by her father, is seen as a signifier of her ongoing devotion to his memory but it contains and conceals another kind of mourning: 'It is the curl of Helen's hair I am afraid for, that she cut from her own head and said I must keep, while she still loved me. I am only afraid of losing that – for God knows! I've lost so much of her already.'[42] In 'breaking out' Margaret manifests both her 'madness' and, by implication, her criminality: that is, she confirms that her suicide was an act of gender transgression, as her mother suspects. Margaret's mother attributes to her daughter the deviousness, cunning and dissimulation which the prison matrons attribute to their charges; she sees Margaret as a recidivist '"picking [her] own wilful way again towards illness"'[43] and, denying the reality of Margaret's distress, insists that her 'illness' is a ruse: '"You keep that card to play as you choose. You are ill when it suits... You are selfish... and wilful."'[44]

The uncanniness of Margaret's encounter with the 'suicide' at Millbank arises not only from a sense that a suicide *cannot* be there, but also from the sense that Margaret *should* be there: that Margaret is to encounter herself when she peers through the inspection flap of the cell: '"It is really I who should have been put there! – not her, not her at all... But didn't you know... that they send suicides to gaol?"'[45] Margaret's conviction that she should be in 'her' place here substitutes Selina for the 'suicide'; anxiety and guilt compel Margaret to wish to take Selina's place in 'the darks' but also betray a sense of the unspoken crime for which Selina has been convicted. Margaret's recognition of the criminal identity from which she is protected by her class is also a kind of affirmation of her shared identity: her 'likeness' not only to Samson but also to Selina. The ghostly quality of the spinster – 'one has to be of their ranks in order to see them at all'[46] – is compounded by that of the convict: '"They might be ghosts!"'[47] If the spinster is a woman without gender, the 'suicide' is a woman who has attempted to leave her gender behind: as Selina says of Margaret: '"You have felt what it's like, to leave your life, to leave your self – to shrug it from you, like a gown."'[48] The heterosexual discourse of the spinster and the pathologising and criminalising discourses of the 'suicide' render Margaret ghostly. These discourses subject Margaret to the 'cycle of prohibition' characteristic of a repressive understanding of power as described by Michel Foucault: 'Renounce yourself or suffer the penalty of being suppressed; do not appear if you do not want to disappear. Your existence will be maintained only at the cost of your nullification.'[49] However, Margaret does seek another existence through the supernatural visual technologies of spiritualism; moreover, the fact that the materialisation of her desires entails 'becoming my own ghost'[50] suggests a complex relationship to visibility.

'Becoming my own ghost': difference visible

In *Affinity*, Margaret's identity as a woman who loves women is written out; it is written over by heterosexual romance through the family script and consigned to oblivion when Margaret burns her private journals. Margaret's fear that her 'difference' will become visible to others is symptomatic of the extent to which she has internalised the edict of invisibility. The material practices of writing and memorialising history are foregrounded from the outset: 'Pa used to say that any piece of history might be made into a tale: it was only a question of deciding where the tale began and where it ended.'[51] Here the essence of narrative is attached to its linear form and its causal logic and yet the very question of the origins and causes of Margaret's 'tale' are confounded or obscured. Margaret's loss is not merely the loss of Helen's love but also the erasure of the significance of that relationship. Helen's attachment to Margaret is written over by a family script which retrospectively understands Helen's visits to the family home as a ruse whose culmination was her marriage to Margaret's brother: '"Of course, we did not know – did we Priscilla – that it was all on Stephen's account that she came here."'[52]

Supported by Helen's private and public silence on their past attachment, this script rewrites Margaret's feelings out of existence: 'I have heard the story told that way so many times, I am half-way to believing it myself.'[53] The relationship takes on a ghostly quality; Margaret refers to her bed as '"haunted, by our old kisses"',[54] testifying to Helen that '"I *have* seemed to see our kisses there sometimes, I've seen them hanging in the curtains, like bats, ready to swoop" [emphasis in original].'[55]

Margaret is tormented by a fear of her difference becoming visible. In this novel, the Panoptical design of Millbank prison, and its mobilising of the disciplinary gaze – '"the women term it *the eye*" [emphasis in original]'[56] – extends beyond the prison walls.[57] Visibility, whether withdrawn or imposed, is a regime used to deny women agency over their own identity; whether exhibited in her cell ('"All the world may look at me, it is part of my punishment"'[58]) or confined in 'the darks' ('"the darkness is the punishment"',[59]) the prisoner is reminded that her identity resides in the owner of the gaze. Margaret's warder is not a matron but her mother, whose surveillance is as punishing: 'She said that; and I knew then that, careful as I have been – still and secret and silent as I have been, in my high room – she has been watching me, as Miss Ridley watches, and Miss Haxby.'[60] The conflation of mother and matron is confirmed more than once; on receiving Miss Haxby's cautionary advice in the view of Miss Ridley, Margaret comments that 'it was like thanking Mother for some piece of hard counsel, while Ellis took the plates away'[61] and later compounds this comparison: 'I said, "Miss Haxby" – but I stumbled over the words, for I had almost said *Mother*! [emphasis in original].'[62] For her mother, Margaret's behaviour is defined as deviant to the extent that it is visible; she chides Margaret for 'grow[ing] so nervous before the maids'[63] and declares that 'she could not bear to have our friends believe [Margaret] weak, or *eccentric* – [emphasis in original].'[64] Margaret fears that her 'difference' will manifest itself in external signs and will thereby compromise or expose her: 'I thought she [Selina] would see some sign about me, something dishevelled or illuminated. – I remembered then fearing the same thing of Mother, when I went back to her from visiting Helen.'[65] Having embarked on her conspiracy with Selina, Margaret is increasingly anxious under the gaze of the prison warders: 'I am frightened the matrons will see it, and guess.'[66] The 'it' at which the matrons might guess here denotes not only the specific secret of her conspiracy with Selina but also the desire which motivates it. Margaret's pact with Selina offers to realise both what she most desires and what she most fears, objects which may be identical: 'People would learn what we had done. *I would be seen*, and recognised [emphasis added].'[67]

Having destroyed the journal which recorded her relationship with Helen, Margaret attempts to write her desires out of existence and to quell the 'twisting thoughts' which 'filled [her] last book':[68] 'I mean this writing not to turn me back upon my own thoughts, but to serve, like the chloral, to keep the thoughts from coming at all.'[69] Margaret evokes the disciplinary mechanisms of the prison as a metaphor for her efforts to restrain and control her past and its meanings: 'His [Mr Shillitoe] knowing nothing, and the women's knowing nothing, that will keep that history in its place. I imagined them fastening my own past shut, with a strap and a buckle . . .'[70] However, there are other discourses capable of quickening into life the very subjectivity which this effacing practice of writing was intended to erase:

> I thought that I could make my life into a book that had no life or love in it – a book that was only a catalogue, a kind of list. Now I can see that my heart has crept across these pages, after all. I can see the crooked passage of it, it grows firmer as the paper turns. It grows so firm at last, it spells a name – *Selina* [emphasis in original].[71]

The discourses of spiritualism, and more specifically the doctrine of 'affinities', authorises subjective and affective identifications in terms beyond those of normative constructions of identity.[72]

Selina describes the concept of affinity as follows:

> '[After death] we will all fly to someone, we will all return to that piece of shining matter from which our souls were torn with another, two halves of the same . . . that other soul, that has the affinity with her soul . . . It may be someone she would never think to look to on the earth, someone kept from her by some false boundary.'[73]

Affinity cannot be contained by the 'false boundaries' of the material world; it is neither sexed nor gendered and so allows for desires other than those sanctioned by heterosexual norms. The seeking of affinity is compelled by the pursuit of likeness and licenses the relinquishing of existing identities:

> 'We have been cut, two halves, from the same piece of shining matter. Oh, I could say, *I love you* – that is a simple thing to say, the sort of thing your sister might say to her husband . . . But my spirit does not love yours – it is *entwined* with it. Our flesh does not love: our flesh is the same, and longs to leap to itself. It must do that or wither! *You are like me* [emphasis in original].'[74]

The likeness which Margaret and Selina share is a likeness of gender which is contrary to the logic of difference on which heterosexuality is premised: that is, the likeness which 'longs to leap to itself'.[75] However, it is also a likeness in difference; they are alike in being apart from conventional society and in having elected to 'leave [the] self'[76] whether as spirit medium or as 'suicide'. The likeness of those gifted with spiritual powers is an identity which only they can recognise and share: 'I might meet someone, sometimes, and I would know they were like me. But that was no good of course, if the person did not know it too – or, worse, if she guessed at it and was afraid.'[77] Within the context of the supernatural, as opposed to the unnatural, difference is legitimised as a gift bestowed rather than a deviance pursued; 'sickness' is the outcome not of its expression but of its suppression. As Selina implores her reluctant client Miss Isherwood: '"If we neglect this thing, then your powers will wither, or else they will twist inside you & make you sick . . . I think you have felt those powers begin to twist a little already, haven't you?"'[78]

Margaret's fear that her inner 'difference' – her 'queer nature'[79] – might betray her by manifesting itself in external and legible signs conveys not only a compound fear of and desire for recognition but also a sense of being somehow changed or transformed by her illicit knowledge of herself:

> I knew my trips to her [Selina] had made me strange, not like myself – or worse, that they had made me *too much like* myself, like my old self, my naked *Aurora* self. Now when I tried to be *Margaret* again, I couldn't. It seemed to me that she had dwindled, like a suit of clothes [emphasis in original].[80]

The identity which is being materialised possesses the spectrality of those who defy the binary logic of visible and invisible: 'I am *evolving* . . . My flesh is streaming from me. I am becoming my own ghost! [emphasis in original].'[81]

The apparitional spinster

When Margaret wonders whether it is 'the same with spinsters as with ghosts' and 'one has to be of their ranks in order to see them at all,'[82] the temptation for the contemporary reader may be to deduce that it is 'the same' with lesbians as with spinsters as with ghosts and to 'see' what Margaret cannot see: that she is 'of their ranks'. However, such a reading might commit what Annamarie Jagose has described, in her discussion of 'lesbian legibility'[83] in *Little Dorrit*, as a 'perspectival error';[84] it would discover in Margaret a lesbian identity which is actually the '*effect* of a later historical moment that not only produces modern taxonomies of sexuality but constitutes us as their most thoroughly interpellated subjects [emphasis added].'[85] Moreover, a retrospective reading of this kind would also occlude the spinster and the specific ways in which she troubles heterosexual categories of gender and sexuality. I wish here to return to the figure of the spinster and to suggest the ways in which readings of the spinster as a 'hidden' lesbian might be implicated in a heteronormative regime of visibility.

As the narrative of *Affinity* suggests, the normative discourses of heterosexual and patriarchal history cannot see the nineteenth-century spinster other than as a woman without sexuality living a vicarious existence through familial attachment to other people's marriages. Such narratives are challenged in Sheila Jeffreys' *The Spinster and Her Enemies: Feminism and Sexuality, 1880–1930* in which she reclaims the spinster as a model of an elective, autonomous and woman-centred existence. Moreover, Jeffreys seeks to make visible a history of lesbian identity hidden within the history of the spinster:

> Any attack on the spinster is inevitably an attack on the lesbian. Women's right to be lesbian depends on our right to exist outside sexual relationships with men. When lesbians are stigmatised and reviled, so, also, are all women who live independently of men.[86]

The spinster as lesbian defies the 'compulsory heterosexuality' which is unable to see her as anything other than a failed heterosexual. Indeed, the 'invisibility' of female same-sex desire and of lesbian identity is a recurring trope in lesbian feminist criticism and theory. For example, in her revisionary lesbian history *Surpassing the Love of Men: Romantic Friendship and Love between Women from the Renaissance to the Present* (1981), Lillian Faderman famously suggests that until the late nineteenth century the invisibility of love between women made it possible for women to engage in and sustain passionate attachments without censure. For Faderman, invisibility provides a refuge from patriarchal masculinity and heterosexuality; by contrast, she argues, the visibility granted by the work of the sexologists of the late nineteenth and early twentieth centuries enabled the policing and suppression of lesbian identity as deviant and pathological. Terry Castle is one critic who has questioned Faderman's inference that women who loved women were invisible to themselves and each other; that is, that intimate relationships between women were no more experienced as sexual by their participants, prior to the advent of sexology, than they were perceived as such by patriarchal culture. In her study of representations of female same-sex desire, *The Apparitional Lesbian: Female Homosexuality and Modern Culture*, Castle asserts that the invisibility to which lesbian identity and female same-sex desire is consigned is, whether consciously or not, wilful: 'When it comes to lesbians . . . many people have trouble seeing what's in front of them';[87] the lesbian is '"ghosted" – or made to seem invisible – by culture itself'[88] because of the threat she is deemed to pose to patriarchy. For Castle the apparitional is expressive of anxieties about lesbian identity, not a manifestation of any instability in the category itself. Indeed, Castle insists on the legibility of the category 'lesbian': 'if in ordinary speech I say, "I am a lesbian," the meaning is instantly (even dangerously clear): I am a woman whose primary emotional and erotic allegiance is to my own sex.'[89]

Heterosexual identity does not suffer from the fear of being rendered problematically 'visible': nor does it need to struggle to accede to an affirmative visibility in its own terms. However, the founding stability and coherence which is assumed to be the possession of heterosexuality can be understood as a fiction constructed through the stigmatised visibility with which homosexuality is threatened and the imposed invisibility with which it is regulated. Indeed, it can be argued that heterosexuality has been privileged by another kind of 'invisibility': that is, the invisibility of the supposedly universal and non-problematic. The emergence of 'the homosexual' as a category of identity in the late nineteenth century is often offered as illustrative evidence of the discursive construction of sexuality; the use of the 'homosexual' as such a case study, however, can tend to obscure the extent to which the norm against which it was defined was an equally novel innovation. As Eve Kosofsky Sedgwick has written:

> Foucault among other historians locates in about the nineteenth century a shift in European thought from viewing same-sex sexuality as a matter of prohibited and isolated genital *acts* . . . to viewing it as a function of stable definitions of *identity* . . . [The period] was prodigally productive of attempts to name, explain, and define this new kind of creature, the homosexual person – a project so urgent that it spawned in its rage of distinction an even newer category, that of the heterosexual person [emphasis in original].[90]

The recognition of the status of 'the homosexual' as a discursive innovation historicises the continuing pathologising and criminalising of acts, desires and identities defined as homosexual. However, while this recognition has effected a shift from the 'unnatural' to the cultural with regard to homosexuality, it also implicitly requires a shift from the supposedly natural to the cultural with regard to heterosexuality: that is, it requires an acknowledgement of heterosexuality itself as an unstable, even incoherent category. The 'failure' of attempts to definitively categorise homosexuality as other to heterosexuality are also testament to the indeterminacy of heterosexuality; Sedgwick refers to 'the plurality and the cumulative incoherence of modern ways of conceptualising same-sex desire and, hence, gay identity; an incoherence that answers, too, to the incoherence with which *hetero*sexual desire and identity are conceptualised [emphasis in original].'⁹¹ 'Ordinary speech'⁹² rarely requires a heterosexual to make the kind of declaration to which Castle refers, but it is evident that if it did there would be no equivalence between Castle's statement of identity and its heterosexual counterpart; in a patriarchal culture founded on the homosocial, a 'heterosexual' is not necessarily an individual whose 'primary *emotional* and erotic *allegiance* [emphasis added]'⁹³ is to the opposite sex. What, then, would it mean to say: 'I am a heterosexual'? In the context of a discussion of Wittig's work, Butler suggests that 'heterosexuality offers normative sexual positions that are intrinsically impossible to embody.'⁹⁴ Hence, when she refers to the 'spectres of discontinuity and incoherence' which are both 'prohibited and produced by the very laws that seek to establish causal or expressive' relations between 'sex, gender, sexual practice and desire',⁹⁵ these 'spectres' embody discontinuities *within* heterosexuality as much as departures from it.

Waters' novel suggests the possibility that the spinster has a sexuality other than that sanctioned by dominant forms of heterosexuality; I would argue that in *Affinity* this possibility mobilises not the production of a retrospective lesbian identity but a more fundamental questioning of categories of sexuality, including the category of heterosexuality itself. As a spinster Margaret is defined by her place outside of the normative regime of reproductive sexuality; she is a woman without access to the means by which to legitimately fulfil her 'natural' destiny as mother: marriage. As a 'spectre of discontinuity'⁹⁶ within the 'heterosexual matrix'⁹⁷ she manifests a kind of 'blindspot' which is the effect of the conflation of heterosexuality with reproductive sexuality (a conflation arguably mimicked by the equation of spinster and lesbian). Writing about the way in which 'nonreproductive sexuality' – which may or may not be a 'homosexual' sexuality – challenges normative reproductive sexuality, Judith Roof has suggested that:

> The reduction of a larger field of sexuality to two categories [heterosexual and homosexual] is partly an effect of narrative's binary operation within a reproductive logic; in this sense there are really only two sexualities: reproductive sexuality, which is associated with difference and becomes metaphorically heterosexual, and nonreproductive sexuality associated with sameness, which becomes metaphorically homosexual.⁹⁸

A nominal heterosexual, the spinster is nevertheless placed within the category of non-reproductive sexuality. Attributing the 'apparitional' qualities of the spinster in *Affinity* exclusively to an incipient lesbian identity risks obscuring the extent to which she troubles categories of *hetero*sexual identity by exposing their instability. Roof argues that 'sexuality's position as licit or illicit depends upon its reproductive use; its intelligibility exists in relation to the reproductive narrative.'[99] The sexualities of the spinster and of the lesbian are rendered unintelligible – and invisible – because they are perceived to be non-reproductive; they confound the reproductive narrative which cannot account for them.

The 'spectres' of discontinuity embodied by female same-sex desire in *Affinity*, I would argue, are symptomatic of an instability and incoherence endemic to normative constructions of heterosexuality. Roof has written that representations of lesbian sexuality signify the 'failure' of a symbolic system and hence are equated with the unaccountable or incomprehensible:

> Operating as points of systematic failure, configurations of lesbian sexuality often reflect the complex incongruities that occur when the logic or philosophy of a system becomes self-contradictory, *visibly fails to account for something*, or cannot complete itself. Simultaneously, lesbian sexuality instigates the overly compensatory and highly visible return of the terms of the ruptured system that mend and mask its gaps [emphasis added].[100]

The 'failure' to which Roof refers, then, is an effect of the inherent contradictions within normative heterosexuality, which rely on constructions of homosexuality to shore up its boundaries. If Margaret's identity cannot be located within identifiable and visible categories, this is not due to a failure of lesbian identity, or of lesbian/feminist authorship; the representation of Margaret's subjective experience of her own identity is all the more powerful because of the way in which it confounds heteronormative categories of sexual and gendered identity.

In conclusion, *Affinity* is not a historical 'coming out' narrative, and not simply because such a motif would have been anachronistic. In the context of a critical interrogation of the 'politics of visibility', Roof has suggested that:

> Together, visibility and invisibility refer obsessively to a knowledge of sexuality that performs a disciplinary function. When visibility is the privileged register of knowledge's proliferation and consumption, it conceals even the telling asymmetry that the sexual identities in question are the only sexual identities that must be rendered visible in the first place.[101]

Roof questions the way in which 'coming out' and 'outing' narratives work within the normative regimes of visibility:

If the lesbian character's visibility is the end product of a narrative struggle between inner and outer that results in knowledge about sexual truth and identity, then coming out stories embody the same reproductive narrative trajectory as dominant cultural stories.[102]

The purported 'invisibility' of female same-sex desire is a complex and paradoxical condition; the 'visibility' denied to female same-sex desire is also implicated in what is authorised as legible, intelligible and legitimate. Invisibility as a trope denoting the cultural and historical absence of representations of female same sex desire cannot easily posit visibility as its remedy; that which is capable of being seen is not merely that which exists but that which is authorised to be read, to be understood, to be legitimised. Butler has argued that 'for heterosexuality to remain intact as a distinct social form, it *requires* an intelligible concept of homosexuality and also requires the prohibition of that conception in rendering it culturally unintelligible [emphasis in original].'[103] It could be argued that the desire for visibility which *Affinity* refuses may be a heteronormative desire: that is, a desire on the part of heterosexuality to have its own status confirmed as normative through the reiterative drama of the visible identification of the homosexual as other. The materialisation of female same-sex desire in *Affinity* defies the prohibition against visibility; however, by remaining 'unintelligible' in heterosexual terms, these 'affinities' subvert the very intelligibility which heterosexuality claims for itself.

Notes

1. See also Rachel Carroll, 'Rethinking Generational History: Queer Histories of Sexuality in neo-Victorian Feminist Fiction', *Studies in the Literary Imagination*, 39: 2 (2006), pp. 135–47.
2. Sarah Waters, *Affinity* (London: Virago, 1999), p. 289.
3. Ibid., p. 348.
4. Judith Butler, *Gender Trouble: Feminism and the Subversion of Identity* [1990] (New York and London: Routledge, 1999), p. xx.
5. Ibid., pp. 315–16.
6. Ibid., p. 209.
7. Ibid., p. 163.
8. Ibid., p. 210.
9. Ibid., p. 240.
10. Yopie Prins, 'Greek Maenads, Victorian Spinsters', in Richard Dellamora (ed.), *Victorian Sexual Dissidence* (Chicago: University of Chicago Press, 1999), p. 46.
11. Waters, op. cit., p. 208.
12. Janet Fink and Katherine Holden, 'Pictures from the Margins of Marriage: Representations of Spinsters and Single Mothers in the Mid-Victorian

Novel, Inter-War Hollywood Melodrama and the British Film of the 1950s and 1960s', *Gender and History*, 11: 2 (1999), p. 233.
13. See Monique Wittig, 'One is Not Born a Woman', in *The Straight Mind and Other Essays* (Boston: Beacon Press, 1992), pp. 9–20.
14. Waters, op. cit., p. 58.
15. Ibid., p. 199.
16. Ibid., p. 199.
17. Ibid., pp. 252–3.
18. Ibid., pp. 161–2.
19. Waters, op. cit., p. 214.
20. See Martha Vicinus, *Independent Women: Work and Community for Single Women: 1850–1920* (London: Virago, 1985).
21. Waters, op. cit., p. 203.
22. Ibid., p. 263.
23. Ibid., p. 96.
24. Ibid., p. 96.
25. Ibid., p. 240.
26. Ibid., p. 244.
27. Ibid., p. 58.
28. Ibid., p. 274.
29. Ibid., p. 22.
30. Ibid., p. 23.
31. Ibid., p. 8.
32. See Michel Foucault, *Discipline and Punish: The Birth of the Prison* [1975], trans. Alan Sheridan (Harmondsworth: Penguin, 1977) and *Madness and Civilisation: A History of Insanity in the Age of Reason* [1961], trans. Richard Howard (London: Random House, 1965).
33. Waters, op. cit., p. 256.
34. Ibid., p. 256.
35. Ibid., p. 257.
36. Ibid., p. 179.
37. Ibid., p. 88.
38. Ibid., p. 177.
39. Ibid., p. 178.
40. Ibid., p. 342.
41. Ibid., p. 29.
42. Ibid., p. 91.
43. Ibid., p. 223.
44. Ibid., p. 252.
45. Ibid., p. 255.
46. Ibid., p. 58.
47. Ibid., p. 20.
48. Ibid., p. 275.
49. Michel Foucault, *The Will to Knowledge: The History of Sexuality: Volume One* [1976], trans. Robert Hurley (1978) (London: Penguin, 1978), p. 84.
50. Waters, op. cit., p. 289.
51. Ibid., p. 7.
52. Ibid., p. 102.

53. Ibid., p. 103.
54. Ibid., p. 204.
55. Ibid.
56. Ibid., p. 23.
57. For a discussion of the architecture of the prison see Lucie Armitt and Sarah Gamble, 'The Haunted Geometries of Sarah Waters' *Affinity*', *Textual Practice*, 20: 1 (2006), pp. 141–59.
58. Waters, op. cit., p. 47.
59. Ibid., p. 182.
60. Ibid., p. 223.
61. Ibid., p. 17.
62. Ibid., p. 267.
63. Ibid., p. 222.
64. Ibid., p. 252.
65. Ibid., p. 189.
66. Ibid., p. 286.
67. Ibid., p. 274.
68. Ibid., p. 30.
69. Ibid., p. 70.
70. Ibid., p. 29.
71. Ibid., p. 41.
72. For a feminist analysis of the discourses and practices of spiritualism, see Alex Owen, *The Darkened Room: Women, Power, and Spiritualism in Late Victorian England* (London: Virago, 1989), Molly McGarry, 'Spectral Sexualities: Nineteenth Century Spiritualism, Moral Panics, and the Making of U.S. Obscenity Law', *Journal of Women's History*, 12: 2 (2000), pp. 8–29 and Marlene Tromp, 'Spirited Sexuality: Sex, Marriage, and Victorian Spiritualism', *Victorian Literature and Culture* (2003), pp. 67–81.
73. Waters, op. cit., p. 210.
74. Ibid., p. 275.
75. Ibid., p. 275.
76. Ibid., p. 275.
77. Ibid., p. 110.
78. Ibid., p. 260.
79. Ibid., p. 315.
80. Ibid., p. 242.
81. Ibid., p. 289.
82. Ibid., p. 58.
83. Annamarie Jagose, 'Remembering Miss Wade: *Little Dorrit* and the Historicizing of Female Perversity', *GLQ: Journal of Gay and Lesbian Studies*, 4: 3 (1998), p. 442.
84. Ibid., p. 424.
85. Ibid., p. 442.
86. Sheila Jeffreys, *The Spinster and Her Enemies: Feminism and Sexuality, 1880–1930* [1985] (Melbourne: Spinifex, 1997), p. 100.
87. Terry Castle, *The Apparitional Lesbian: Female Homosexuality and Modern Culture* (New York: Columbia University Press, 1993), p. 2.
88. Ibid., p. 4.

89. Ibid., p. 15.
90. Eve Kosofsky Sedgwick, *Epistemology of the Closet* (Berkeley and Los Angeles: University of California Press, 1990), pp. 82–3.
91. Sedgwick, op. cit., p. 82.
92. Castle, op. cit., p. 15.
93. Ibid., p. 15.
94. Butler, op. cit., p. 155.
95. Ibid., p. 23.
96. Ibid., p. 23.
97. Ibid., p. 9.
98. Judith Roof, *Come as You Are: Sexuality and Narrative* (New York: Columbia University Press, 1996), p. xxix.
99. Ibid., p. 35.
100. Judith Roof, *A Lure of Knowledge: Lesbian Sexuality and Theory* (New York: Columbia University Press, 1991), p. 5.
101. Roof, *Come As You Are*, op. cit., pp. 146–7.
102. Ibid., p. 106.
103. Butler, op. cit., p. 98.

Chapter 2

Telling tales out of school: spinsters, scandals and intergenerational heterosexuality in Zoë Heller's *Notes on a Scandal*

A school is a fitting location for a depiction of intergenerational sexuality given the prominence of motifs of sexual tutelage and pedagogic hierarchy in representations of such relationships. It is also the time-honoured professional location of the spinster, whose reputation as a 'surplus woman' from the nineteenth century onwards is offset by employment in the task of social reproduction through ancillary attachment to other people's families. However, where an intergenerational sexual relationship between an adult male and a younger female aligns with pedagogic, generational and gendered hierarchies, the sexual relationship between a mature, married mother and an adolescent boy depicted in Zoë Heller's 2003 novel *Notes on a Scandal* troubles such sexual and gendered structures of power. Feminist activists and theorists have worked hard to challenge discourses and practices which normalise inequities of power in heterosexual relationships; 'intergenerational' relationships between adult men and women are placed in a spectrum whose nadir is the sexual abuse of girls by adult men, including fathers. As such, it seems unlikely that a literary depiction of a sexual relationship between a mature man, father and husband and an adolescent girl would escape feminist censure on ideological grounds. As a mature woman, mother and wife, Sheba's sexual liaisons in *Notes on a Scandal* challenge assumptions to do with women's, and especially mothers', sexual agency, but to what extent can this subversion of gendered power justify what in other contexts would be seen as an abuse of generational power? A confessional narrative, enlisting first-person address and employing the device of the private journal, would seem an appropriate literary strategy for an account of a sexual experience likely to provoke public disapproval and outrage and hence to produce personal guilt and shame. However, the confession which the narrative foregrounds is not that of the female heterosexual sexual transgressor, Sheba Hart, but that of her confidante, Barbara Covett. As her name implies, Barbara takes up a vicarious position in relation both to Sheba's affluent and expansive family life and to her secretive sexual adventures. As such, Barbara's investment in the narrative she offers to recount is suspect and indeed, through an act motivated by thwarted desire and vengeful spite, Barbara is revealed to be complicit in Sheba's public exposure and downfall. In effect, troubling questions about female heterosexual agency are displaced through the production of a more familiar and less threatening stereotype of non-normative female heterosexuality: the spinster as socially marginal, emotionally suspect and sexually repressed. In other words, in *Notes on a Scandal*, the satirical momentum of a narrative ostensibly investigating deviant female heterosexuality finds its displaced target in a figure who has long functioned as a coded repository for homophobic ridicule.

From 'spinster' to 'singleton' and back again: the sexuality of the 'single woman'

Generational, and indeed class, differences are often the satirical focus of Zoë Heller's comedy of manners, differences not only between Sheba and her teenage working-class pupil, Connolly, but also between the sometimes chaotic affluence of Sheba's privileged family life and the scrupulous respectability of Barbara's singular lower-middle-class existence. Set in 1996, Sheba is 42 years old at the time of her affair with Connolly; Barbara is 'of an age … at which retirement is a plausible option',[1] as the headmaster, Pabblem, puts it in an effort to secure Barbara's retirement as a compromised solution to her complicity in Sheba's misdemeanour. Barbara is, then, of a generation which was of an age to take advantage of the 'sexually permissive' late 1960s and early 1970s and, in the context of the Second Wave of the women's movement, to understand a detachment from marital and familial convention as empowering and emancipatory. The fact that Barbara's values seem to belong to an earlier time and are perhaps more in line with those of her parents' generation does not detract from the novel's social and historical acuity; on the contrary, it reflects the way in which 'the 1960s' have become a universalising experience through retrospective mythologising, rather than a lived reality. What is more notable is the way in which Barbara is depicted as a spinster in this novel and the way in which the pathologising, and even criminalising associations that this apparently outdated term possesses are mobilised anew in a late twentieth-century fiction.

In 1862, W. R. Greg famously pronounced on the 'disproportionate and quite abnormal' number of unmarried women, diagnosing women's single status as 'both productive and prognostic of much wretchedness and wrong', resulting in a female existence which is 'independent and incomplete'.[2] A demographic reality becomes an ideological crisis given the discrepancy between the actuality of the unmarried state for many women and the dominant Victorian discourses of middle-class femininity, which privileged the marital and familial hearth and home as a woman's proper sphere. Contemporary and subsequent women's rights and feminist activists and scholars have documented the productive and meaningful role which many single women have historically assumed. Indeed, as Alison Oram has observed 'a specific politics of spinsterhood existed in late nineteenth-century and early twentieth-century suffrage feminism'[3] which dignified and politicised spinsterhood as elective, strategic and fulfilling. However, the stigma of the 'surplus' woman, whose unfulfilled reproductive potential renders her redundant in a way that does not extend to the lifelong bachelor, persists. The generations of women 'denied' husbands by the two world wars of the twentieth century have been met with a more compassionate response, but the sense that spinsterhood is on some level a tragic plight remains. The 'wretchedness and wrong' diagnosed by Greg is attributed to the thwarting of women's 'natural' maternal instincts; the advent of sexology, and its popularisation in the first decades of the twentieth century, left a perhaps more insidious legacy – the pathologising of the spinster's sexuality. While emerging discourses of sexology acknowledged the existence of female sexual desire in ways that countered its denial or repression in earlier ideologies their emphasis on sexual hygiene and normative function rendered its expression through reproductive sexuality mandatory both for individual and societal health. Alison Oram has commented on the 'pathologising of spinsters' sexuality'[4] by the discourses of sexology which made marriage and motherhood imperative in new terms, albeit it with familiar ideological effect: 'These new "sciences" placed a premium upon marriage, motherhood and heterosexual fulfilment for women's psychological happiness, a condition spinsters were unable to attain.'[5] Sheila Jeffreys makes explicit the ideological implications of this imperative for those who chose to resist or were unable to comply: 'The sexologist offered the "freedom" only to marry and engage willingly in sexual intercourse. Spinsterhood, lesbianism, celibacy and heterosexual practices apart from sexual intercourse were condemned.'[6] As Janet Fink and Katherine Holden have noted, the popularisation of assumptions underlying sexological discourses can be held accountable for the production of abiding, disparaging and even hateful modern stereotypes of the unmarried woman as 'miserable old maid' or 'rigid frustrated spinster'.[7] These discourses also contribute to the sexualisation of the spinster – or more properly, the equation of the spinster with problematic or repressed sexuality. Once a woman defined by her marital state she now becomes, following Foucault, a default sexual type, albeit defined by her desexualised state. In modern parlance the 'spinster' does not merely denote marital status but a failure to acquire sexual experience; in previous eras the two might be thought of as synonymous but with the detachment of female sexual experience from marriage, and the equation of the former with personal fulfilment and liberation, 'spinster' has become an outmoded term used to denote a woman out of step with her times. Moreover, with the equation of female sexual experience and personal liberty – the somewhat conflicted legacy both of the sexual liberation of the 1960s and 1970s and of the Second Wave of the women's movement – the mature woman without sexual experience is pitied, suspected and demeaned in new ways.[8] The slippage in the connotations of the term are captured by Jeffreys: 'Now, when women are expected to engage in sex with men whether married or not, the word 'spinster' is generally reserved for those who do not.'[9] This heterosexual sexual imperative is a new way to police and coerce women's sexuality; if its expression was once repressed, it now seems compulsory. The complex relationship between the Second Wave and 'postfeminism', whether understood as uneven continuation or reactionary repudiation, is manifest in the figure of the 'singleton', the specific literary legacy of Helen Fielding's *Bridget Jones's Diary*, a significant progenitor of the 1990s and 2000s 'chick lit' boom. Where 'sex and the single girl' could be seen as pioneering literary territory for popular fiction for women in the Second Wave era, here sexual agency and pleasure is subordinated, albeit with self-conscious irony, to the project of securing commitment from a male partner and remedying the personal misery of being a 'singleton'.[10] In her landmark text *Independent Women: Work and Community for Single Women: 1850–1920*, Martha Vicinus described the 'passion for meaningful work, so often underestimated and misunderstood' as 'the sacred center of nineteenth-century single women's lives and communities';[11] if such a vocation contained an element of sublimation this served to dignify rather than demean. By contrast the singleton's career is often revealed to be a poor substitute for her stalled personal 'career' and any investment in it is ultimately exposed as delusion manufactured by the mythical 'have it all' feminism.

Heller's Barbara may seem very removed from Fielding's Bridget but in a certain sense there is a continuity; Barbara, as a 'senior singleton', has as thoroughly internalised negative constructions of her single state as Bridget and suffers comparable agonies of shame and desperation. As an experienced teacher Barbara is, by all accounts, a highly effective professional enjoying a degree of hard-earned seniority in her workplace; her occupation and experience do not expose her to the personal humiliations suffered by Bridget, but there is a sense in which her working life is made to reflect her own perceptions of her single status, ensuring that she remains captive to the world of family, and by extension marriage, from which she is removed.

Teaching has long been seen as an appropriate employment for unmarried women, and indeed in previous eras was one of the few respectable occupations open to women unable to rely on the economic support of their families. As Heather Julien has observed, the instruction of children – whether in a school or as a private governess – has been seen as 'continuous with and related to the primary work of mothering'.[12] As such, teaching provides the spinster with compensatory access to the maternal role denied her by her unmarried state; the selflessness of mothering gives way to the perhaps greater self-abnegation of caring for other people's children. This vicarious relation to the family is further complicated by the compromised class status of the female teacher or governess – 'a lady "in disguise" as a worker' or as 'workers disguised as ladies'.[13] The competing discourses of female emancipation and pathologisation are evident in key literary representations of unmarried women as teachers, from the stoicism of Charlotte Brontë's eponymous heroine in *Jane Eyre* (1847) and Lucy Snowe in *Villette* (1853), both fond and dismissive of the frivolous femininity of their charges, to Henry James's implicitly hysterical governess in *The Turn of the Screw* (1989), fixated both on her absent master and the ghost of the flagrant Quint, and culminating with the scandal which serves to ruin the lives and careers of the protagonists of Lillian Hellman's *The Children's Hour* (1961). Discourses of suspicion serve to cast into doubt the vocation of the unmarried female teacher and here the discourses of sexology seem to find a double target: the spinster, whose sexuality is already diagnosed as problematically frustrated, now becomes the target of anxieties about contagion and corruption. As Julien writes: 'Anti-spinsterism vilified single women teachers as narrow-minded, sexually "thwarted" and even predatory.'[14] In a discussion of the representation of male and female homosexuality in films of the late Hollywood Production Code era, Julia Erhart suggests that 'libel, slander [and] gossip' act as the 'names of homosexuality';[15] gossip and insinuation play an equally important role in *Notes on a Scandal*. Barbara is herself the agent, not the target, of gossip relating to sexual misconduct in the comprehensive school in which she teaches; it is heterosexual transgression which is subject to legal and criminal intervention. Contrary to one trend in the depiction of the spinster teacher, Barbara is not depicted as the source of sexual danger to her pupils, but rather Sheba, the wife and mother. But insinuation is deployed against Barbara by narrative strategies which prompt us to bring a hermeneutics of suspicion not only to the compromised reliability of her narration but also to the question of her sexuality.

Consorting and conspiring: the covetous spinster

Barbara Covett is a mature professional woman, unmarried and without children; the independence, autonomy and vocational satisfaction such an existence might offer is undercut, however, by her perception of herself as a figure more likely to attract pity and ridicule than command respect and admiration. Barbara does not embrace her unmarried state as figuring freedom and choice, as outlined in Suzette A. Henke's affirmative account of the twentieth-century spinster: 'She has freely chosen to eschew the categories of traditional womanhood and her choice implicitly subverts received ideas about social order, family relationship, and interdependence.'[16] Rather, it would seem that Barbara has thoroughly internalised the disparaging and pathologising constructions of the female single state. 'Spinster' might seem an outdated term to employ in the postfeminist era but its post-sexology negative associations are apparent in Barbara's self-perception. Moreover, Barbara's social unease at her unattached status makes her susceptible to media-manufactured fantasies of coupledom and she is, like Fielding's Bridget Jones, both scathing of and deeply envious of the 'Smug Marrieds'.[17] Barbara describes Sheba's married life with Richard – 'the dinner parties, the French holidays, the house buzzing with colleagues and children and ex-wives and family friends'[18] – as 'the stuff of newspaper "Living" sections'.[19] So closely does this 'intoxicating . . . [and] raucous domesticity'[20] evoke the upper-class bohemia conjured by lifestyle publishing that Barbara begins to doubt its authenticity: 'Sooner or later I always grew incredulous. This was all make-believe, wasn't it? Surely the family ceased to exist when I wasn't there?'[21] Sheba's home-life seems designed to taunt and tantalise Barbara, whose satirical commentary is so suggestive of a sublimated yearning to belong. The most unlikely candidate for a romantic date – her colleague Brian Bangs – nevertheless inspires a ready fantasy of escape from the single life. The terms in which she describes the life from which she seeks to be liberated reveal the contempt in which she holds her own existence: 'I pictured myself shedding my old, unfortunate self and stepping forth into the light and air of the regular world. I would cease to be the shut-in biddy waiting around for an invitation from my one, married friend.'[22] Barbara's contempt extends to her single peers, who she perceives as belonging to a common type: one defined not only by its alienation from what she perceives to be the warmth, intimacy and purpose of married and family life but also by its alienation from its own kind. The unhappily single, in Barbara's view, recoil from each other as carriers of the stigma with which they know themselves to be infected: 'Lonely people are terrible snobs about one another, I've found. They're afraid that consorting with their own kind will compound their freakishness.'[23] Brian is quickly restored to his status as object of satirical contempt when his 'date' with Barbara turns out to be a pretext to pursue, by indirect means, his crush on Sheba. As a bachelor accused of harbouring pitiful delusions about his capacity to remedy his single state, Brian is certainly one of Barbara's 'kind'. In this way, the stigma extends equally to single men, but as a mature single woman Barbara is subject – or subjects herself – to specifically gendered stereotypes. Tellingly, Barbara's unease with her single state is not assuaged but rather exacerbated by female companionship. Even the cherished companionship of her now estranged friend Jennifer Dodd compounds a cruelly disparaging self-image:

> Alone, each of us was safely unremarkable – invisible, actually – as plain women over the age of forty are to the world. Together, though, I always suspected that we were faintly comic: two screamingly unhusbanded ladies on a day out. A music-hall act of spinsterhood.[24]

While Barbara's behaviour does attract critical, and even slanderous, comment at times in the novel, there is little evidence to suggest that others share her judgement of herself as a spinster; it would seem that she is her own audience as far as her 'turn' as a figure of ridicule is concerned. The first-person narrative employed in this novel certainly reinforces the 'hall of mirrors' effect an unreliable narrator can induce; a closed world consisting only of distorted reflections of herself. This narrative strategy arguably serves to pathologise Barbara; her very actions and experience being attributable to her own internal distortions, rather than the cultural and historical context which forms her. Indeed, the narrative draws on some familiar tropes to render singleness absurd, pitiful and even pathological. In time-honoured fashion, Barbara is a cat owner whose emotional investment in her pet is depicted as disproportionate and even hysterical; Portia's death, and Sheba's inadequate response to it, is a pivotal event in the genesis of Barbara's self-described 'very reprehensible behaviour'.[25] A stern disciplinarian at work and a pragmatic confidante to Sheba, Barbara's solitary outbursts of emotion are depicted as exceeding their cause and socially disruptive; the volume of her sobs of frustration in trying to choose a suitable outfit for her first family dinner with Sheba prompts the tenant above to bang warningly on the floor. Later she strikes her own head against the steering wheel of her car, oblivious to the impression made on passers-by.

Barbara's unreliability as a narrator is integral to the narrative's ironic effects. Her sublimated investment in the narrative she recounts compromises her objectivity; moreover, a vicarious relation to the lives, and especially the family lives, of others serves both to discredit Barbara's perspective and to reinforce the sense that a spinster's life can only be ancillary. Somewhat like the fictional literary editor of Vladimir Nabokov's 1962 *Pale Fire*, Barbara's experiences and perspectives quickly exceed their status as 'footnotes' to the ostensible story. Her claims for narrative authority only serve to qualify the narrative objectivity of her account: 'I am presumptuous enough to believe that I am the person best qualified to write this small history. I would go so far as to hazard that I am the *only* person [emphasis in original].'[26] It becomes quickly apparent that Barbara's capacity for self-knowledge is in question. Her attachment to Sheba is shadowed in the novel by Barbara's history of attachments to other women but it is the narrative strategy itself, in *Notes on a Scandal*, which lays insinuating siege to Barbara's sexuality, offering the reader an implied knowledge to which Barbara herself does not have access.

Barbara is a woman whose history of passionate attachments to other women is disclosed in such a way as to implicitly pathologise and even criminalise. Sheba is not the first female colleague with whom Barbara has established a passionate friendship; Sheba, like Jennifer Dodd before her, is first 'rescued' from an alliance with an unsuitable colleague and then assumed as the object of an exclusive friendship. Jennifer would seem to be the willing and reciprocating recipient of Barbara's attachment, given the evidence of their shared holiday, but their estrangement casts Barbara as abnormally possessive and demanding. Barbara's incomprehension at Jennifer's withdrawal is itself incriminating in a narrative which has schooled us to doubt rather than sympathise with Barbara's testimony: 'Beyond some mysterious references to my being "too intense", she refused to furnish *any* explanation for her decision . . . she actually threatened to take out a legal injunction against me if I did not leave her alone [emphasis in original].'[27] When Barbara encounters Jennifer and her new boyfriend his 'aggressive posture'[28] and 'insolent and challenging'[29] manner culminate in an embrace suggestive of sexual rivalry:

> Evidently in some sort of fury, he turned to Jennifer, grasped her by the shoulders and kissed her. The aim, it seems, was to assert his proprietorial

rights over my friend. When he finally released her, he fixed me with a horrible smile and made an obscene gesture.[30]

In pitting Barbara as a dangerous rival in a struggle to claim Jennifer, Jason's reaction seems homophobic in its venom and yet the narrative persists in depicting Barbara as a trespasser requiring forcible expulsion. In this context the 'certain personal difficulties ... experienced with staff members'[31] in her first teaching post in a private school in Scotland also act as insinuating evidence of predatory behaviour. When Barbara's rival, Sue, instigates rumours implying 'some sort of Sapphic love affair'[32] Barbara claims to be neither surprised or troubled: 'I was not distressed on my account. I have been on the receiving end of this sort of malicious gossip more than once in my career and I am quite accustomed to it by now.'[33] The persistence of the rumours, combined with Barbara's belittling dismissal of 'Sapphic' love, conspire to paint a portrait of a woman unable to see what is self-evident to others: the reality of her desires. Barbara evidently does not identify as lesbian, and her attachments to women are anyway complex and ambivalent, but it does seem that the narrative depicts her, by strategies of insinuation, as a repressed lesbian; in this way the homophobic and heteronormative conflation of the spinster and the lesbian is perpetuated. Feminist scholars such as Martha Vicinus have sought to recover the spinster from historical contempt and Jeffreys and others have found in the 'spinster' a hidden history of lesbian existence. In an era in which constraints on the public expression of lesbian identity and desire in mainstream British culture are less rigid and punishing, the spinster as 'repressed lesbian' can be depicted in newly pathologising ways: as someone whose thwarted sexuality is internal, not external, in origin and hence attributable to personal pathology, not societal responsibility. She is both blamed for her own repression and constructed as the source of a deceitful, manipulative and ultimately illegitimate desire.

School for scandal: intergenerational heterosexuality

In *An Education*, the 2009 film adapted from Lynn Barber's memoir, a precocious teenage girl and her aspirational parents are 'seduced' by an older man whose charm and apparent affluence seem to fulfil a fantasy of social mobility.[34] The girl temporarily forfeits her grammar-school education and her career as a star pupil being coached for Oxbridge entry to undertake a more glamorous and worldly 'education'. This film illustrates both the conflation of sexuality, education and social mobility and the normalisation of intergenerational sexuality between an older man and younger woman or girl; while her affair violates school codes of conduct, it is also the focus of envy and, moreover, her suitor's behaviour is in no way depicted as perverse or pathological. In *Notes on a Scandal*, Sheba's offer to provide one-to-one tutoring is prompted by a discovery that Connolly's special needs programme precludes him from participating in art classes; while some of their public rendezvous take place in locations which could be claimed to have edifying effects (such as Hampton Court and the National Portrait Gallery) her desire to expand Connolly's educational horizons is exposed as a romantic delusion, serving to provide a rationalisation for unorthodox encounters. Connolly's participation in what seems a rather self-serving pretext is equally expedient; moreover, the narrative focus is less on Connolly's upward mobility than on Sheba's downward trajectory. As Barbara comments: 'Until she met Connolly, Sheba had never had any intimate contact with a bona fide member of the British proletariat.'[35] Sheba's fascination with Connolly's working-class family life – the unexpected cleanliness of his home, the thinness of the walls in council properties, the synthetic fabric of his bedding – is distinctly condescending, but her class identity is also compromised by her attempts to play her part; she is embarrassed to be discovered rummaging in a high-street fashion shop for cheap 'sexy' underwear.

St George's comprehensive is in many ways a site of arrested development for the novel's protagonists. In describing it as a 'holding pen for Archway's pubescent proles'[36] Barbara reveals not only a latent contempt for her charges but also a sense of working beneath her station. A strict adherent of discipline and a sceptic with regard to education's socially transformative powers, her subject and her approach to it align her with conservative positions on schooling; history is not only a 'hard' humanities subject compared to the expressive art of Sheba's pottery, but one whose teaching has proved the flashpoint for ideological battles over education. As a traditionalist in a 'progressive' setting, Barbara is out of place; her sense of grievance at her enforced departure from a post at a fee-paying institution in Dumfries confirms a sense of her perceived natural home. St George's is depicted as a closed world as much for its staff as for its pupils. The staff room is riven by interpersonal tensions little different to those of a sixth-form common room: fractious cliques, unrequited crushes and competition for status and influence. Mild insubordination and satirical mockery of headmaster Pabblem's sanctimonious regime provides a comforting collective identity; as Barbara puts it, there is 'a certain pleasure in the cosy predictability of things being unsatisfactory'.[37] While Barbara may aspire to be above this staffroom culture, she is evidently an ardent player, subjecting the oblivious Sheba to a barrage of snubbing, blanking and theatrically judgemental looks as a punishment for her alliance with a rival. Like the pupils, the staff are subject not only to the regime of term and timetable but also of homework and detention; Barbara is summoned to the headmaster's office when her 'report' on an outbreak of indiscipline fails to make the grade. Barbara could be understood as the bright but mutinous 'star pupil' at St George's; working in an institution which fails to reflect her own sense of her deserved social station, her energies become locked in a battle with the head whose authority she does not find credible. 'Expelled' by her chosen exclusive school, she is also 'expelled' from St Georges when compelled to take early retirement to evade disciplinary action or even prosecution for her complicity in Sheba's affair. By contrast, Sheba is the underachieving privileged pupil with a seemingly constitutional failure to graduate. The daughter of a celebrated and formidable economist, she fails to complete her own degree studies and her teaching is depicted as unskilled and amateurish. Indeed, Sheba's formal education is diverted by her marriage to her university tutor – a relationship which returns us to the motif of sexuality and tutelage.

Sheba's marriage to an older male academic is depicted as an extension of her role as daughter to her intellectual father: 'The rules for being a hand maiden to a great, pompous man were more or less instinctive to her.'[38] The generational difference between Sheba and her husband – 'Sheba had mentioned that her husband was older than her; I was taken aback to discover by how much'[39] – is one which reminds us of the ways in which marriage is implicated in patriarchal hierarchies of power; the transition from her father's daughter to her older husband's wife is here one of continuity rather than difference. Barbara's surprise perhaps originates from a presumption about Sheba's power and agency as a sexually attractive woman; in an era in which women's sexual agency and choice is asserted by postfeminist discourses and exploited by the mass market, Sheba's 'failure' to choose a partner who is her equal in allure seems a dereliction of duty. Linda Alcoff has written that 'Cross-generational relations between old men and young women are the subject of so many approving cultural representations that they may seem to typify one of the normative scenarios for "romance".'[40] Intergenerational sexual relationships between older men and younger women or girls are normative in terms of gendered power; feminist theorists and activists have fought hard to wrest exploitative and abusive relationships between men and girls from a spectrum which threatens to normalise them. While Sheba is an adult above the age of consent when she begins her relationship with Richard she is nevertheless in an unequal power dynamic. The age differential between Sheba and Connolly is much more pronounced and, crucially, he is below the age of consent; as a consequence, Sheba is charged with 'indecent assault on a minor'[41] following the exposure of her affair with Connolly. There is nothing to suggest the use of force or coercion but the laws of consent criminalise the relationship on account of Connolly's age alone. In what ways, then, can Sheba's actions be theorised in feminist terms?

In *Interrogating Incest*, Vicki Bell writes that 'To desire someone younger than oneself, with less access to power than oneself, is certainly not an abnormal desire. It is the predominant construction of masculine desire in the contemporary form of heterosexuality.'[42] Sheba's desire for someone younger than herself is not a predominant construction of female heterosexual desire; popular cultural constructions of such desire have tended to be salacious and implicitly demeaning, suggesting a consumerist desire for status (through patronage and the possession of a 'toy boy') or a predatory sexual agency (the older woman as stealthy 'cougar');[43] in this way they are symptomatic of trends in postfeminist media culture which equate sexual agency with empowerment and desire with consumerism. However, the object of Sheba's sexual desire is not of high sexual status and her affair exposes her to ridicule not envy. Indeed, Sheba's affair does little to challenge gendered relations of power; if anything it serves to reinforce them. The scandal of the title of the novel finds its stage not in the courts, despite the dramatic potential such an event would offer, but in the tabloid media coverage of the case which transforms Sheba into a 'celebrity deviant'[44] and confirms popular perceptions of intergenerational relationships between older women and younger men or boys. The affair is so closely aligned with normative male heterosexual fantasies of sexual initiation by an older woman as to render the crime seemingly victimless. Feminist analyses of legal discourses and practices to do with the prosecution of child sexual abuse have challenged the ways in which female victims are depicted as seducing their abusers; such constructions render the abuser the victim of a 'knowing' child's actions and attribute blame to the victim as a morally or sexually corrupting agent. Male victims of female-perpetrated child sexual abuse, even after the 'discovery' of widespread child sexual abuse in the late 1970s and 1980s, have had to contend with a disbelief grounded in presumptions about women's capacity to abuse; the reality of female-perpetrated child sexual abuse challenges ideological constructions of femininity and female sexuality as passive and equations between male sexuality and penetration, and between penetration and abuse. The construction of the minor as the seducer persists in representations of boys in intergenerational sexual relationships as willing, active and even fortunate. Connolly in *Notes on a Scandal* is depicted as calculating and persistent in his pursuit of his teacher and as suffering no apparent harm as a consequence of their relationship. There is a tension between, on the one hand, reading Connolly as a boy victim and resisting narrative strategies to compromise his status as a child and, on the other hand, acknowledging Connolly as an apprentice man, exercising sexual power. Given the emphasis placed on sexual experience as demarcating an irreversible induction into knowledge and culpability, his implied lack of sexual 'innocence' serves to reinforce the implication that he is not an 'innocent victim'. In an infamous passage from *The History of Sexuality*, Foucault uses the example of the legal and medical examination of a farmhand who had molested a child as an illustration of how what he calls 'inconsequential bucolic pleasures'[45] became the object of state apparatus. Paraphrasing Foucault, we might suggest that female–male intergenerational sexuality in *Notes on a Scandal* is, in contrast to feminist perspectives on male–female equivalents, depicted as an 'inconsequential *metropolitan* pleasure', taking place as it does in some choice London locations, including a well-known site of same-sex male sexual liaisons, Hampstead Heath. Foucault's reference to 'simple-minded adults and alert children',[46] which arguably risks belittling the offence by excusing the perpetrator and displacing responsibility to the figure of the supposedly 'seductive child', is here mapped onto a narcissistic pottery teacher and an assiduous teenage boy.

As a male on the threshold of majority, Connolly exercises a certain sexual power which sustains gendered power relations. An emotional power is at work in public and private contexts in which Connolly withholds intimacy, becomes sullen, uncommunicative and passively aggressive. Sheba refuses to see his sexualised sketch of her as objectifying or pornographic but is offended when he makes sexually demeaning remarks during an intimate encounter: '"You're worried your vadge has gone loose."'[47] Their relationship follows some stereotypical patterns in terms of gendered behaviour with Sheba idealising and romanticising the relationship and rationalising Connolly's insensitive behaviour in terms that preserve both her image of him as vulnerable and needy and her sense of her own class power; on discovery of Connolly's hackneyed artistic rendition of her as a 'Foxy Lady' Sheba is 'not alarmed. On the contrary, she was pleased and rather flattered. In the brutal atmosphere of St George's, the gesture struck her as eccentrically innocent.'[48] By contrast, Connolly's actions can often be interpreted as expedient and designed to achieve ends to do not with sustained intimacy but with sexual access. Barbara's comments typify this interpretative tension, since they both suggest that 'power' is not the exclusive possession of the adult, but also perpetuate the notion of the victim as 'knowing' and hence guilty:

> The sort of young person who becomes involved in this kind of imbroglio is usually pretty wily about sexual matters. I don't mean just that they're sexually experienced – although that is often the case. I mean that they possess some instinct, some natural talent, for sexual power play.[49]

Indeed Barbara pronounces Connolly's initial overtures, as recounted by Sheba, 'harassment' and advises that Sheba report him to the headmaster to be disciplined.

Sheba's rationalisations of Connolly's insensitive behaviour suggests a willingness to tolerate what might be described as unreconstructed masculinity. Sheba's romanticisation of his soft porn fantasies and her interpretation of his unselfconscious sexual pursuit of her as an expression of a refreshingly uncomplicated working-class masculinity could be placed within the context of the emergence of the 'new lad' and his complex relationship to 'postfeminist' culture. Sheba's youth coincides with a very politicised era in terms of sexual politics; as the wife of an academic in a 'new' university it would seem unlikely for her not to be exposed to feminist ideas. However, there is no evidence of any engagement with the identity politics of the Second Wave; in a sense her 'retreatism'[50] – her embrace of marriage and family in preference to economic or professional opportunities or sexual freedoms – anticipates trends in postfeminist popular culture. In particular, Sheba's attempt to cast conformity as rebellion suggests a resistance to injunctions to escape historic norms which is defensively defiant: '"I told myself that it was subversive of me to be doing something so conventional."'[51] Sheba's relationship with Connolly can be understood as relating to issues of age and generation. Sheba's early marriage to an older man has paradoxical effects in terms of her generational identity; in one sense she 'loses' a period of early adulthood more often experienced as one of growing independence but in another sense her youth is artificially prolonged. In this sense her relationship with Connolly might be understood as an attempt to recapture her lost youth or to live out a kind of second adolescence. In this sense, Sheba might be counted among other literary representations of mid-life crisis acted out through intergenerational sexuality. Margaret Morganroth Gullette has argued that:

> Behind every story of pedophilia is a drama of normal human regret at growing older in the body, distorted by the protagonist's illusory attempt to circumvent his aging in *this* particular way, by trying to possess youth vicariously through the bodies of the young [emphasis in original].[52]

In this 1984 publication Gullette appears to use term 'pedophilia' rather problematically, simply to denote desire for the young, rather than to prescribe a specific sexually abusive behaviour or type. Sheba is unusual, by virtue of her gender, in this company, which includes Thomas Mann's Aschenbach in *Death in Venice* (1912) and Vladimir Nabokov's Humbert Humbert in *Lolita* (1955). However, the implications of ageing in relation to sexual appeal does not seem to preoccupy Sheba, who is depicted by Barbara as strikingly attractive in her early forties. Sheba's relationship with Connolly can also be understood as symptomatic of her extended youth as a result of her association, through her husband, with an older generation among whom she is always the younger woman:

> 'If anything, I think I've artificially prolonged my youth by being with Richard. I've been allowed to stay a child, don't you see? . . . I got old without knowing it, still imagining myself Daddy's best girl . . . Richard had been protecting me from confronting my own middle age.'[53]

Sheba's attraction to Connolly is rationalised through a complex set of male identifications: specifically, aversion to her 'progressive' male peers and identification with the unreconstructed fantasies of an older male generation. Sheba is flattered, rather than offended, by Connolly's presumption – 'no one, before Connolly, had ever truly *pursued* her [emphasis in original]'[54] – and attributes the absence of overtures from men of her own generation to the 'kind of men she had consorted with'.[55] Richard's colleagues are depicted as having adopted a code of sexual conduct informed by fear of feminist rebuke: 'They were all terrified at the thought of being "cheesy" or insensitive . . . Even when they told you that your dress was nice, they put it in quotation marks in case you took offence and slapped their faces.'[56] Feminism is here depicted as repressive and punitive and men as its beleaguered victims. Sheba's memory of the hostility underlying the sexual advances of a visiting professor captures the misogyny at work in some male heterosexual behaviour; however, when placed in the context of the 'kind of men'[57] fearful of making sexual faux pas, it seems to imply that feminism is itself responsible for producing sexual aggression: 'She had sensed something resentful about him, as if he begrudged her for having the power to attract him. The moment she resisted – or hesitated, actually – he had become very nasty and rude.'[58] In this context, Connolly's appeal lies in the fact that he is neither 'scared [nor] angry with her'.[59] With progressive or enlightened masculinity unmasked as hypocritical or dismissed as fearfully emasculated, the possibility of a sexual affair with a peer is altogether precluded. Moreover, in defending her own behaviour Sheba reveals an identification with, and perhaps nostalgia for, an older generation of men unconcerned about the sexual politics of their desires and unapologetic in their pursuit:

> 'You know when feminists get angry about older men chasing younger women? I never could get behind all that. I always sympathized with the old goats. And now I'm glad I did, because I see for myself what it is that can drive you mad about a beautiful young body.'[60]

Underlying Sheba's reckless persistence in her sexual relationship with Connolly – culminating in encounters in both family homes – is a seeming sense of entitlement to sexual pleasure. The transformation of a right to freedom of sexual expression into an entitlement to sexual pleasure is one way of charting the transition from feminism to post-feminism; for Second Wave feminism the assumption of sexual agency is the countermove to the struggle against sexual appropriation. In popular postfeminist discourses, sexual agency is equated with personal liberty and personal liberty sexualised to the degree that, as Rosalind Gill has argued, sexual agency becomes 'compulsory'.[61] Sheba's actions, despite their transgressive potential, take place in a kind of void as far as sexual politics are concerned; seemingly oblivious to the ways in which she is arguably exploiting a position of nominal power, she resists any attempt to bring her to consciousness of culpability. Conversely, nor does she attempt to articulate her actions in feminist terms: neither as a response to the suppression of her identity in successive relationships with paternal men (her father and husband) nor as subversively inverting the conventional gendered hierarchy at work in intergenerational relationships.

Intergenerational sexuality, feminism and queer theory

In the index to Eve Kosofsky Sedgwick's *Epistemology of the Closet*, the entry under 'pedagogy' reads '*See also* pederasty', and the entry for 'pederasty' reads '*See also* pedagogy';[62] this tautological indexing is indicative of a complex discursive conflation. References to 'pederasty' address a range of practices including 'child-love',[63] sexual choice 'within or between generations'[64] and the 'Greek pederastic or initiation model'.[65] The Greek precedent is evidence of the ways in which both intergenerational sexuality and same-sex practices have been historically and culturally constructed; here sexual relationships between men and boys are not just permitted but idealised as fulfilling an educative purpose. Indeed, the 'pedagogic-pederastic'[66] model fulfils a significant homosocial function, serving to perpetuate male hierarchies of power through the forging of intimate bonds between men. Citing Allan Bloom, Sedgwick suggests that 'the history of Western thought is importantly constituted and motivated by a priceless history of male–male pedagogic or pederastic relations.'[67] The 'pedagogic-pederastic'[68] model raises important questions with regard to the different ways in which intergenerational sexuality is analysed in feminist and queer theoretical frameworks. Firstly, it is evident that the 'pedagogic-pederastic'[69] model to which Sedgwick refers is highly gendered. It does not apply to female–male or female–female adult–minor relationships; adult women are not in the same relation to patriarchal power as men and hence girls cannot be apprenticed in its inheritance in the same way. Secondly, feminist theorists and activists have been at the forefront of efforts to identify and address child sexual abuse as a form of sexual oppression implicated in gendered power; in this context, the generational power difference seems exploitative at best and abusive at worst. Consent is a key issue in analysing child sexual abuse, with child protection activists arguing that no child can truly consent to sex with an adult. However, the age of consent laws have been used to criminalise same-sex practices which in heterosexual contexts would escape censure; hence a scepticism about the effects of state regulation on sexual freedom is understandable. Moreover, and finally, some theorists suggest that child sexuality is being denied and repressed through an emphasis on victimisation in child sexual abuse discourses. Indeed, when Steven Angelides refers to the '*feminist* erasure of child sexuality [emphasis added]'[70] in his essay 'Historicizing Affect, Psychoanalyzing History: Pedophilia and the Discourse of Child Sexuality', he aligns feminism with the forces of sexual regulation and posits it as complicit in disciplinary regimes of sexuality. If Heller's *Notes on a Scandal* invites the reader to view Sheba's prosecution as a legal absurdity, the reader of A. M. Homes's *The End of Alice* is left in no doubt about the abusive nature of its narrator's relationships with girls. However, Homes's novel enters more ambiguous territory in its depiction of a sexual relationship between a nineteen-year-old female college student and a twelve-year-old boy in which the categorical distinction between intergenerational sexuality and abuse is disturbingly blurred; *The End of Alice* provides the focus for the next chapter which will explore the tensions between differing feminist and queer perspectives on child sexuality in more detail.

Notes

1. Zoë Heller, *Notes on a Scandal* (London: Penguin, 2003), pp. 232–3.
2. Quoted in Martha Vicinus, *Independent Women: Work and Community for Single Women: 1850–1920* (London: Virago, 1985), pp. 3–4.
3. Alison Oram, 'Repressed and Thwarted, or Bearer of the New World? The Spinster in Inter-War Feminist Discourses', *Women's History Review*, 1: 3 (1992), pp. 416–17.
4. Ibid., p. 414.
5. Ibid.
6. Sheila Jeffreys, *The Spinster and Her Enemies: Feminism and Sexuality, 1880–1930* [1985] (Melbourne: Spinifex, 1997), p. 185.
7. Janet Fink and Katherine Holden, 'Pictures from the Margins of Marriage: Representations of Spinsters and Single Mothers in the Mid-Victorian Novel, Inter-War Hollywood Melodrama and the British Film of the 1950s and 1960s', *Gender and History*, 11: 2 (1999), p. 236.
8. For a discussion of literary representations of the postwar spinster see: Hope Howell Hodgkins, 'Stylish Spinsters: Spark, Pym, and the Postwar Comedy of the Object', *Modern Fiction Studies*, 54: 3 (2008), pp. 523–43 and Estella Tincknell, 'Jane or Prudence? Barbara Pym's Single Women, Female Fulfilment and Career Choices in the "Age of Marriages"', *Critical Survey*, 18: 2 (2006), pp. 31–44.
9. Jeffreys, op. cit., p. 175.
10. See Imelda Whelehan, *The Feminist Bestseller: From* Sex and the Single Girl *to* Sex and the City (New York and Basingstoke: Palgrave Macmillan, 2005).
11. Vicinus, op. cit., p. 1.
12. Heather Julien, 'School Novels, Women's Work, and Maternal Vocationalism', *NWSA Journal*, 19: 2 (Summer 2007), p. 118.
13. Ibid., p. 122.
14. Ibid., p. 121.
15. Julia Erhart, '"She Could Hardly Invent Them!" From Epistemological Uncertainty to Discursive Production: Lesbianism in *The Children's Hour*', *Camera Obscura*, 35 (1995), p. 87. Erhart is referring to three films: *Victim* (1961), *Tea and Sympathy* (1956) and *The Children's Hour* (1961).
16. Suzette A. Henke, 'The Ideology of Female (Re)Production: The Spinster in Twentieth-Century Literature', *Works and Days: Essay in the Socio-Historical Dimensions of Literature and the Arts*, 6: 1–2 (1988), p. 177.
17. Helen Fielding, *Bridget Jones's Diary* (London: Picador, 1996), p. 40.
18. Heller, op. cit., p. 122.
19. Ibid.
20. Ibid., p. 123.
21. Ibid., p. 124.
22. Ibid., p. 179.
23. Ibid., p. 114.
24. Ibid., pp. 114–15.
25. Ibid., p. 171.
26. Ibid., pp. 7–8. In a discussion of interwar female detectives in fiction, Kathy Mezei suggests that the spinster is 'uniquely situated as an instrument of

surveillance precisely because of her marginal and indeterminate position.' 'Spinsters, Surveillance, and Speech: The Case of Miss Marple, Miss Mole, and Miss Jekyll', *Journal of Modern Literature*, 30: 2 (2007), p. 104. However, whereas the Misses Marple, Mole and Jekyll are ultimately celebrated for exercising spinsterly surveillance in support of the social order, Barbara's assumption of epistemological authority is depicted as compromised and illegitimate.

27. Heller, op. cit., p. 35.
28. Ibid., p. 35.
29. Ibid.
30. Ibid.
31. Ibid., p. 39.
32. Ibid., p. 140.
33. Ibid.
34. *An Education* (USA, Lone Scherfig, 2009, screenplay Nick Hornby and Lynn Barber).
35. Heller, op. cit., p. 45.
36. Ibid., p. 20.
37. Ibid., p. 87.
38. Ibid., p. 124.
39. Ibid., p. 99.
40. Linda Martín Alcoff, 'Dangerous Pleasures: Foucault and the Politics of Pedophilia', in Susan J. Hekman (ed.), *Feminist Interpretations of Foucault* (University Park, PA: Pennsylvania State University Press, 1996), p. 116.
41. Heller, op. cit., p. 4.
42. Vikki Bell, *Interrogating Incest: Feminism, Foucault and the Law* (London: Routledge, 1993), p. 158.
43. This term was popularised by the launch in 2009 of an American television drama, *Cougar Town*, in which Courteney Cox plays a divorced woman in her forties who dates younger men.
44. Heller, op. cit., p. 166.
45. Michel Foucault, *The Will to Knowledge: The History of Sexuality: Volume One* [1976], trans. Robert Hurley (1978) (London: Penguin, 1978), p. 31.
46. Ibid.
47. Heller, op. cit., p. 151.
48. Ibid., p. 29.
49. Ibid., p. 83.
50. See Diane Negra, 'Quality Postfeminism? *Sex and the Single Girl* on HBO', *Genders*, 39 (2004), n.p.
51. Heller, op. cit., p. 108.
52. Margaret Morganroth Gullette, 'The Exile of Adulthood: Pedophilia in the Midlife Novel', *NOVEL: A Forum on Fiction*, 17: 3 (1984), p. 215.
53. Heller, op. cit., p. 126.
54. Ibid., p. 31.
55. Ibid.
56. Ibid.
57. Ibid.
58. Ibid.

59. Ibid., p. 32.
60. Ibid., pp. 160–1.
61. Rosalind Gill 'Empowerment/Sexism: Figuring Female Sexual Agency in Contemporary Advertising', *Feminism and Psychology*, 18: 1 (2008), p. 40.
62. Eve Kosofsky Sedgwick, *Epistemology of the Closet* (Berkeley and Los Angeles: University of California Press, 1990), p. 256.
63. Ibid., p. 8.
64. Ibid., p. 31.
65. Ibid., p. 134.
66. Ibid., p. 139.
67. Ibid., p. 55.
68. Ibid., p. 139.
69. Ibid.
70. Steven Angelides, 'Historicizing Affect, Psychoanalyzing History: Pedophilia and the Discourse of Child Sexuality', *Journal of Homosexuality*, 46: 1–2 (2003), p. 100.

Part Two: Transgressive female heterosexuality

Chapter 3

Queering Alice, killing Lolita: feminism, queer theory and the politics of child sexuality in A. M. Homes's *The End of Alice*

The narrator of A. M. Homes's controversial 1996 novel *The End of Alice* is an unrepentant perpetrator of child sexual abuse incarcerated in a high-security US correctional facility for the brutal sexualised murder of a twelve-year-old child: the Alice of the title. His compelling narrative voice uncomfortably insinuates the reader 'among our kind',[1] to use his term; we are positioned to occupy the subjective perspective of those belonging to his 'profession'[2] or 'calling',[3] and made party to the narrator's memories and fantasies of abusive and violent sexual encounters with pre-pubescent girls. This narrative interpellation is sufficient in itself to account for the recoil and resistance experienced and expressed by critics and readers on first encounter with this novel.[4] However, further discomfort awaits the reader when his narrative recounts his correspondence with an unnamed nineteen-year-old female college student who he depicts as another 'of his kind':[5] that is, a prospective perpetrator of sexual abuse, whose seduction of a twelve-year-old boy proceeds under the apparent tutelage of the veteran abuser and is described in graphic detail to the discomfort of the reader. While the novel is unambiguous in its depiction of its narrator's sexuality as abusive and violent, it also depicts the twelve-year-old Alice as an active if ambivalent sexual agent, testing out her emergent sexuality with an adult whose capacity to harm she does not anticipate. Matthew, the twelve-year-old boy, is also a willing participant in the sexual experiments initiated by his teenage neighbour. But here generational difference is less marked; both are positioned within the spectrum of adolescence, albeit at opposing ends. The graphic or provocative depiction of sexual acts deemed to be illicit or perverse has long served as a signifier of an avant-garde literary tradition, in texts from Georges Bataille's 1928 *Story of the Eye* to Anthony Burgess's 1962 *A Clockwork Orange*. Bourgeois sexual norms are often the target of such scandalous texts and, from a feminist standpoint, the recurring use of a woman's body to signify those norms is highly problematic, arguably reducing sexualised violence to a figurative signifier for something other than the actual abuse or exploitation of girls and women. A feminist counter-narrative of sexual abuse, however, privileges the voice of the silenced victim-survivor and insists on the political materiality of acts of sexual abuse. Hence, at first sight, *The End of Alice* departs quite radically from feminist imperatives with regard to child sexual abuse, which focus on the testimony of the female victim/survivor. Indeed, in its exploration of ambiguities of consent where child/adult sexuality is concerned the novel might seem to suggest that 'intergenerational' sexual relationships are not necessarily abusive.

Intergenerational is a term which can be used to describe sexual relationships between individuals of different ages, including those below the age of consent; it implies that such relationships can be consensual and non-harmful. From a feminist perspective the term seems problematic for its apparent failure to differentiate the non-consensual, the coercive and the abusive and for the way in which it elides hierarchies of gender; it does, perhaps, generate anxieties about attempts to rationalise or excuse the sexual exploitation of children and adolescents by adults. However, what this term does do is focus critical attention on the 'age of consent' as a legal concept which is historically and discursively constructed. It is evident from a feminist perspective that the age of consent has served patriarchal mandates, serving less to mark a girl's entry into sexual majority than her entry into the marriage market. But it is also evident that the construction of a distinct category of homosexual consent has criminalised expressions of same-sex desire between adolescents and young adults. Queer theorists have explored the relationship between intergenerational sexuality and heteronormative imperatives; where for feminism the normalisation of sexual relationships between men and girls is deeply suspect, for queer theory the specific forms of censure to which consensual same-sex intergenerational sexuality is subject is equally demanding of interrogation. This chapter is an attempt to conceptualise some of the complex issues which Homes's novel raises. My thesis, in brief, is that feminist perspectives on child sexuality continue to be shaped by radical feminist critiques of child sexual abuse which are premised on rigid gendered hierarchies of power and which see the sexual abuse of children as 'a manifestation of the oppression of females inherent in patriarchy'.[6] By contrast the 'queer child', as theorised by Natasha Hurley and Steven Bruhm, is one who 'doesn't quite conform to the wished-for way that children are supposed to be in terms of gender and sexual roles.'[7] As examples, Hurley and Bruhm suggest not only 'the child who displays interest in sex generally', including 'same-sex erotic attachments', but also, and significantly, the child who '[displays interest] in cross-generational attachments'.[8] Queer theoretical perspectives on child sexuality in relation to heteronormativity raise important questions for feminism but they also bring into relief persistent tensions between feminist and queer perspectives. I would like to tentatively suggest that A. M. Homes's *The End of Alice* brings a queer sensibility to a subject matter which has been claimed as a feminist prerogative. As such the discomfort it causes the feminist reader is worthy of investigation.

I wish to approach *The End of Alice* in a slightly oblique fashion by focusing on its intertextual relationship with two key texts which have also acted as recurring reference points in contemporary discourses on child sexuality: Vladimir Nabokov's 1955 *Lolita* and Lewis Carroll's 1865 *Alice's Adventures in Wonderland* and 1872 *Through the Looking-Glass*.

'Small ghosts': feminism, *Lolita* and child sexual abuse

The literary affinities between Homes's *The End of Alice* and Nabokov's *Lolita* are irresistible. There are strong narrative analogies; both recount a fugitive flight across the American landscape by car and posit the motel room as the sight of a child's 'end', and both are pseudo-psychiatric confessions written from within carceral captivity. Where Humbert Humbert in *Lolita* addresses the 'ladies and gentlemen of the jury',[9] presenting a range of spurious evidence including a set of 'lovely, glossy-blue picture postcards'[10] and retrospective constructions of letters, diaries and journals long since lost or destroyed, the narrator of *The End of Alice* similarly assembles 'my archive, my autobiography'[11] in anticipation of the interview with a parole board panel with which the novel concludes: 'They're telling my story and they're getting it wrong.'[12] Both confessions contain candid if fleeting admissions of self-knowledge – 'I know who I am'[13] – amid extensive self-justification: both admit to having 'stolen sex'[14] from young girls. In *The End of Alice* one of the narrator's child victims, procured from a children's shoe shop, accidentally knocks herself unconscious and hence provides an opportunity for the narrator to undertake an assault without resistance; Humbert similarly persists in his belief that Lolita is oblivious to his first covert exploitation: 'I felt proud of myself. I had stolen the honey of a spasm without impairing the morals of a minor.'[15] Both express a contempt and revulsion for mature female sexuality in terms which combine misogynistic sentiment with authorial satirical comment on bourgeois femininity. Humbert's girl bride Valeria is transformed by her induction into marital sexuality into a 'large, puffy, short-legged, big-breasted and practically brainless *baba* [emphasis in original]'.[16] The suburban wife and mother is similarly parodied by the narrator in *The End of Alice*: 'They are brainless-bat-full in the belfry, the last lost generation of homemakers, trained to be deaf, dumb and blind.'[17] The depiction of the 'homemaker', whether of the 1950s or the 1990s, as both signifier and victim of the reactionary forces of conformism is not beyond feminist recuperation but the accompanying aversion to the mature female body seems irredeemably misogynistic: 'uncorked, uncovered, they reek of sexual steam . . . I want it green, before it is ripe, before is has an odor easily discerned.'[18] In other words, the sexual abuse of girls becomes a displaced expression of hatred for adult women. Homes's *The End of Alice* consciously echoes one of the most contentious and disputed claims made by Humbert in Nabokov's novel: his attempt to evade responsibility for his own actions by projecting his own sexual agency onto his victim. When the narrator of *The End of Alice* declares, after his first sexual encounter with Alice, that 'in this rare case, it was she who took me',[19] his words echo those of his more famous literary precursor, Humbert Humbert who in *Lolita* similarly claimed: 'I am going to tell you something very strange: it was she who seduced me.'[20]

The critical reception history of *Lolita* tells us much about the necessity for feminist campaigns to recognise child sexual abuse as a crime against girls. The word 'Lolita' has entered public currency not as a way of denoting the sexual victimisation of children, but, as Abigail Bray has put it, as 'naming the sexual deviance of girls'.[21] For all that literary critics have recognised the unreliability of Humbert's narrative voice many have remained complicit in his construction of Lolita in the image of his own desire. As Eric Goldman has put it: 'From Humbert's perspective . . . it is essential to establish Lolita's experiences as utterly perverse so that he can feel exonerated from the charge of perverting her.'[22] Nabokov's intended ironies are called to account by his defenders in order to exonerate the author of charges of obscenity, but seemingly forgotten when it comes to Lolita's character. As Todd Bayma and Gary Allen Fine put it: 'By discrediting the victim, reviewers could more plausibly defend assertions of reader identification with Humbert and so make involvement in his narrative enjoyable.'[23] In a kind of narcissistic mirroring, critics seem to adopt Humbert's perspective in order to defend Nabokov – and implicitly themselves – against a moral slur whose source is found to be Lolita herself. Hence Lionel Trilling, the leading New York intellectual and liberal humanist critic, suggested: 'Perhaps [Humbert's] depravity is the easier to accept when we learn that he deals with a Lolita who is not innocent, and who seems to have very few emotions to be violated.'²⁴ Lolita is 'not innocent' according to Trilling simply because she has sexual experience.

By contrast, Elizabeth Patnoe's 1995 article 'Lolita Misrepresented, Lolita Reclaimed' exemplifies a radical feminist position which seeks to challenge the ideological erasure of sexual abuse evident in the novel's reception; it does so by reclaiming Lolita through a revisionary reading and by mobilising a discourse of experiential testimony. Patnoe writes:

> As if it is not enough that Humbert repeatedly violates Lolita and that she dies in the novel, the world repeatedly reincarnates her – and, in the process, it doubles her by co-opting, fragmenting, and violating her: it kills her again and again.²⁵

Her conflation of material and textual violence is further evident in her decision to incorporate into her published article a colleague's graphic disclosure of her abuse at the hands of her own father, adding:

> Is this shocking to you? Do you feel that in my writing it and your reading it, this person's trauma has been re-enacted? It has – through her, through and for me, and for you. And I imposed this trauma on you, thrust it into your eyes without your consent.²⁶

Hence, Patnoe contests readings of Lolita as deviant girl by emphasising her status as a victim of sexual violence – and does so by mobilising an understanding of representation as itself an instrument of violence. The insertion of a first-person testimony of sexual abuse within an analysis of a highly self-referential and ironic postmodern text casts into relief two very different approaches to truth claims: the first seeking to establish the primacy of experiential truth in the face of ideological distortion or denial, the second reflecting and reproducing the discursive provisionality of 'truth' when mediated by subjectivity and narrative. Moreover, the first is framed within a feminist politics.

A number of theorists have reflected on the factors impacting on the emergence of child sexual abuse – and of the child abuser – as objects of public anxiety and state intervention in the 1980s and, as Carol Smart notes, child sexual abuse remains 'a contested discursive field'.²⁷ However, Sara Scott has argued that 'feminism can claim with considerable justification to have been the point of origin for contemporary concern over child sexual abuse.'²⁸ More specifically, child sexual abuse has been theorised in powerful and persistent ways by radical feminist frameworks originating in Second Wave activism. Anne Seymour provides an incisive summary when she writes:

> The radical feminist perspective considers sexual abuse of children to be a manifestation of the oppression of females inherent in patriarchy ... Child sexual abuse is an expression of male power over females and, as such, is seen as a logical extension of the nature of patriarchy.[29]

This emphasis on sexuality as the site of female oppression and on violence as central to the functioning of patriarchal power explicitly genders the power dynamic at work in child sexual abuse. In her book *Interrogating Incest*, Vikki Bell refers to the 'perpetual asymmetry'[30] of abuse; the presumption that sexual abuse is a 'crime committed overwhelmingly by men against women'[31] renders the possibility of a female perpetrator ideologically inconceivable. But it is just this prospect which *The End of Alice* forces the reader to confront. Homes's first person narrative not only compels the reader to occupy the narrative perspective of a convicted child abuser; the depiction of his female adolescent correspondent as an apprentice abuser challenges both the feminist politics of identification and also the gendering of sexual power implicit in radical feminist analyses of child sexual abuse.

It is here that the novel's intertextual relationship with *Lolita* serves to unsettle established feminist positions. As Kasia Boddy has noted, 'the most imitated aspect of *Lolita* is its narrative voice'[32] and indeed the narration of *The End of Alice* is, like *Lolita*, literary, erudite and flamboyant – that of an aesthete and provocateur. The motif of the old-world sensibility caught in a contemptuous fascination with the avidity of American consumerism and its ideal target – the American child – is also evident in Homes's late twentieth-century fiction and expressed though linguistic hauteur; the narrator castigates the 'stinted, stilted language of youth'[33] and the 'leaden, forced, falsified'[34] prose of the 'overly undereducated'.[35] However, while stylistic affinities identify the narrator as Humbert's plot double, plot analogies also extend to the girl herself. In *Lolita*, Humbert's obsession with girls can be attributed to an unconscious attempt to resurrect the lost love of his youth, Annabel, who dies at a young age of typhus. However, in *The End of Alice* it is the girl whose first object of childhood desire is killed by lightening at summer camp; indeed, camp figures large in the imaginations of both narrators as a space of fantasy and envy, given its capacity to sequester children from the view of predatory adults. In *Lolita* Humbert encourages Lolita to play tennis so that he can enjoy 'the indescribable itch of rapture'[36] which the sight of her playing induces. In *The End of Alice* tennis lessons are the ruse by which the girl gains access to the twelve-year-old Matthew's life, a strategy which the narrator recognises as practised by those of his profession: 'It is clear that she has been looking for years, searching out the places where all variety and versions of her chosen kind are on display, where one can browse, where it is easy to shop unnoticed.'[37] It is the college girl – 'that horror of horrors'[38] – who, having just crossed the threshold from girl to woman, is the object of Humbert's especial disdain: 'There are few physiques I loathe more than the heavy low-slung pelvis, thick calves and deplorable complexion of the average coed.'[39] But it is the very same figure, as uncomfortable in her own skin as Humbert is in inspecting it, who the narrator in *The End of Alice* appoints as his 'good soldier',[40] enlisted to 'hunt him down'[41] until she has 'found her man'.[42]

The narrator's construction of the girl as one of his kind – subjecting the boys in her neighbourhood to a calculating campaign of sexual surveillance – is at odds with feminist constructions of female sexual agency as empowering. In her classic 1984 essay 'Pleasure and Danger: Towards a Politics of Sexuality', Carole Vance warns against an exclusive emphasis on sexuality as a site of oppression *or* pleasure:

> Sexuality is simultaneously a domain of restriction, repression, and danger as well as a domain of exploration, pleasure, and agency. To focus only on pleasure and gratification ignores the patriarchal structure in which women act, yet to speak only of sexual violence and oppression ignores women's experience with sexual agency and choice.[43]

Here female agency is equated with pleasure and male oppression with danger; however, the deployment of female sexual agency for oppressive ends is foregrounded in *The End of Alice*. Aligned with the veteran abuser's perspective, the girl's intentions seem calculating and exploitative: 'Her boy had been under observation for several years – he was of course not her first; there had been other, earlier experiments – but this was to be, she hoped, the first complete conquest.'[44]

Matthew, like Alice, is twelve years old and so both are minors according to contemporary laws of heterosexual consent. However, both are depicted, in this novel, as active sexual agents in their encounters with adults, Alice initiating and Matthew willingly participating in sexual encounters with the narrator and the girl respectively. The intertextual parallel with *Lolita* might prompt caution as to the extent to which this consent is the projection of adult fantasy; moreover, the possibility of genuine child 'consent' to any instance of intergenerational sexuality, given the inherent inequality of power, is highly disputed. However, in *Lolita*, Humbert acknowledges that Lolita's apparent 'consent' is coerced and compromised. He employs bribes and threats, offering treats and pocket money as a reward for Lolita's compliance and threatening juvenile reformatory if these strategies are not successful; the impact of the latter is reliant on Lolita's internalisation of her own purported criminality. Moreover, he acknowledges that she sobs 'every night, every night'[45] of her abduction and admits her vulnerability as 'a lone child, an absolute waif'.[46] It is the narrator of *The End of Alice* who is imprisoned for the murder of a child, but it is Humbert who is haunted by the living phantom of a violated childhood, experiencing an 'oppressive, hideous constraint as if I were sitting with the small ghost of somebody I had just killed'.[47]

By contrast, it is the precocious Alice – who has poems by Sylvia Plath and Emily Dickinson inked on the soles of her sneakers – who seems to set the rules of the game which she plays with the man she discovers naked by a lake on her grandmother's property. By tying her willing adult victim to a tree she is able to play out frontier fantasies and indulge her sexual curiosity simultaneously; empowered by class privilege she punishes him as 'my captive, my prisoner'[48] for 'trespass[ing] on my land'.[49] The narrator is similarly restrained – tied to the bed of his rented cabin – when Alice straddles him like a '"precious pony"',[50] never breaking the play script to acknowledge the sexual nature of their contact and offering him a bucket of oats and an apple for his efforts. In flight from his crime in Philadelphia and seeking to cure himself through seclusion, the narrator knows himself as the guilty party and imagines himself under surveillance and entrapped by a secretly wired Alice, so fully does she assume the part of his fantasy. His car journey with Alice to visit her hospitalised grandmother echoes Humbert's abduction of Lolita but here is licensed by her family; moreover, it is Alice who later conceals herself in the trunk of his car.

Lolita's sexual experience in Nabokov's novel has been used to excuse his abusive behaviour by constructing her as a 'seductive child'; she becomes the source of 'sexual danger and mendacity'[51] in a way which is congruent with attitudes toward child sexuality prior to the child sexual abuse crises of the 1980s. Alice's sexual curiosity and experiments as a child in *The End of Alice* are not used to excuse the narrator's behaviour; even the narrator himself, somewhat disingenuously recognises an adult responsibility despite his own arousal:

> Although undoubtedly I've not said it before, I do firmly believe it is up to an adult to ignore the attempted flirtations of the young, to allow the child to express her powers of persuasion in a seemingly safe setting. She is asking for it, if only to learn, to practice such; it doesn't necessarily mean that she really wants it or even knows what *it* is. She is in fact compelled by the culture. For the first time in my life I feel vaguely paternal [emphasis in original].[52]

It is the narrator, as a marginalised and socially insignificant itinerant, whose presence coincides with Alice's need for a 'seemingly safe'[53] object on which to play out her desires. By contrast, in *Lolita*, Humbert exploits his socially legitimate paternal powers to sexually exploit his dead partner's daughter; as Linda Kauffman notes: 'Perhaps the novel's most profound paradox is that Humbert cannot violate Lolita sexually until he assumes the societally sanctioned role of stepfather.'[54]

However, Alice's sexuality as a child does expose the problematic conflation of 'innocence' and 'victimhood'. If 'innocence' where child sexuality is concerned is equated with a lack of sexual knowledge then Alice is not 'innocent'. But, as the literary fate of Lolita has shown, this state of sexual experience, however child-like, makes Alice vulnerable to the apportioning of blame or guilt for her own fate. As Sara Scott has written: '"innocence" is used to incite revulsion and operates as a double-edged sword because innocence – or the tension between innocence and "knowledge" – is part of what is sexualized by abusers, and because it stigmatizes the "knowing" child as spoiled.'[55] When Alice's sexuality is played out with an adult who has confided violent sexual crimes against children to the reader the effects are deeply sinister and disturbing. However, the dynamics of power are further complicated by the revelation that the narrator was himself a child victim of sexual abuse by his disturbed mother. His vicious murder of Alice is triggered by a traumatic memory through which he has learned to associate menstrual blood with his own misplaced guilt, as a child, for his mother's death. The knowledge of the narrator's history as an abused child in no way mitigates the crime he commits against Alice; his frenzied assault and sexual mutilation of her body are recounted in graphic detail. But again the evidence of female perpetrated child sexual abuse is at odds with some feminist frameworks which assume male perpetrators and female victims.

To return to the girl, the generational gap between her and her twelve-year-old neighbour is much less pronounced than with the narrator and Alice; she and Matthew occupy either end of the spectrum of adolescence, he entering it and she struggling to depart it. As Jo Croft has written of adolescence, 'typically conceived as a transitional, in-between and conflict-ridden category, its relationship to the unswerving linearity of physical chronologies is apparently uneasy';[56] it is posited 'paradoxically, both as an epoch of sexual uncertainties and as an anchor for the most normative accounts of sexuality.'[57] In this context, it might be possible to conceive of the girl and Matthew as peers, albeit distant ones, within the parameters of child and adolescent sexuality, to the effect that neither is exploited or exploiter. But this may be to evade the girl's culpability as an adult and the boy's vulnerability as a child. However, if the girl's relationship with Matthew is transgressive – breaking as it does a number of age-related taboos and social responsibilities – then the fact that it seems less inherently harmful might be attributed to the fact of her sex and, more specifically, presumptions about female sexuality as innately passive. The relationship between the feminist focus on the 'perpetual asymmetry of abuse' and the perception that female perpetrated child sexual abuse is less harmful is complex. If the binary construction of male sexuality as active and female sexuality as passive makes female-perpetrated child sexual abuse difficult to conceive, it also compromises the status of the male child as a victim. Both Matthew in *The End of Alice* and Connolly in Zoë Heller's *Notes on a Scandal* alike are depicted as taking an expedient view of the sexual interest shown in them by adult women, possibly perpetuating a male fantasy of heterosexual initiation. If, as Alcoff has written, 'Cross-generational relations between old men and young women . . . seem to typify one of the normative scenarios for "romance",'[58] then cross-generational relationships between mature women and younger men typify a normative scenario for male heterosexual initiation. Indeed, *The End of Alice* depicts child/adult sexuality in ways which are not exclusively defined by radical feminist frameworks on child sexual abuse; ambiguities of agency and power allow for the acknowledgement of child sexuality and prompt an unsettling of gendered hierarchies of power.

'Curiouser and curiouser': the queer ends of child sexuality

Lewis Carroll's 'Alice' has played a significant role in revisionary readings of eroticised children; more specifically, Charles Dodgson's photographic portraits of Alice Liddell have been drawn into the frame of problematic images in an era following the child sexual abuse crises of the 1980s. 'Alice' seems to have joined 'Lolita' in the lexicon of literary girls whose status as victims of male sexual exploitation has been the object of feminist projects of reclamation. Hence the title of Homes's novel – *The End of Alice* – is sufficient in itself to instill a degree of dread in the reader as regards its subject matter. The novel's epigram from Carroll – 'A stopped clock is right twice a day' – confirms the intertextual allusion. While revisionary readings of Dodgson's relationship with girls may have marked the 'end' of a particular kind of Alice,[59] Alice has re-emerged as a literary mascot of a different kind of work on child sexuality, influenced by Foucault and informed by queer politics. Where the radical feminist reclamation of the 'real' Alice constructs her as an unknowing victim of an exploitative gaze, the contemporary queer appropriation of the fictional Alice celebrates her as a knowing agent.

Curiouser is the title of a collection of essays on the 'queerness of children' edited by Steven Bruhm and Natasha Hurley. Alice's encounters with the absurdity of normative laws and customs and her radical indeterminacy as a child in an adult world – at once too big and too small – make her a suitably transgressive standard bearer for this collection. This is the textual Alice, whose curiosity is philosophical and subversive, rather than the extra-textual Alice whose translation into the vocabulary of child pornography renders her an unwitting victim. Alice's girlhood is central to feminist rereadings; her appropriation as a 'queer child' has the effect of revealing the extent to which this girlhood is also a heterosexual construction.

A number of theorists have noted the ways in which prevailing feminist analyses of child sexual abuse are rooted in radical feminist frameworks and, more specifically, in frameworks for the critique of rape and pornography. In her book *Interrogating Incest*, Vikki Bell writes:

> In contrast [to Foucault], feminism has tended to see the question of adult–child sex as more or less the problem of rape . . . As a consequence of this, the problem has been assimilated into feminist discourse as a problem of sexual violence. Thus feminist analyses have not really addressed the notion of consent nor discussed consensual adult–child relations (and consensual incest).[60]

Moreover, radical feminist campaigns against child sexual abuse and child pornography have sometimes found uneasy allies; political and religious conservatives may attribute such abuse to moral decline, the permissive society and the breakdown of the traditional family but both they and their feminist counterparts alike make arguments in support of greater state control of sexuality, including censorship, and more vigorous applications of the criminal law. As Frigga Haug has commented:

> Antagonists as well as protagonists came from opposite political camps including feminists fighting for women's rights on the one hand, side by side with the moral majority rallying for 'law and order', marriage and the family, and both asking for more state intervention in this field.[61]

Theorists resisting the actions proposed by such movements include those who take a Foucauldian perspective on sexuality and power, contesting any attempt by the state to govern or control sexuality as an exercise in disciplinary power. For example, Amy Adler, in her article 'The Perverse Law of Child Pornography', argues that 'child pornography law represses sexual representations of children in child pornography, but it also produces a new kind of sexual representation of children – child pornography law.'[62] Adler argues that legal discourses designed to prohibit the sexual exploitation of children through pornography have the paradoxical effect of producing the very object they aim to outlaw: the sexualised child. As Adler puts it: 'The legal tool that we designed to liberate children from sexual abuse threatens to enslave us all, by constructing a world in which we are enthralled – anguished, enticed, bombarded – by the spectacle of the sexual child.'[63] Adler suggests that 'child pornography law explicitly requires us to take on the gaze of the pedophile';[64] such a claim powerfully suggests the productive power of repressive discourse, but in some ways it seems to shift the 'moral panic' attending the paedophile to the law itself which is attributed an almost conspiratorial agency. The potential tensions between such a Foucauldian analysis of the paradoxes of power and a feminist standpoint on the reality of abuse are illustrated in Abigail Bray's critique. Bray's concern is that the feminist identification of images of childhood as sexualised and as problematic will be dismissed as unwittingly symptomatic of the 'pedophilic' gaze which Adler suggests is produced by repressive legislation: 'A binary distinction between the abnormal gaze of a paedophile and the normal gaze of the "reasonable adult" operates to pathologise a perception that the mass media sexualise girls.'[65] Interestingly, Adler concludes her analysis of what she sees as the absurdities of child pornography law with a quote from Carroll's *Through the Looking Glass*: '"What do you suppose is the use of a child without any meaning?"'[66] This allusion evokes the 'ends' which the figure of the child is made to serve in her role as a vehicle for an adult struggle over meaning. In the context of child pornography law 'child sexuality' is the property of both the paedophile's desire and the law's jurisdiction – what it is not is the property of the child. In other words, child sexuality is explored as a discursive effect of competing regimes of adult power. In her important essay 'Dangerous Pleasures: Foucault and the Politics of Pedophilia', Linda Martín Alcoff seeks to reconcile feminist and Foucauldian perspectives on child sexual abuse. Alcoff writes that while 'Foucault never sanctioned coercive acts against children, he rejected the view that sexual relations between adults and children are always harmful for the children involved.'[67] Such a position presents difficulties for feminist readers trained to regard defences of child/adult sex as implicit rationalisations of the exploitation of girls by men. However, feminist theorists, including Linda Alcoff, Vikki Bell, Sara Scott and Carol Smart, have begun to bring Foucauldian frameworks to radical feminist positions on children and sexuality. As Alcoff notes, Foucault's position on child/adult sexual relations seems compromised,[68] but his observations concerning the historical and discursive processes by which deviant sexual types are constructed is one which other theorists have extended. In her efforts to 'disentangle a repudiation of sex between adults and children with a repudiation of children's sexuality',[69] Alcoff acknowledges the challenges in reconciling 'two very disparate sets of literature': one 'concerned with the crisis of childhood sexual abuse' and the other with 'increasing problems of homophobia and rightist sexual repression'.[70] The question of childhood sexuality is framed in different ways by feminist and queer perspectives; the tensions that emerge between these 'disparate literatures' can be understood in the context of competing priorities. By bringing Foucauldian perspectives to bear on child sexual abuse, Alcoff, Bell, Scott and Smart have questioned the ways in which radical feminist frames of analysis and political strategies might become complicit in discourses of power. Scott observes that one outcome of such questioning is the 'recognition that "breaking the silence" in relation to the sexual abuse of children does not necessarily lead to liberatory outcomes for either children or women, and has in fact had unintended consequences in the spawning of disempowering discourses.'[71] The discursive processes by which 'deviant' sexual types are constructed has been a founding concern of queer theory; Steven Angelides has extended this analysis to the figure of the paedophile, arguing that that 'paedophilia, like ... modern homosexuality, is a decidedly Western invention of the late nineteenth century.'[72] However, he notes a disparity in the development of these 'types':

> In stark contrast to the discourse of homosexuality, then, an individual practising intergenerational sex in the late nineteenth and early twentieth centuries was infrequently labelled a 'paedophile'. Of principal concern to sexologists were sexual deviations with respect to the aim or gender of object choice, not the age of the object choice.[73]

Angelides argues that 'homophobia played a pivotal role'[74] in this process, arguing that 'the image of the predatory paedophile was homosexualised and enlisted in the process of constructing subordinated or negated masculinities':[75]

> This was a defensive projection of a homophobic and heteronormative discourse that served, on the one hand, to deflect attention away from the fact that child sex abuse had been exposed as a problem inherent to dominant and not marginal forms of masculinity and male sexuality and, on the other, to halt the advancing campaigns for homosexual equality.[76]

Where intergenerational sexuality between a mature woman and male minor is concerned (as depicted in Heller's *Notes on a Scandal*) patriarchal discourses either normalise the relationship as heterosexual initiation in line with male fantasy or pathologise the woman as deviant in gendered terms; in neither scenario is the boy constructed principally as a victim and in both his presumed sexual agency implicitly protects him from that status. By contrast, the sexual innocence of boys where same-sex intergenerational sexuality is concerned becomes a privileged property in need of state-sanctioned protection; hence the vulnerability of (male) child sexuality (to men) is mobilised in resistance to the equalisation of laws of consent.

In *The End of Alice*, the narrator insists on the heterosexual nature of his desires, hypocritically drawing on the naturalising discourses of reproductive sexuality to legitimise his actions: 'Call me old-fashioned ... I am interested in the coupling that throughout history has propagated the human race.'[77] His attitude to his 'profession',[78] here in the context of a dream that he is being quizzed on the popular American television show *What's My Line*, parodies the construction of the paedophile as a 'type': 'We are not an organization, a political machine, we have no common goal and are therefore considered too diffuse, pathetic, and self-centred to cause a revolution.'[79] However, a fantasy of liberation during an Independence Day fireworks display returns to this possibility:

> Revolution! ... Regiments of proud perverts have been rounded up, recruited from every back-room bar, brothel, and jolly house up and down your stinky streets, and they're here now on the distant shore preparing to charge these steely gates.[80]

Segregated with other 'sexual types' away from other high-security prisoners, the narrator and his 'kind' become the very image of moral panic fears. In this way, the narrator taunts the reader with the assertion that he and his kind are engaged in an implicit contract with the 'normal' world, as repositories of forbidden desires:

> You are breaking your promise, the very terms of our agreement – the one that puts me in here and lets you stay out there – if I commit the crimes for you, you must be good to me. You and I, we're in this together, best not to forget.[81]

He posits the paedophile as a scapegoat, carrying the stigma for a crime which is then constructed as other to, rather than inherent in, conventional society: 'What I'm getting at is that, with so many of us locked up, you'd think it would stop. That it continues means that it is you and not me.'[82] The narrator does not seem to regard his sexual relationship with his male cellmate Clayton as at odds with his heterosexual identity; it is depicted as a strategic act of survival within the prison environment. He understands this relationship in terms which draw on his own perception of heterosexual power hierarchies: 'This is not exactly punishment; it is not torture. It is an experience I deserve (need). I am the woman ... In order to survive I must relax.'[83] He draws analogies between his own 'consent' and that of his captive victims: 'I thought of my girls and their unsuspecting parts. Surprised, temporarily taken aback, horrified by my inspection, but always beneath the gentility of my touch, the firmness of my hand, my tongue, my member, they surrendered.'[84] In this way, the power dynamic of his relationship with Clayton is the vehicle through which he gains insight into the experience of his victims: 'I allow it ... I have no will. I will always allow it ... I close my eyes, ignore him, and think about my girls, all my girls.'[85] However, unlike his victims he is able to reassert his power; reacting with homophobic violence to his own pleasure at Clayton's touch, he rapes him and in doing so converts him into a victim within the brutalised sexual economy of the prison: 'I'll not be the pussy anymore. A man, a man again, reclaimed. I have the power ... It's all over, anyone can have him now.'[86] In this act he reveals a misogynist contempt for the penetrable female body – 'How odd it must be to have at your center a great gap, a poisonous pit'[87] – and a homophobic recoil at what he perceives to be the 'feminising' effects of homosexual sex. The narrator is not 'homosexualised' as an abuser in the sense of being depicted as posing a threat to boys or their heterosexual identity. However, the fact that his 'apprentice' is a heterosexual female plays games with his vicarious identification with her desire for a minor: 'She'll have me fucking the boy, essentially fucking myself, which is all too familiar, slightly degrading, and hardly enough fun.'[88]

Roger Moody has suggested that debates about intergenerational sexuality have long been a feature of libertarian movements: 'There is also a virtually unbroken tradition, from the 'new educationists' of the nineteenth century, through utopian socialism, to the libertarianism of the sixties, which links free love, self-awareness and the dissolution of barriers between adults and children, to social equality.'[89] Such movements predate the emergence of the child sex abuse crises of the late twentieth century; one consequence of the latter is that is difficult to view adult advocacy of child/adult sexuality with anything other than suspicion. These movements offer radical critiques of the power relationship between adults and children but the belief that children might be empowered through sexual experiences with adults is one that is now hard to countenance. In feminist contexts, an understanding of sexuality as a site of power means that male/female intergenerational sexuality is seen only in terms of exploitation and abuse, whereby generational power differentials are compounded by gender. Nevertheless, Moody's thesis is supported by Alcoff's observation that even in the work of founding Second Wave feminists such as Andrea Dworkin, Shulamith Firestone and Kate Millett, the figure of the sexually liberated child persists as a signifier of utopian thought. However, Alcoff makes an important distinction between child sexuality and child/adult sexuality:

> It is not transformative to posit a future where children have sex with adults: this is our uninterrupted past and present. A truly transformative future would be one in which children could be, for the first time, free from the economy of adult sexual desire and adult sexual demands.[90]

Moody makes his assertion in the context of an essay exploring 'Man/Boy Love and the Left' in a collection entitled *The Age Taboo: Gay Male Sexuality, Power and Consent*; in his introduction to this collection Daniel Tsang acknowledges the anxieties that the 'man/boy love' paradigm provokes and seeks to address these concerns by emphasising the rights of the less powerful partner:

> The primary issue, it should be made clear, is *not* the right of men to have sex with boys ... Rather the real issue is the liberation of young people, so that they are empowered to make their own decisions regarding all aspects of their lives, including their sexuality [emphasis in original].[91]

However, his definition of paedophilia – 'sexual attraction or experience between an adult and pre-pubertal child'[92] – now seems dated at best and deeply problematic at worst; his usage could be understood as symptomatic of the changing meanings of the term but for those troubled by the man/boy love paradigm it may seem to confirm anxieties that child consent is subsumed to adult desire. Kathryn Bond Stockton, writing some decades after Tsang, offers some historical contextualisation for defences of 'man/boy love': 'Given that children and teens have not found it safe by and large to express their same-sex longings to peers (without the fear of ridicule, rejection, or bullying), to what extent has man/boy love, at least for a century, in some contexts, functioned as a substitute lateral relation for men and boys?'[93] In her discussion of the 'gay child's "backward birth"',[94] Stockton perhaps implies that the adult advocate or defender of child/adult sexuality may be speaking less as an adult than on behalf of the child they once were. She writes that the 'queer child' is one who is 'remarkably, intensely unavailable to itself in the present tense';[95] since categories of non-heterosexual identity are the prerogative of adults only it is only through adults that s/he can express his/her identity. This shift in theoretical attention away from 'man/boy love' to the 'queer child' is evident in Bruhm and Hurley's collection *Curiouser: On The Queerness of Children* in which a number of autobiographical essays testify to memories of same-sex relationships with adults as offering a safe induction into sexual identity in a homophobic world.

Evidently, the male homosexual paradigm of 'man/boy love' does not map readily onto gendered heterosexual relationships; or rather its effects have very different meanings in feminist contexts. The 'pedagogic-pederastic'[96] model to which Eve Kosofsky Sedgwick refers serves to ensure the transmission of patriarchal power through homosocial bonds. As Bruhm and Hurley note 'According to Foucault . . . pederastic behaviour properly conducted was the boy's means to social and philosophical accession.'[97] The pederastic relationship – between an adult man and a male adolescent – is also seen as providing 'accession' to a gay male identity. Feminist perspectives have also seen child/adult sex as providing an induction but into a power regime in which the girl is divested of power both as a child and as an apprentice woman. For example, Vikki Bell observes how feminist analyses understand incestuous abuse as exemplary rather than exceptional: 'an extreme form of the training that all girl children receive. The normalising aim of such training is feminine, subordinate girls and women.'[98] Conversely, the patriarchal normalisation of intergenerational relationships between mature men and girls, including those ratified by marriage, is in stark contrast to the criminalisation of not only adolescent but also young adult gay male sexuality through differentials in the heterosexual and homosexual ages of consent. Age of consent laws have constructed what counts as an intergenerational relationship in different ways for heterosexual and homosexual people regardless of actual consent by individual agents. For feminists the sexuality of girls is in need of protection from abuse by adult men in a patriarchal culture; for gay rights and queer activists the campaign is against the repression of queer children's sexuality in a homophobic world. The confluence of different contextual influences and political priorities has constructed intergenerational sexuality as the site of specific tensions between feminist and queer perspectives. The term itself is contested and originates in queer contexts where it foregrounds ambiguities of generational and sexual identity – ambiguities which feminist frameworks for the analysis of child sexual abuse might see as problematic.

This tension can best be illustrated by comparing the standpoints taken by Abigail Bray and Steven Angelides. In the course of her incisive and powerfully argued analysis of child sexual abuse controversies, Bray writes that 'many celebrations of "child loving" or "intergenerational intimacy" within queer theory remain surprisingly indifferent towards feminist critiques of the cultural and sexual politics of paedophilia.'[99] The conflation of 'child-loving' – a paradigm seeming to foreground adult agency and more properly located in the libertarian politics of the 1970s – with 'intergenerational' overlooks the new ways in which queer theory is approaching child sexuality; nor does it acknowledge the good reasons that queer theorists may have to challenge some of the heteronormative assumptions about child sexuality. Bray's critique seems to vindicate the concern that Bruhm and Hurley express, that 'discussions of queerness and child sexuality all too quickly invoke the specter of the pedophile, which all too quickly destroys one's political credibility.'[100] However, Bruhm and Hurley also question the 'cultural and psychoanalytic fantas[y]' that 'sex between a child and an adult, regardless of the gender of either party, is inevitably traumatic and debilitating for the child.'[101] Since feminists have worked so hard to challenge the denial of child sexual abuse as a fantasy, including Freud's disavowal of the seduction theory, the way in which this assertion is formulated does seem provocative. Conversely, the 'feminist erasure of child sexuality'[102] provides the focus for one in a series of publications by Steven Angelides on the discursive construction of child sexual abuse. Angelides acknowledges the efforts of feminists to 'reverse the tendency to blame the victims of child sexual molestation'[103] and also recognises that 'many pedophile groups, employing the rhetoric of gay liberation, positioned themselves as the representatives of an oppressed minority akin to homosexuals.'[104] However, Angelides attributes a hegemonic power to feminism and holds it responsible for prevailing assumptions about childhood, sexuality and 'innocence':

> Whereas the pre-1980s witnessed the coexistence of contradictory notions of childhood – as sexual *and* innocent – the post-1980s have been characterised by a conscientious effort to resolve this representational dynamic. The dominant post-1980s figuration of children in terms of asexual innocence differs significantly from that of earlier decades. One side of the contradiction has been repressed or disavowed as overt representations of child sexuality have been eliminated by the hegemonic feminist discourse of child sexual abuse [emphasis in original].[105]

Angelides acknowledges that the specific framework which has prevailed in the analysis of child sexual abuse is a radical feminist one, and this raises interesting questions in relation to its reliance on a specific model of power. However, his attribution of hegemonic power to feminism seems to imply that patriarchal power has been overcome. Furthermore, the conflation of feminism and radical feminism overlooks Foucauldian feminist critiques of the latter, including work examining the relationship between child sexuality and the discourse of 'innocence'. Where Bray attributes a hegemonic power to queer theory, Angelides does the same to feminism. Bray accuses queer theory of overlooking issues of gendered power; Angelides suggests that feminism has been complicit in the imposition of heteronormative ends on queer childhoods.

Integral to this queer work on childhood sexuality is an understanding of childhood innocence as having a heteronormative dimension. As Bruhm and Hurley write: 'There is currently a dominant narrative about children: children are (and should stay) innocent of sexual desires and intentions. At the same time, however, children are officially, tacitly, assumed to be heterosexual.'[106] Hence, Bruhm and Hurley define the 'queer child' as one who confounds this construction; s/he is not simply one who expresses same sex desires but also one who 'displays interest in sex generally, in same-sex erotic attachments or in cross-generational attachments.'[107] And here we return to the feminist sticking point. Alice and Matthew might be termed 'queer children' by this definition, despite the heterosexual nature of their encounters, but the use of 'cross-generational' as a signifier for transgressive sexuality seems to risk the elision of the consensual and the coerced.

'I know who you are': the end of *The End of Alice*

In Homes's novel the girl's campaign to seduce an underage boy, as recounted vicariously by the narrator, provides a discomforting narrative trajectory; the reader is compelled towards an end from which she simultaneously recoils. I want to conclude by reflecting on what becomes of this deeply ambivalent narrative momentum as the novel approaches its own end.

The End of Alice is a highly self-referential narrative and not only in its intertextual allusions to Nabokov's *Lolita* and Carroll's Alice; its narrator repeatedly draws attention to the way in which reality is mediated by his own narrative. The narrator candidly admits that his role as 'translator'[108] of the girl's testimony is a 'free' one: 'She writes of the memory of one particular afternoon – or perhaps I write for her.'[109] The narrative is punctuated with ironically authenticating admissions of incomprehension – 'While my intention is not to interrupt the proceedings, you should be aware that I have no idea of what they're talking about'[110] – but these do not resolve a suspicion as to the extent to which the narrator may be the author of the girl's narrative: 'I remain convinced that my interpretation, my translation, is a more accurate reflection of her state of mind, far exceeding that which she is able to articulate independently.'[111] This presumption is congruent with the narrator's imposition of his will on other children: 'God, they are so annoying when they believe they can think for themselves.'[112] It is evident that the narrator's account of the girl's life is overwritten by the projection of his own fantasies, such as when he imagines her engaging in same-sex encounters at summer camp. In this way, the girl becomes the vehicle for the narrator's sexual fantasies about female children, but this identification becomes more complicated where her pursuit of Matthew is concerned; the girl's gender and sexuality would not seem to make her an ideal candidate for his 'apprentice' and indeed the narrator expresses disgust at the way in which he is made to relive, rather than escape, the sexual intimacy with male bodies which takes place in his prison confinement. It might be tempting to dismiss the girl's sexual encounters with an underage boy as the projection of the narrator's fantasy, but this is difficult to sustain due to their ultimate failure to follow his preferred script.

The narrator depicts himself and the girl as 'partners in this subtle crime'[113] but his conflation of her with the dead Alice suggests a different role: 'Confused. I am confusing her with another one. I am lost in time. I begged myself not to play this game, she is not that girl but some other one. Are they all the same?'[114] Moreover, the girl's voice dramatically breaks through the narrator's ventriloquised version when she declares: '*I know who you are and I know what you did . . . Her street. I live on her street* [emphasis in original].'[115] This may not come as a surprise given the narrator's status as a celebrity criminal whose childhood toys are on display in a Museum of Criminal Culture. The shock – both for the narrator and the reader – is in the revelation of a personal agenda on the girl's part; she goes on to reveal that, growing up on the same street as his victim, her childhood was haunted by the narrator's crime: 'I live differently because of you, there is no such thing as safety.'[116] Moreover, she describes her relationship with the twelve-year-old Matthew as an 'experiment': 'I needed him, needed someone who didn't scare me.'[117] In other words, she is revealed not as an apprentice perpetrator but as an indirect victim, a role which the narrator's unconscious substitution of her for Alice confirms. The girl's apparent power as Matthew's seducer is undermined when she is sexually threatened by one of Matthew's peers, Aaron; she is only saved from an attempted rape when his mother calls him in to dinner. When Matthew's father in turn sexually coerces her the narrative seems to revert to more familiar patterns of gendered power. Her words of resignation echo those of the imprisoned narrator, despite the fact that he is captive where she is nominally free: 'Despite my best efforts, I am always the one who gets fucked. It won't ever be any different, some things don't change – I suppose I have to learn to enjoy it.'[118]

The disclosure of a mitigating motive, a traumatic memory and ongoing sexual victimisation may serve to explain, even vindicate, the girl's actions; moreover, the emergence of an 'authentic' unmediated voice perhaps transforms her narrative into a victim's testimony. To return to Carole Vance's terms, where the girl's sexual agency initially seemed the source of socially transgressive pleasures, it now becomes the domain of familiar dangers; in this way, the novel acknowledges the indirect victimisation of girls and women in a culture of endemic sexual violence. However, it could also be argued that the dramatic conversion of the girl from perpetrator to victim brings to an end the reader's discomforting confrontation with a provocative depiction of non-normative female heterosexuality; in perhaps the final irony of the novel, the girl's victim status relieves the reader of the more troubling prospect of her deviance as a heterosexual woman.

Notes

1. A. M. Homes, *The End of Alice* (London: Granta, 1995), p. 13.
2. Ibid., p. 12.
3. Ibid., p. 90.
4. The head of a leading UK child protection charity declared *The End of Alice* 'the most vile and perverted novel I have ever read'. Quoted in Kasia Boddy, 'Regular Lolitas: The Afterlives of an American Adolescent', in Jay Prosser (ed.), *American Fiction in the 1990's: Reflections of History and Culture* (London and New York: Routledge, 2008), p. 171.
5. Homes, op. cit., p. 13. I will refer to the narrator's unnamed female correspondent as 'the girl', deploying his language in recognition that her identity is mediated through him.
6. Anne Seymour, 'Aetiology of the Sexual Abuse of Children: An Extended Feminist Perspective', *Women's Studies International Forum*, 21: 4 (1998), p. 416.
7. Steven Bruhm and Natasha Hurley, 'Curiouser: On the Queerness of Children', in Steven Bruhm and Natasha Hurley (eds), *Curiouser: On the Queerness of Children* (Minneapolis, MN and London: University of Minnesota Press, 2004), p. x.
8. Ibid., p. x.
9. Vladimir Nabokov, *Lolita* [1955] (London: Penguin, 1995), p. 9.
10. Ibid.
11. Homes, op. cit., p. 174.
12. Ibid., p. 195.
13. Ibid., p. 146.
14. Ibid., p. 183.
15. Nabokov, op. cit., p. 62.
16. Ibid., p. 26.

17. Homes, op. cit., p. 77.
18. Ibid., p. 133.
19. Ibid., p. 206.
20. Nabokov, op. cit., p. 132.
21. Abigail Bray, 'The Question of Intolerance: "Corporate Paedophilia" and Child Sexual Abuse Moral Panics', *Australian Feminist Studies*, 23: 57 (2008), p. 324.
22. Eric Goldman, '"Knowing" Lolita: Sexual Deviance and Normality in Nabokov's *Lolita*', *Nabokov Studies*, 8 (2004), p. 94.
23. Todd Bayma and Gary Alan Fine, 'Fictional Figures and Imaginary Relations: The Transformation of Lolita from Victim to Vixen', *Studies in Symbolic Imagination*, 20 (1996), p. 167.
24. Trilling, quoted in Linda S. Kauffman, 'Framing Lolita: Is There a Woman in the Text?', *Special Delivery: Epistolary Modes in Modern Fiction* (Chicago and London: University of Chicago Press, 1992), p. 59.
25. Elizabeth Patnoe, 'Lolita Misrepresented, Lolita Reclaimed: Disclosing the Doubles', *College Literature*, 22: 2 (1995), n.p.
26. Ibid.
27. Carol Smart, 'A History of Ambivalence and Conflict in the Discursive Construction of the "Child Victim" of Sexual Abuse', *Social and Legal Studies*, 8: 3 (1999), p. 392.
28. Sara Scott, 'Surviving Selves: Feminism and Contemporary Discourses of Child Sexual Abuse', *Feminist Theory*, 2: 3 (2001), p. 349.
29. Seymour, op. cit., p. 416.
30. Vikki Bell, *Interrogating Incest: Feminism, Foucault and the Law* (London: Routledge, 1993), p. 71.
23. Ibid., p. 71.
32. Boddy, op. cit., p. 165.
33. Homes, op. cit., p. 28.
34. Ibid., p. 153.
35. Ibid.
36. Nabokov, op. cit., p. 230.
37. Homes, op. cit., p. 17.
38. Nabokov, op. cit., p. 65.
39. Ibid., p. 175.
40. Homes, op. cit., p. 22.
41. Ibid., p. 23.
42. Ibid., p. 46.
43. Carole Vance, 'Pleasure and Danger: Toward a Politics of Sexuality', in Sandra Kemp and Judith Squires (eds), *Feminisms* (Oxford: Oxford University Press, 1997), p. 327.
44. Homes, op. cit., p. 21.
45. Nabokov, op. cit., p. 176.
46. Ibid., p. 140.
47. Ibid.
48. Homes, op. cit., p. 189.
49. Ibid.
50. Ibid., p. 290.
51. Smart, op. cit., p. 398.

52. Homes, op. cit., p. 209.
53. Ibid.
54. Kauffman, op. cit., p. 70.
55. Scott, op. cit., p. 354.
56. Jo Croft, 'Writing the Adolescent Body', in Jan Campbell and Janet Harbord (eds), *Psycho-Politics and Cultural Desires* (London: UCL Press, 1998), p. 190.
57. Ibid., p. 190.
58. Linda Martín Alcoff, 'Dangerous Pleasures: Foucault and the Politics of Pedophilia', in Susan J. Hekman (ed.), *Feminist Interpretations of Foucault* (University Park, PA: Pennsylvania State University Press, 1996), p. 116.
59. See Katie Roiphe's novel, *Still She Haunts Me* (New York: Delta, 2001).
60. Bell, op. cit., p. 155.
61. Frigga Haug, 'Sexual Deregulation or, the Child Abuser in Neoliberalism', *Feminist Theory*, 2 (2001), p. 57.
62. Amy Adler, 'The Perverse Law of Child Pornography', *Columbia Law Review*, 101: 2 (2001), p. 272.
63. Ibid., p. 210.
64. Ibid., p. 213.
65. Bray, op. cit., p. 333.
66. Adler, op. cit., p. 273.
67. Alcoff, op. cit., p. 100.
68. See Chapter 2 for a fuller discussion of Foucault's comments on child sexual abuse.
69. Alcoff, op. cit., p. 129.
70. Ibid., p. 119.
71. Scott, op. cit., p. 356.
72. Steven Angelides, 'The Emergence of the Paedophile in the Late Twentieth Century', *Australian Historical Studies*, 36: 126 (2005), p. 272.
73. Ibid., pp. 272–3.
74. Ibid., p. 286.
75. Ibid., p. 295. See also Vikki Bell, 'The Vigilant(e) Parent and the Paedophile: The *News of the World* Campaign 2000 and the Contemporary Governmentality of Child Sexual Abuse', *Feminist Theory*, 3: 1 (2002), pp. 83–102.
76. Angelides, op. cit., p. 295.
77. Homes, op. cit., p. 14.
78. Ibid., p. 12.
79. Ibid.
80. Ibid., p. 142.
81. Ibid., p. 70.
82. Ibid., pp. 68–9.
83. Ibid., p. 8.
84. Ibid., p. 56.
85. Ibid., p. 102.
86. Ibid., pp. 148–9.
87. Ibid., p. 176.
88. Ibid., p. 100.

89. Roger Moody, 'Man/Boy Love and the Left', in Daniel Tsang (ed.), *The Age Taboo: Gay Male Sexuality, Power and Consent* (Boston and London: Alyson Publications/Gay Men's Press, 1982), p. 147.
90. Alcoff, op. cit., p. 133.
91. Daniel Tsang, 'Introduction', in Tsang, op. cit., p. 10.
92. Ibid., p. 8.
93. Kathryn Bond Stockton, *The Queer Child, or Growing Sideways in the Twentieth Century* (Durham, NC and London: Duke University Press, 2009), p. 62.
94. Ibid., p. 6.
95. Ibid., p. 6. Stockton writes: 'For this queer child, whatever its conscious grasp of itself, has not been able to present itself according to the category "gay" or "homosexual" – categories deemed too adult, since they are sexual, though we do presume every child to be straight.'
96. Eve Kosofsky Sedgwick, *Epistemology of the Closet* (Berkeley and Los Angeles: University of California Press, 1990), p. 139.
97. Bruhm and Hurley, op. cit., p. xxiv.
98. Bell, op. cit., p. 68.
99. Abigail Bray, 'Governing the Gaze: Child Sexual Abuse Moral Panics and the Post-feminist Blindspot', *Feminist Media Studies*, 9: 2 (2009), p. 177.
100. Bruhm and Hurley, op. cit., p. xxiii.
101. Ibid., p. xxii. A similar assertion is made by Ellis Hanson in his reading of the 'gothic conundrum' of the 'sexual child' in Henry James's *The Turn of the Screw*: 'The erotic innocence of children is founded on the presumption that they cannot possibly understand or experience sexual desire except as trauma.' 'Screwing with Children in Henry James', *GLQ: Journal of Lesbian and Gay Studies*, 9: 3 (2003), p. 374.
102. See Steven Angelides, 'Feminism, Child Sexual Abuse, and the Erasure of Child Sexuality', *GLQ: Journal of Lesbian and Gay Studies*, 10: 2 (2004), pp. 141–77.
103. Ibid., p. 147.
104. Ibid., p. 146.
105. Ibid., pp. 154–5.
106. Bruhm and Hurley, op. cit., p. ix.
107. Ibid., p. x.
108. Homes, op. cit., p. 11.
109. Ibid., p. 28.
110. Ibid., p. 83.
111. Ibid., p. 153.
112. Ibid., p. 49.
113. Ibid., p. 132.
114. Ibid., p. 143.
115. Ibid., p. 152.
116. Ibid., p. 156.
117. Ibid., pp. 155–6.
118. Ibid., p. 167.

Chapter 4

Unauthorised reproduction: class, pregnancy and transgressive female heterosexuality in Alan Warner's *Morvern Callar*

Alan Warner's 1995 novel *Morvern Callar* begins and ends with acts of unauthorised reproduction on the part of its eponymous young working-class narrator: the first is cultural and the second sexual. The novel opens with Morvern's discovery of the dead body of her older middle-class boyfriend who has committed suicide in the home that they share in a small Scottish port; Morvern overwrites his name on the unpublished manuscript which he leaves behind, submits it to a London-based publisher and uses the advance to fund a youth-oriented package holiday for herself and her best friend Lanna. The novel ends, following Morvern's return to her home town from a second excursion to the rave clubs of a Mediterranean resort, with the revelation of her pregnancy with 'the child of the raves'.[1] In the first act of unauthorised reproduction Morvern violates the legitimising name of her unnamed boyfriend, appropriating his intellectual property and the capital which it accrues. In the second, Morvern violates the principles of patrilineal law, property and inheritance embodied in conventions of legitimacy through her pregnancy with a child whose paternity is not attributed. This chapter will suggest that a continuity between social and sexual reproduction in Warner's novel plays a key role in the construction of Morvern as a transgressive figure. The significance of Morvern's pregnancy will provide a focal point for reflection on the heteronormative construction of female reproductive sexuality and the role of class in its regulation.

The conflation of reproductive sexuality with heterosexuality and of non-reproductive sexuality with homosexuality has been integral to the construction of heterosexuality and homosexuality as distinct categories of sexuality; as Judith Roof has put it, 'sexuality's position as licit or illicit depends upon its reproductive use.'[2] Indeed, discourses and practices intent on the regulation of sexuality have worked to equate the 'natural' and the 'normal' with the reproductive; sexual desires or practices without reproductive potential have been subject to suppression and criminalisation as 'unnatural' and 'abnormal'. In the course of a discussion of the 'naturalised primacy of heterosexuality' in Freud, Roof suggests that:

> The reduction of a larger field of sexuality to two categories is partly an effect of narrative's binary operation within a reproductive logic; in this sense there are really only two sexualities: reproductive sexuality, which is associated with difference and becomes metaphorically heterosexual, and nonreproductive sexuality associated with sameness, which becomes metaphorically homosexual.[3]

Evidently, not all heterosexual practices can result in conception and equally same-sex desires do not preclude a capacity to reproduce; however, this 'metaphorical' conjunction is persistent and serves not only to perpetuate the premises from which homophobia proceeds but also to obscure the complexity of the relationship between heterosexuality and reproductive sexuality. Not every act of heterosexual reproduction is socially sanctioned, never mind privileged; one only need consider the history of illegitimacy to appreciate that reproductive sexuality is itself subject to normative regimes.[4] The social stigma and penalties of illegitimacy have historically been attached both to the mother and child, but not to the father; evidently, gender hierarchies play an integral role in the policing of reproductive sexuality. While the stigma of illegitimacy may seem to have receded in the latter part of the twentieth century, the figure of the 'lone mother' has become the object of renewed social anxieties which are expressive of complex and contradictory attitudes towards women's sexual and maternal autonomy. The lone mother represents a fissuring of the category of motherhood into socially sanctioned and socially stigmatised forms; here the institution of marriage serves as the legitimising agency, making explicit its status as a patriarchal institution. The prevailing discourses of lone motherhood at work in the mid-1990s, when Warner's novel was published, make apparent the key role that class plays in such constructions; the economic imperatives inherent in the policing of the reproductive sexuality of the working-class woman reveal reproduction as a form of labour in service to the national economy. At the end of Warner's novel, having apparently exhausted the financial legacy both of her dead boyfriend's book advance and his father's inheritance, Morvern returns alone to the depressed post-industrial economy of the port pregnant with a child whose paternity is not disclosed. Morvern's pregnancy has been interpreted as signifying both her defiance of, and capture by, patriarchal constructions of gender; I wish to focus on the role of class in the production of meanings attributed to this 'child of the raves'.[5]

'Lost in silence': guilt by dissociation

Critical reception of Warner's novel has identified his protagonist's narrative voice as a source of unease as much, if not more, than the trangressive acts she commits since it offers little indication of intention, motivation or remorse. One might expect a first-person narrative charting the aftermath of a young woman's discovery of her boyfriend's dead body, following a seemingly unanticipated suicide, to be characterised by a charged interiority, especially given the prolonged periods of silence and solitary withdrawal which characterise her existence; by her own admission Morvern is 'a right queer-case for not talking'.[6] However, one of the distinctive features of Morvern's narrative voice is a persistent and peculiar sense of dissociation not only from external events but also from her own feelings: 'A sort of wave of something was going across me. There was fright but I'd daydreamed how I'd be'.[7] This sensation of 'something ... going across'[8] is a recurring motif throughout the narrative and serves to infer different emotions in different contexts, including sexual arousal, betrayal, shock and grief.[9] Feeling or emotion is depersonalised and its origin located elsewhere; in this way a persistent disjunction between agency and affect is established. Carole Jones has argued that 'through the flat, emotionless voice she [Morvern] appears disengaged, an observer of herself in the scene, giving the impression she is not quite occupying her own body'[10] and John Caughie has suggested that Warner 'gives to Morvern a voice which describes every action from the same perspective, without seeming to inhabit any of them or confer value on them.'[11] Moreover, more than one critic has made recourse to literary analogy in order to account for Morvern's disposition; both Duncan Petrie and Roderick Watson compare Morvern to the notoriously anomic protagonist of Albert Camus's 1942 novel *The Outsider*, a narrative which begins with a bereavement and centres on a murder committed without apparent motive or remorse; Watson suggests that 'the spirit of *Morvern Callar* is closer to the unforced existential detachment of Camus's *L'Étranger* in sunny Algiers than to Banks's Gothic glee or Irvine Welsh's violent nihilism'[12] and Petrie suggests that 'Morvern's hunger for experience ... mirror[s] Meursault's own enjoyment of everyday experience despite his apparent indifference to bigger emotional and moral issues.'[13] While this parallel profitably expands the contexts within which Warner's novel can be considered it is, perhaps, also symptomatic of a struggle to find a frame of reference within which to make sense of Morvern's subjectivity as it is rendered in this narrative. The apparent unaccountability of Morvern's reaction to her boyfriend's death is a recurring subtext in critical responses to the novel; the sense that there is something improper, inappropriate and fundamentally lacking about her response has prompted critics to pathologise her personality. For example, Jones remarks that 'Morvern is arguably, then, an independent, empowered, liberated, if slightly psychotic woman'[14] and Watson suggests that 'an oddly unfocused sweetness' has the effect of 'defus[ing] what might otherwise come across as a psychopathic dissociation'.[15] The reference to Camus's novel is helpful in terms of categorising narrative voice, but in terms of character this parallel infers a criminality which is not in proportion to Morvern's actions; Meursault is guilty of murder but Morvern is not responsible for her boyfriend's death. It could be argued that she conceals his death and disposes of his body *as if* she had committed a crime but there is no suggestion of guilt or shame in her behaviour. Her 'crime' is perhaps more of a gendered nature. Meursault is guilty of an offence against society as well as against the person of his victim; he has violated moral and social codes in not only taking the life of another human being, but in showing no just cause or remorse for his actions. However, Morvern's crime is in part an offence against gendered constructions of identity: it is a failure of femininity. This failure takes two forms; the first concerns her apparent lack of affect. Morvern does not demonstrate the susceptibility to overwhelming emotion conventionally attributed to women; not only does she not exhibit grief in the expected way, but she maintains a stubborn autonomy and persistence in her subsequent actions, relying on no one other than herself and pursuing her solutions in a single-minded fashion. The second concerns her failure to properly commemorate the identity of her dead boyfriend; arguably, his masculinity is compromised by her omission. The unnamed boyfriend – known only by the deifying pronoun 'Him'[16] in the narrative – is in most ways the more empowered partner; he is older, economically privileged and – as a writer – promised a stake in language and posterity. Indeed, his suicide note stipulates: 'I ONLY ASK YOU TO GET IT [the manuscript] PUBLISHED. I'LL SETTLE FOR POSTHUMOUS FAME AS LONG AS I'M NOT LOST IN SILENCE (capitals in original).'[17] In overwriting his name on the title page of his manuscript and submitting his work under her own, Morvern fails to honour the masculine proper name; 'He' is 'lost' to the silence which has been Morvern's chosen provenance. Meursault is apprehended and prosecuted; his crime is publicly named and, in some way, his own masculinity is reaffirmed by his assertion of will in defiance of public morality; by contrast, Morvern's dissimulation is never exposed or remedied and her boyfriend's literary property is not restored. The novel ends with a narrative device – pregnancy – often deployed to signify redemptive closure. However, Morvern is not pregnant with the boyfriend's child; indeed, no man is granted paternity of the 'child of the raves'.[18] Morvern's illegitimate pregnancy seems an extension of, rather than compensation for, her initial act of appropriation; she is now additionally guilty of appropriating reproductive property. I wish to investigate more closely the transgressive nature of Morvern's crimes against 'property'; moving away from the pathologising of her subjectivity, I wish to suggest that discourses of class, combined with those of gender, have been instrumental in constructing Morvern's relationship to social and sexual reproduction as deviant.

'Working in the meat': regimes of labour and leisure

Morvern's compulsion to evade public scrutiny in relation to her boyfriend's death gives rise to one of the most provocative and darkly comic scenes in the novel. Morvern does not notify anyone of her boyfriend's suicide, concealing his corpse in the attic to avoid the risk of its discovery; finally she elects to dispose of his body by dismembering it, later burying it in the mountains which overlook the port where she lives. In one sense this scene typifies the apparent absence of affect which some critics have sought to pathologise. However, it is also notable for the way in which it suggests the alienating effects of labour. Sinister continuities with the world of work persist in times and spaces designated as distinct from the workplace: here the home and later the holiday.

At the superstore where Morvern has been employed since a teenager, she works expertly and efficiently to monitor and renew supplies of fruit and vegetables on display on the shop floor, and to dismantle and dispose of the empty boxes and pallets which are left behind. However, this impersonal proficiency also extends into the private domestic space of her flat, where Christmas presents are dispatched briskly and without apparent sentiment: 'I lined up the presents from Him to me then just tore them all open one after another like apple boxes at the work.'[19] Morvern's management of her boyfriend's corpse is recounted dispassionately – 'He was heavier than a six-wheeler loaded with tatties'[20] – as a job of work to which she is clearly equal: 'I used the goldish lighter on a Silk Cut while knocking off from the job for a bit.'[21] Indeed, a direct parallel is suggested between her work 'in the meat'[22] at the butcher's counter and her capacity to plan the disposal of her boyfriend's body with the aid of 'the new meat knife and the gardening saw':[23]

> I used to work in the meat. You cleaned up each night. Afterwards you smelled of blood and it was under your nails as you lifted the glass near your

nose in the pub. You pulled the bleeding plastic bag of gubbins, cut open by bones, to the service lift. Blood spoiled three pairs of shoes. You were expected to supply your own footwear.[24]

Morvern demonstrates resourcefulness in devising a technique to ensure that her boyfriend's remains can be transported to their resting place without trace or discovery: 'What you do is divide the limbs and wrap them in a good few layers of binliner and absorbent hessian sacking bound again and again with strips of thick parcel tape.'[25] Burying the parcels in the mountains above the port, Morvern again reflects on how her job has prepared her to conduct this task with apparent equanimity: 'Soil was all under my nails like at work.'[26]

Warner's novel foregrounds Morvern's experience of alienating labour and indeed she is inscribed into class narratives by both her foster father, Red Hanna, and her boyfriend; from very different class positions both position her as a victim of economic injustice. A lifelong trade union activist, Red Hanna projects his own despair about his future onto his foster daughter: 'Here's you, twenty-one, a forty-hour week on slave wages for the rest of your life.'[27] Narrative tropes to do with the stoic suffering and heroic solidarity of industrial labour are exemplified in Red Hanna's account of the tragic fate of his workmate, known as The Stick; fatally crushed between two empty fish wagons, he dies only months away from retirement, despite the combined efforts of 'railway, fishermen, piermen, fellows from the ice factory'.[28] Red Hanna draws the following conclusion from this example: 'The hidden fact of our world is that theres no point in having desire unless youve money . . . In plain language, I'm fifty-five: a wasted life.'[29] By contrast, as a middle-class man of independent income who does not appear to need to work, the boyfriend occupies a position of economic privilege very unlike that of his girlfriend's foster father and yet in his suicide note he also depicts Morvern as a victim of class inequality. Moreover, he accounts himself both complicit and capable of providing a remedy: 'LIVE THE LIFE PEOPLE LIKE ME HAVE DENIED YOU. YOU ARE BETTER THAN US [capitals in original].'[30] The category of class on which these narratives of oppression and reparation rely is implicitly gendered; class affiliation is defined in relation to waged male labour and conferred on women via heterosexual attachment (within the family or through marriage). Morvern's relationship to these institutions is oblique, given that she was fostered as a child and is not married, but by writing her into these scripts the men in her life claim her as their own by appointing her to their class identity. However, the conventional distinction between labour and leisure implied in traditional accounts of class (leisure being the privilege of the upper classes and the elusive reward of the working classes) is confounded in Morvern's experience, which suggests a more complex relation to class and its subversion.

From childhood, Morvern dreams of the Mediterranean blue of the sea seen in holiday brochures; on discovering the amount available to her through her dead boyfriend's cash card, her first act is to book a holiday for herself and her best friend Lanna. The Spanish resort to which they fly is then implicitly constructed as the location of Morvern's fantasised escape from the economic and social realities of the port. However, the worlds of labour and leisure are not as distinct as one might expect. Tellingly, on her outward journey Morvern mistakes a T-shirted airport worker for a holidaymaker in a bar;[31] the boundaries between the worlds of work and recreation, and the timescales of shift work and flight schedule, merge in the transitional space of the departure lounge. Moreover, in his depiction of the recreational nihilism and industrialised leisure of Morvern's youth-oriented package holiday, Warner suggests that the regimes of alienated labour extend beyond the workplace.

In her home town, Morvern inhabits an environment in which a culture of nihilistic working-class masculinity dominates. Petrie refers to the 'insecurity, self-loathing, abuse and exploitation defining the psyche of the Scottish "hard man"'[32] and these qualities are given often outlandish expression in Warner's novel; for example, the Panatine, having already sliced a nerve in his arm while working as a butcher, severs a finger while forcing entry into his own house after injecting whiskey into his temples and liquid LSD into his pupils. This culture of recreational self-destruction is also evident in the resort which is supposed to offer an escape from the world of work. Approaching a group of young drinkers, Morvern notes that 'the guys mustve been in motorcycle accidents; they had plaster and gauze stuck all over their arms.'[33] However, she soon discovers that these injuries are self-induced symptoms of enthusiastic entry into a 'sunburn competition',[34] to which end olive oil, silver foil and prescription lenses are employed to magnify the damage. Later, Morvern witnesses a saw being drawn across a boy's bare arm in return for free alcohol in a drinks promotion campaign: 'Right, half a pint, the barman goes and he drew the saw on its own weight over the lad's arm. A pint, went the barman as he pushed the saw forward. You saw the white scratches on the tanned skin.'[35] This reckless disregard extends to the natural and built environment. An enraged holidaymaker lobs a bottle at a cicada from his balcony window in an effort to extinguish 'that loud electric drill sound they make';[36] the sounds of nature are industrialised in a setting in which men, freed from the imperatives of waged labour, seem to be employed in waging war against nature. A group of men 'working busily at some baby palm trees in the central reservation' are revealed to be not road maintenance workers but fellow holidaymakers: 'They were carefully ripping out the trees then flinging them across the tarmac.'[37] Morvern's first sight of the beach – 'Every bit sand was covered in people'[38] – is rather balefully suggestive of the production line: 'I watched the bodies get carried up on the winch till they fell to the water.'[39] The experience of open-air swimming, both in the Highlands and the Mediterranean, is the object of some of the most rhapsodic passages in Warner's novel, with Morvern testifying to the 'loveliness' of being 'In Nature'.[40] However, her first encounter with the sea at her holiday resort is also an unwitting exposure to the industrialisation of nature. Seeking respite from the heat and noise of the resort at night, Lanna and Morvern make their way towards the water in the dark, only to find the ground beneath their feet 'shaking';[41] they have inadvertently stumbled on the reclamation of a landfill site, itself the by-product of accelerated consumption generated by the tourist industry. Its conversion into the more profitable category of beach is complete by the next morning, when Morvern witnesses sunbathers rushing to 'claim a patch'[42] of the newly laid sand. The disciplinary regimes of work also extend to the recreational games organised by the Youth Med couriers; assembled in sex-segregated lines, instructed by megaphone and bullied into 'ice-breaking' intimacies, the youngsters are as regimented in their leisure as they presumably are in the working lives which have funded this excursion. Partnered with a member of opposite sex, tied into a black canvas sack and forced to exchange swimming costumes under threat of being thrown into the pool, the young holidaymakers experience coercion and humiliation in the guise of fun. This experience of compulsory heterosexuality moves the taciturn Morvern to some of her most emphatic assertions: 'I says, What a utter total nightmare',[43] 'Is that not called murder? I whispered'[44] and 'This is like living hell on earth, I says into the darkness'.[45]

The summary which Carole Jones provides of the plot of Warner's novel is characteristic of the way in which the narrative – and its implied class politics – is commonly abbreviated: '*Morvern Callar* is the story of a young woman who, after the suicide of her boyfriend, appropriates the novel he leaves behind and the profits from it to fund a Mediterranean rave spree.'[46] However, Morvern travels to the Mediterranean not once but twice, the second time funded by an unexpected windfall which is quite legitimately her own; it consists of the boyfriend's father's legacy, which he has bequeathed to her in his will. Moreover, while Morvern's initial appropriation of her boyfriend's unpublished manuscript undoubtedly entails imposture it nevertheless fulfils the spirit, if not the letter, of his suicide note which licenses her to 'LIVE THE LIFE PEOPLE LIKE ME HAVE DENIED YOU [capitals in original].'[47] I would suggest that the nature of Morvern's transgression lies not so much in her financial (mis)appropriation as in the way in which she disposes of these funds. Jones's reference to Morvern's 'spree'[48] is key here, the term denoting an excessive and perhaps undeserved indulgence in consumption.

In *Morvern Callar*, the publication contract and the legacy both constitute forms of capital whose value is oriented towards future accumulation: the former a bid for posterity in print but also success in the literary marketplace and the latter an act presumably intended (on the part of the boyfriend's father) to preserve and extend class status through inherited wealth. Morvern uses these funds to purchase commodities of great value to her as a young working woman: time and leisure. Her own existence is dominated by the time-managing regimes of low-skilled labour (shift work and paydays), regimes which have foreshortened her childhood and education: 'You ruin your chances at school doing every evening and weekend.'[49] In *Class, Self, Culture* Beverly Skeggs writes that 'the working class have a long history of being represented by excess, whilst the middle-class are represented by their distance from it, usually through associations with restraint, repression, reasonableness, modesty and denial.'[50] Indeed, when viewed from a class perspective defined by restraint, Morvern's pursuit of pleasure liberated from economic constraints would seem personally profligate and financially irresponsible. Morvern does not make any efforts to preserve or accumulate the figures which appear on the ATM screen or printed on a cheque. She does not invest in property nor aspire to social mobility; she makes no attempt to trade in her class identity and indeed her generosity both to friends and fellow service industry workers (including waitresses and taxi drivers in the resorts she visits) seems motivated by a sense of class solidarity. This pattern of expenditure is perhaps expressive of the futility of escape: the amounts in question may not be sufficient to effect long term change. However, Morvern's spending is also suggestive of a defiance of the economy of profit; in a sense, she *destroys* capital by spending it in ways which deprive it of its personal accumulative potential.

Morvern's actions are pathologised in analyses which focus on her individual subjectivity but I have argued that they can also be understood as symptomatic of broader structural and economic inequalities; I have sought to foreground questions of class but also to suggest that Morvern's actions challenge gendered constructions of labour and leisure, production and consumption. Significantly, Morvern's pregnancy on return from her second Spanish sojourn has also been interpreted as a symptom of economic excess; when both Cristie Marsh and Carole Jones, writing in different contexts, describe Morvern as 'penniless and pregnant'[51] her pregnancy is implicitly constructed in class terms.

'The child of the raves': unauthorised sexual reproduction

As a narrative device, pregnancy is often deployed to evoke both a sense of trajectory into the future and to imply a kind of redemption, with the unborn child serving to retrospectively vindicate or justify the conditions of its conception; for example, Watson refers to Morvern as 'pregnant and full of *unearned* and unmediated hope, almost a kind of grace [emphasis added]'.[52] More specifically, in fictional pregnancies the identity of the woman who has conceived is subsumed by larger and more abstract narrative imperatives, to whose interests her own agency is subordinated. Pregnancy becomes metaphorical, serving to expediently 'carry' a symbolical meaning which acts to evacuate the political, economic, corporeal and affective realities of women's experience. The non-realist registers at work in Warner's novel have invited readings of his narrative as 'mythic odyssey'.[53] Morvern's pregnancy is often foregrounded in such readings but in a symbolic register which displaces social and economic realities in favour of archetypal meanings; for example, Jones suggests that her pregnancy 'imposes a feminine interruption that resists the finality of death, inserting an alternative vision of a cycle of life beyond the singular individual'.[54] Moreover, in 'Return of the Goddess: Contemporary Music and Celtic Mythology in Alan Warner's *Morvern Callar*', John LeBlanc suggests that 'Morvern becomes pregnant with ... the future hopes of the Scottish nation, the fruit of the ordeal she has undergone.'[55] While myth may deploy universalising and naturalising language, it is no less implicated in ideology and especially so in relation to racial and ethnic constructions of national identity, in which women's reproductive sexuality plays such a crucial role.[56]

In her essay 'Deconstructing Motherhood', Carol Smart writes that:

> Motherhood is not a natural condition. It is an institution that *presents* itself as a natural outcome of biologically given gender differences, as a natural consequence of (hetero)sexual activity, and as a natural manifestation of an innate female characteristic, namely the maternal instinct [emphasis in original].[57]

The 'naturalising' of motherhood has ideological effects which serve to reinforce presumptions about sexed, sexual and gendered categories of identity, all of which rely on the binary oppositions (male and female, heterosexual and homosexual, masculine and feminine, respectively) implicated in normative constructions of reproductive sexuality. 'Motherhood' is itself a complex term which entails a range of differing roles – genetic, gestational, social – which may not necessarily be undertaken by a single individual.[58] Pregnancy is routinely incorporated within 'motherhood' in its ideological sense, with the 'expectant mother' being interpellated into her prescribed role in advance; such discourses are also mobilised by anti-abortion movements against women who choose to terminate a pregnancy, with the foetus constructed as a child whose rights are privileged over those of the woman on whose body it is dependent. This conflation of pregnancy and motherhood – which itself assumes that the first leads inevitably to the latter – impedes a consideration of pregnancy in its own right. Feminist work on reproductive technologies has done much to deconstruct motherhood and to expose the ways in which it is culturally mediated. In her essay 'Shooting the Mother: Fetal Photography and the Politics of Disappearance', Carol Stabile argues for an increased attention to pregnancy as *'work* women may, or may not, choose to undertake [emphasis added]'.[59] Stabile argues that

> although feminists must insist that pregnancy is not identical with mothering, they must also insist that both are 'biosocial' experiences – that pregnancy, like mothering, is something that occurs within a specific social, economic, cultural, and historical environment and that the experience of pregnancy, as such, is structured by social relations.[60]

I wish to focus on the ways in which the representation of pregnancy, and the meanings it mobilises as a narrative device, are 'structured by social relations',[61] especially in relation to class.

Reflecting on the struggle to establish motherhood as a social and legal institution, Carol Smart identifies the campaigning efforts of two groups: feminists and philanthropic organisations. While the former sought to codify a discourse of motherhood in which mothers were active and expert agents, the latter 'sought to impose specific standards of motherhood on *working class women* through health education, child protection legislation, and various activities associated with poor relief, such as demands for maternity benefits that would have 'strings' attached [emphasis added].'[62] Hence the 'rise of specific normative expectations of white, British motherhood'[63] impacted disproportionately on working-class women. Later discourses, especially those to do with eugenics, compounded this sense of national imperative to regulate the reproductive sexuality of working-class women. As Clare Hanson has written of the 1930s: 'The belief that social class was biologically determined led many to advocate the monitoring and control of reproduction as the most effective means of improving the health and efficiency of the nation.'[64] More recently, Imogen Tyler has analysed 'historically familiar and contemporary anxieties about sexuality, reproduction and fertility and "racial mixing"'[65] in the construction of the 'chav mum' in popular media discourses, including tabloid journalism and television comedy. Tyler writes that this figure 'is used instrumentally to classify bodies according to more or less desirable forms of reproduction.'[66] Moreover, she suggests that the 'chav mum' is

> haunted by another figure, that of the infertile white middle-class middle-aged woman. For whilst the chav mum represents a highly undesirable reproductive body, this figure can also be read as symptomatic of an explosion of anxiety about dropping fertility rates among the white middle class.[67]

The young working-class unmarried mother is pitted against the older middle-class woman struggling to conceive; where the former's supposed profligacy, both economic and sexual, is constructed to provoke disgust and disapproval, the latter's plight is constructed to evoke sympathy, albeit mixed with judgement and cautionary warning. This juxtaposition can be traced to the early 1990s, the context in which Warner's novel was published. The tensions and contradictions at work in the ways in which motherhood has been constituted are made explicit in the polarised discourses about motherhood and work in the 1990s: in the idealisation of motherhood in postfeminist discourses of retreat to the home and family and in the demonising of the 'lone mother'.

Motherhood plays a key role in the 'retreatism' which Diana Negra finds at work in the postfeminist popular culture of the 1990s and early 2000s. She argues that this era has witnessed

> perhaps the most intense cultural coercion for women to retreat from the workplace since the post-World War II period ... the particular target of such discourse is the well-educated professional white woman who, unencumbered by feminist dogma about her entitlement to non-familial personal rewards, abstains from paid work in a display of her 'family values.'[68]

Persistent and avowedly anti-feminist agendas are at work in this movement, but allied in historically specific ways with a 'backlash' politics which holds the women's movement and its legacy responsible for women's disillusionment with the promise of workplace and domestic equality. As Laura Tropp puts it, 'contradictory discourses about women's ability to have it all by achieving motherhood while maintaining a successful professional career and personal life circulate in the popular press and culture';[69] women's failure to 'have it all' is attributed either to essentialist models of gender or to the false promises of feminism rather than to the limitations of masculinist and capitalist models of success and career into which the 'have it all' myth has been readily incorporated. White, middle-class women's 'return' to motherhood within normative familial and marital constraints have generated what Judy Kutulus calls the 'baby-longing plot'[70] in popular cultural narratives, in which a woman's struggle to conceive is experienced as the price paid for prioritising career over motherhood. By contrast, in the early 1990s the figure of the 'lone mother' was simultaneously subject to persistently negative public discourses in both British and North American contexts, in which she was castigated as 'deviant and problematic'.[71] Smart writes that 'after the 1970s it is the lone mother (whether divorced or never married) who is reconstituted more firmly as a burden on the state, as an inadequate mother to her children and as damaging to the moral fibre of society.'[72] However, the economic and class terms by which the lone mother is problematised were compounded in the early 1990s by the popularisation of Charles Murray's controversial theory of the 'underclass'; in 1993 Murray pronounced illegitimacy 'the single most important problem of our time'.[73] Indeed, Sasha Roseneil and Kirk Mann, in their critique of the gendered politics of underclass theory in British contexts, declare 1993 'the year of the lone mother'[74] in ironic recognition of the hateful pitch at which hostile media coverage of lone motherhood had arrived. Mann and Roseneil write that 'the most obvious way in which "the underclass debate" is concerned with gender is in the central place allocated to the lone mother in explanations of its *reproduction* [emphasis added].'[75] The lone mother is deemed to be engaged in a form of *unauthorised* reproduction outside of the legitimising institution of marriage; where reproductive sexuality has been seen in classic Marxist terms as a form of social reproduction (of the labour force) here the lone mother, especially if unmarried, is seen as productive only of future economic dependents.

Hence, when both Marsh and Jones refer to Morvern as 'penniless and pregnant',[76] this phrasing arguably mobilises a discourse to do with class and reproductive sexuality; this discourse posits the unmarried working-class woman as at once an economic and sexual delinquent, her illegitimate sexual reproduction understood as a burden to the economy rather than a contribution to its social reproduction. For Marsh pregnancy is the price which Morvern pays for 'indulg[ing] in what she thought would be unfulfilled dreams'[77] and for Jones it 'signif[ies] her failure to permanently escape from gender and identity, as well as the place of her entrapment'.[78] In this sense, Morvern's pregnancy is its own punishment, containing her within ideological scripts which are informed by both gender and class.

Unauthorised reproduction

I want to conclude by returning to the analogy between social and sexual reproduction with which this chapter opened. Warner's novel does not depict Morvern's experience of birth or motherhood;[79] in some ways this renders her pregnancy all the more open to symbolic interpretations divorced from social and economic reality. However, by disclosing her pregnancy in terms which defy conventions of legitimacy – as the 'child of the raves'[80] – the transgressive quality of Morvern's heterosexuality is foregrounded. Jenny Teichman describes the illegitimate child as '*one whose existence is the result of an unsanctioned sexual act* [emphasis in original]'.[81] Indeed, the policing of conventions and laws pertaining to legitimacy provide a focal point for the patriarchal regulation of female heterosexuality. As Jenny Bourne Taylor writes:

> The creation of a distinction between legitimate and illegitimate children is clearly central to both the definition and establishment of patriarchal power, of the ascendancy of the name and genealogy of the father over that of the mother, of the *transmission of property and established power* [emphasis added].[82]

Like Taylor, Teichman also argues that the 'legitimacy/illegitimacy distinction' is integral to forms of social arrangement which 'link sexuality, reproduction, lineage and naming, and inheritance'.[83] In Warner's novel, issues of property, naming and inheritance become highly charged in relation to Morvern's appropriation of her dead boyfriend's manuscript; I would argue that in this act and in her illegitimate pregnancy alike Morvern confounds what Taylor calls 'the ascendancy of the name and Law of the Father'.[84] In his essay 'Mothers and Authors', Mark Rose observes that:

> As even a cursory invocation of the representation of authorship as analogous to procreation suggests, authorship is a gendered category. Indeed, even today the principle that an author has a right to have his name attached to a work he has created is known as the 'right of paternity.'[85]

The boyfriend's 'right of paternity' has been doubly violated and Morvern is 'unauthorised' in her reproduction both of an appropriated manuscript and of a 'fatherless' child. In making this analogy I have sought to examine the ways in which Morvern's transgressions can be seen as both subversive of normative heterosexuality and as hostage to the discourses by which it is regulated. Questioning the 'unchallenged assumption of a uniform heteronormativity from which all heterosexuals benefit',[86] Cathy J. Cohen has noted the way in which 'heteronormativity works to support and reinforce institutional racism, patriarchy, and class exploitation'.[87] In this chapter questions of class have been foregrounded in order to make explicit its role in the construction of both normative and 'deviant' heterosexualities; I have suggested that the representation of pregnancy in *Morvern Callar* – and its critical reception – can be analysed as illustrating the issues at stake in the regulation of female reproductive sexuality and the uneven distribution of heterosexual privilege.

Notes

1. Alan Warner, *Morvern Callar* (London: Vintage, 1995), p. 229.
2. Judith Roof, *Come as You Are: Sexuality and Narrative* (New York: Columbia University Press, 1996), p. 35.
3. Ibid., p. xxix.
4. See also Rachel Carroll, 'Queer Beauty: Illness, Illegitimacy and Visibility in Dickens's *Bleak House* and Its 2005 BBC Adaptation', *Journal of Adaptation in Film and Performance*, 2: 11 (2009), pp. 5–18.
5. Warner, op. cit., p. 229.
6. Ibid., p. 36.
7. Ibid., p. 1.
8. Ibid.
9. Ibid., pp. 25, 105, 168 and 188.
10. Carole Jones, *Disappearing Men: Gender Disorientation in Scottish Fiction 1979–1999* (Amsterdam and New York: Rodopi, 2009), p. 169.
11. John Caughie, '*Morvern Callar*, Art Cinema and the "Monstrous Archive"', *Scottish Studies Review*, 8: 1 (2007), p. 109.
12. Roderick Watson, *The Literature of Scotland: The 20th Century* (London: Macmillan, 2007), p. 272.
13. Duncan Petrie, *Contemporary Scottish Fictions: Film, Television and the Novel* (Edinburgh: Edinburgh University Press, 2004), p. 98.
14. Jones, op. cit., p. 168.
15. Watson, op. cit., p. 271.
16. Warner, op. cit., p. 1.
17. Ibid., p. 82.
18. Ibid., p. 229.
19. Ibid., p. 3.
20. Ibid., p. 51.

21. Ibid., p. 52.
22. Ibid., p. 11.
23. Ibid., p. 80.
24. Ibid., pp. 11–12.
25. Ibid., p. 81.
26. Ibid., p. 88.
27. Ibid., p. 44.
28. Ibid., p. 46.
29. Ibid., p. 45.
30. Ibid., p. 82.
31. Ibid., pp. 116–17.
32. Petrie, op. cit., p. 92.
33. Ibid., p. 126.
34. Ibid., p. 127.
35. Ibid., p. 129.
36. Ibid., p. 146.
37. Ibid.
38. Ibid., p. 125.
39. Ibid.
40. Ibid., p. 104.
41. Ibid., p. 131.
42. Ibid., p. 136.
43. Ibid., p. 139.
44. Ibid., p. 140.
45. Ibid., p. 142.
46. Jones, op. cit., p. 162.
47. Warner, op. cit., p. 82.
48. Jones, op. cit., p. 162.
49. Warner, op. cit., p. 10.
50. Beverly Skeggs, *Class, Self, Culture* (London: Routledge, 2004), p. 99.
51. Cristie L. Marsh, *Rewriting Scotland: Welsh, McLean, Warner, Banks, Galloway and Kennedy* (Manchester and New York: Manchester University Press, 2002), p. 77 and Jones, op. cit., p. 178.
52. Watson, op. cit., p. 272.
53. Petrie, op. cit., p. 97.
54. Jones, op. cit., pp. 179–80.
55. John LeBlanc, 'Return of the Goddess: Contemporary Music and Celtic Mythology in Alan Warner's *Morvern Callar*', *Revista Canaria de Estudios Ingleses*, 41 (2000), p. 150.
56. Writing in an American context, Cathy J. Cohen points out that 'many of the roots of heteronormativity are in white supremacist ideologies which sought (and continue) to use the state and its regulation of sexuality, in particular through the institution of heterosexual marriage, to designate which individuals were truly fit for full rights and privileges of citizenship.' Cathy J. Cohen, 'Punks, Bulldaggers, and Welfare Queens: The Radical Potential of Queer Politics?', *GLQ: Journal of Lesbian and Gay Studies*, 3 (1997), p. 453.
57. Carol Smart, 'Deconstructing Motherhood', in Elizabeth Bortolaia Silva

(ed.), *Good Enough Mothering? Feminist Perspectives on Lone Motherhood* (London and New York: Routledge, 1996), p. 37.
58. See Michelle Stanworth, 'Reproductive Technologies and the Deconstruction of Motherhood', in Michelle Stanworth (ed.), *Reproductive Technologies: Gender, Motherhood and Medicine* (Cambridge: Polity, 1997), pp. 10–35.
59. Carol Stabile, 'Shooting the Mother: Fetal Photography and the Politics of Disappearance', in Paula A. Treichler, Lisa Cartwright and Constance Penley (eds), *The Visible Woman: Imaging Technologies, Gender and Science* (New York and London: New York University Press, 1998), p. 191.
60. Ibid., p. 192.
61. Ibid.
62. Smart, op. cit., p. 45.
63. Ibid., p. 39.
64. Clare Hanson, 'Save the Mothers? Representations of Pregnancy in the 1930s', *Literature and History*, 12: 2 (2003), p. 59.
65. Imogen Tyler, 'Chav Mum Chav Scum', *Feminist Media Studies*, 8: 1 (2008), p. 18.
66. Ibid., p. 29.
67. Ibid., p. 30.
68. Diana Negra, 'Quality Postfeminism? *Sex and the Single Girl* on HBO', *Genders*, 39 (2004), n.p.
69. Laura Tropp, '"Faking a Sonogram": Representations of Motherhood on *Sex and the City*', *Journal of Popular Culture*, 39: 5 (2006), p. 861.
70. Judy Kutulus, '"Do I look like a chick?": Men, Women, and Babies on Sitcom Maternity Stories', *American Studies*, 39: 2 (1998), p. 26.
71. Ann Phoenix, 'Social Constructions of Lone Motherhood: A Case of Competing Discourses', in Elizabeth Bortolaia Silva (ed.), *Good Enough Mothering? Feminist Perspectives on Lone Motherhood* (London and New York: Routledge, 1996), p. 176.
72. Smart, op. cit., p. 54.
73. Mary McIntosh, 'Social Anxieties About Lone Motherhood and Ideologies of the Family: Two Sides of the Same Coin', in Elizabeth Bortolaia Silva (ed.), *Good Enough Mothering? Feminist Perspectives on Lone Motherhood* (London and New York: Routledge, 1996), p. 148.
74. Sasha Roseneil and Kirk Mann, 'Unpalatable Choices and Inadequate Families: Lone Mothers and the Underclass Debate', in Elizabeth Bortolaia Silva (ed.), *Good Enough Mothering? Feminist Perspectives on Lone Motherhood* (London and New York: Routledge, 1996), p. 192.
75. Kirk Mann and Sasha Roseneil, '"Some Mothers Do 'Ave 'Em": Backlash and the Gender Politics of the Underclass Debate', *Journal of Gender Studies*, 3: 3 (1994), p. 329.
76. Marsh, op. cit., p. 77 and Jones, op. cit., p. 178.
77. Marsh, op. cit., p. 77.
78. Jones, op. cit., p. 178.
79. Morvern's story is continued in Warner's subsequent novel *These Demented Lands* (London: Jonathan Cape, 1997).
80. Warner, op. cit., p. 229.
81. Jenny Teichman, *Illegitimacy: A Philosophical Examination* (Oxford: Basil Blackwell, 1982), p. 79.

82. Jenny Bourne Taylor, 'Representing Illegitimacy in Victorian Culture', in Ruth Robbins and Julian Wolfreys (eds), *Victorian Identities: Social and Cultural Formations in Nineteenth Century Literature* (London: Routledge, 1996), pp. 121–2.
83. Teichman, op. cit., p. 84.
84. Jenny Bourne Taylor, 'Nobody's Secret: Illegitimate Inheritance and the Uncertainties of Memory', *Nineteenth-Century Contexts*, 21 (2000), p. 570.
85. Mark Rose, 'Mothers and Authors: Johnson V. Calvert and the New Children of Our Imaginations', in Paula A. Treichler, Lisa Cartwright and Constance Penley (eds), *The Visible Woman: Imaging Technologies, Gender and Science* (New York and London: New York University Press, 1998), p. 225.
86. Cohen, op. cit., p. 452.
87. Ibid., p. 455.

Part Three: Reproducing heterosexuality

Chapter 5

'First one thing and then the other': rewriting the intersexed body in Jeffrey Eugenides' *Middlesex*

The narrative of Jeffrey Eugenides' 2002 comic epic of Greek American identity, *Middlesex*, journeys through time and space from Greco-Turkish hostilities in Smyrna in 1912, to the 1967 'race riots' in Detroit, through to post-unification Berlin in 2001. However, this reconstructed family history is also mapped against the narrator's retrospective account of an ambiguously sexed identity. Intersexuality demonstrates both the indeterminacy of 'sex' as a category by which to define bodies and identities and the normative violence to which deviant bodies are subject. Indeed, the medical and surgical management of intersexed bodies can be considered symptomatic of a heteronormative imperative; as Alice Domurat Dreger has put it, 'a significant motivation for the biomedical treatments of hermaphrodites is the desire to keep people straight.'[1] The refusal of 'corrective' surgery is pivotal to the life history recounted in *Middlesex*. However, I will argue that this act of apparent resistance to medical orthodoxy serves less to contest the binary logic of sexed, gendered and sexual identities than to preserve a normative sexed identity as male and sexual identity as heterosexual. Eugenides' Pulitzer Prize-winning novel seems to be expressive of a broader cultural and theoretical interest in the discontinuities of sex, gender and sexuality; *Middlesex* gives a memorable fictional voice to one of 'those "incoherent" or "discontinuous" gendered beings' who, as Judith Butler puts it, 'fail to conform to the gendered norms of cultural intelligibility by which persons are defined.'[2] However, this chapter will consider the ways in which a nominally transgressive narrative can nevertheless remain captive to normative discourses.

Dreger describes 'hermaphrodite studies' as a 'lively storytelling genre in medicine'[3] whose authors attracted a degree of celebrity on account of the sensational case histories they published. More recently, the emergence of advocacy movements campaigning for the rights of intersexed people has inaugurated of a new genre of 'storytelling': the testimonies of intersexed people, often recording traumatising encounters with the medical establishment. Hence, this genre of life-writing has become the site of highly charged claims for self-determination, authorship and agency. Storytelling is a significant motif in Eugenides' acutely self-reflexive novel; this chapter aims to explore the narrative strategies within which Cal's intersexed body is framed. The intersexed body problematises the notion of origin in relation to sexed and hence gendered and sexual identity. However, fictions of origin – whether cultural, generational or genetic – dominate the narrative of *Middlesex*. I wish to interrogate the retrospective logic at work within *Middlesex* and to explore the ways in which it serves to *contain* the contingencies of sex, gender and sexuality suggested by the intersexed body.

Border crossings: cultural and sexed hybridity

Cal Stephanides, the narrator and protagonist of *Middlesex*, is a third generation Greek American whose cultural heritage provides ample opportunities for the author to playfully evoke the mythological meanings of the figure of the hermaphrodite. Self-reflexive allusions to classical mythology abound in this ebulliently metafictional novel. Cal is conceived following her parents return from a theatrical production of *The Minotaur*, studies Ovid's *Metamorphoses* at school and is cast as Tiresias in a student production of *Antigone*. Later, as a teenage runaway living amid the sexual counter-cultures of San Francisco, he re-enacts the myth of Salmacis and Hermaphroditus for the titillation of the punters in Bob Presto's club, the Sixty Niners.[4] Cal is a diminutive for Calliope, the muse of heroic epic and indeed the narrator claims, in a rather disingenuous apology, an epic status for his story: 'Sorry if I get a little Homeric at times. That's genetic too.'[5] In this aside, cultural and genetic constructions of heritage and inheritance are humorously conflated. Indeed, parallels between the kinds of national, ethnic and racial border crossings which Cal's forebears undergo and the sexed and gendered border crossings which Cal encounters as an intersexed person are a recurring motif in this novel:

> My grandparents had fled their home because of a war. Now, some fifty-two years later, I was fleeing myself ... A ship didn't carry me across the ocean; instead, a series of cars conveyed me across a continent. I was becoming a new person, too, just like Lefty and Desdemona, and I didn't know what would happen to me in this new world to which I'd come.[6]

This analogy is not without precedent, as Judith Halberstam has noted in relation to transsexuality: 'Metaphors of travel and border crossings are inevitable within a discourse of transsexuality. But they are also laden with the histories of other identity negotiations, and they carry the burden of national and colonial discursive histories.'[7] The crossing of borders is, of course, not in itself a subversive act. Indeed, the Stephanides' American story charts an assimilationist imperative which first challenges but then compounds racial and ethnic hierarchies. The fate of the family restaurant business – Hercules Hot Dogs – is instructive here. Located within an African American neighbourhood as a consequence of the segregationist effects of urban housing policy, it is the last white-owned business to be destroyed by fire during the 1967 'race riots' in Detroit. However, the subsequent insurance settlement enables the family to join the 'white flight' from the city and only accelerates their economic and social mobility, such that Cal's parents are able to place her in a private girls' school and thereby evade the racial desegregation of the public school system. Middlesex Boulevard is the location of Cal's teenage family home. In this least desirable of the sought-after white neighbourhoods in Grosse Point, the Stephanides live happily alongside an orthodox Jewish family; both are subject to the 'points system' by which real estate agents police racial boundaries, but both enjoy the privileges of a hard-won, if somewhat provisional, 'whiteness'. The complex, contradictory and contested nature of normative constructions of national and racial identity are embodied in Middlesex as a location. Similar tensions are at work in the narrative depiction of intersexed identity – the 'middle sex' to which the title more punningly refers.

The conflation of cultural and sexed hybridity in the border crossing analogy is reinforced when Cal reflects on his origins in this way: 'I'm the descendant of a smuggling operation, too. Without their knowing, my grandparents, on their way to America, were each carrying a single mutated gene on the fifth chromosome.'[8] His grandparents' passage not only allows them to undergo a transformation of national identity but also of familial identity; in 1912 they leave the burning shores of Smyrna brother and sister, to dock in America as husband and wife. This union is itself implicated in ethnic and racial discourses given that it is attributed to, and implicitly explained by, the shortage of marriageable Greek women. Desdemona and Lefty's incestuous marriage is retrospectively identified by Cal as the genetic cause of his intersexed state. This deduction is not simply a reflection of one branch of medical opinion.[9] It is also symptomatic of a narrative logic which serves to fix the indeterminacy of intersexed identity by reference to a founding origin. Cal attributes his intersexed state to their consanguineous union – and so establishes genetic determinism as the driving force of his retrospective narrative, which is neatly reduced to the 'roller-coaster ride of a single gene through time'.[10] The generational narrative acts as a carrier for a genetic narrative, whereby Cal's identity is destined to be determined by the past; in this way his possible futures are foreclosed by an inheritance which is written into his genes:

> I'm quickly approaching the moment of discovery: of myself by myself, which was something I knew all along and yet didn't know ... the discovery of the mutated gene that had lain buried in our bloodline for two hundred and fifty years, biding its time ... it started the chain of events that led to me, here, writing in Berlin.[11]

In *Middlesex*, a theory of genetic inheritance – only one medical hypothesis among many seeking to explain the incidence of intersexed births – serves as the premise for a complex and compelling narrative strategy: one which rewrites what Cal 'didn't know' into something 'known all along'.[12]

'First one thing and then the other'

The course of Cal's life story is anticipated in the opening of the novel:

> I was born twice: first, as a baby girl, on a remarkably smogless Detroit day in January of 1960; and then again, as a teenage boy, in an emergency room in Petoskey, Michigan, in August of 1974 ... But now, at the age of forty-one, I feel another birth coming on.[13]

This arresting, proleptic prelude to the action of the narrative correctly raises an anticipation that Cal's identity will be medically mediated. However, the process by which his identity is determined is much more protracted and ambiguous than is suggested in this narrative sleight of hand. By focusing on the process by which Cal 'becomes' intersexed, I will explore how the retrospective logic at work in this narrative is complicit in a heteronormative temporality.

In his essay '"The Glans Opens Like a Book": Writing and Reading the Intersexed Body', Iain Morland writes that: 'Intersex bodies have genetic, hormonal, and anatomical configurations that cannot be adequately apprehended by hegemonic discourses of sexual difference.'[14] More specifically, these bodies confound the binary logic of sexed identity. The cultural and historical construction of gender has been compellingly demonstrated over the decades by feminist and gender theorists.

More recently, queer theorists – and most prominently Judith Butler – have questioned the rhetorical manoeuvre by which this argument has sometimes been made, namely the differentiation of gender, as culturally mediated, from sex, as biologically fixed.[15] The cultural construction of 'sex' is made all too apparent in the medical management of intersex bodies. Intersex theorists have noted how the birth of an intersexed infant is conventionally interpreted as presenting a 'medical emergency';[16] the appearances of ambiguities in, or discrepancies between, genetic, hormonal and anatomical definitions of sex is deemed to warrant rapid and radical surgical intervention, even though the intersexed condition does not necessarily in and of itself pose a threat to the baby's immediate or even future health. Such interventions pose important ethical questions given that they constitute medically unnecessary cosmetic surgery on a subject unable to give consent, and given that such initial surgeries are often a prelude to lifelong medical interventions whose side effects can include irreversibly impaired sexual function. Cheryl Chase is one of the most eloquent of theorists and activists who have articulated a critique of this practice: 'Pediatric surgeries literalize what might otherwise be considered a theoretical operation: the attempted production of normatively sexed bodies and gendered subjects through constitutive acts of violence.'[17] Indeed, advocates of intersex rights have made analogies between female genital mutilation (FGM) and what they term infant genital mutilation (IGM), some noting that while Western opposition to FGM sits comfortably within latent colonial assumptions, acceptance of IGM within Western medical practice reveals a very culturally entrenched commitment to normative constructions of sexed identity. The medical and surgical management of intersexed bodies is, then, a highly charged issue within intersex theory and activism. I will consider Cal's refusal of 'corrective' surgery as a teenager in Eugenides' novel in this context and question the extent to which it can be aligned with a queer critique.[18]

Intersexed conditions are various and the particular form which Eugenides fictionalises offers specific narrative opportunities. Many intersexed conditions are apparent at birth in the form of ambiguous external genitalia. However, Cal is diagnosed as having a 5-Alpha-reductase deficiency, a condition in which an individual's genitals appear female at birth but undergo an apparent male to female transformation at puberty. A powerful motif in the life-writing of intersexed people is the discovery in later life of a hidden sexed history, in the form of surgery performed in infancy and concealed throughout childhood.[19] By contrast, Cal's condition enables Eugenides to construct a narrative in which intersexed identity is experienced within a temporal and teleological structure: as having a 'before' and 'after', as departing from an origin to arrive at a given destination, as crossing a border upheld by a binary logic. Or as Cal puts it, in another knowingly classical reference: 'Like Tiresias, I was first one thing and then the other.'[20] This logic echoes the retrospective tendency which intersex theorists have discovered in conventional medical discourses of intersex. Its management is premised on the assumption that a true sexed identity *does* exist – and that it must be restored. This restitution narrative, as Dreger has described it (borrowing from Arthur Frank in *The Wounded Storyteller*), informs the terms by which patients, or more often their parents, are advised. Genitals are described as being 'unfinished' or 'incomplete' and surgery offered as simply finishing a process of development begun in the womb. Eugenides' narrative strategies share the paradoxical relationship to origin which Morland attributes to normalising surgery, which 'purports to reconstitute a sexed original which is somehow prior to the intersexed original, prior to the origin and arrival in the world of the human subject, the intersex individual.'[21]

The third birth to which Cal alludes in the opening of the novel refers in one sense to his anticipated emergence as the author of a life history to rival its historical antecedents: 'When this story goes out into the world, I may become the most famous hermaphrodite in history.'[22] His aspiration towards authorship arguably has its roots in his interviews with Dr Luce, the medical celebrity to whom Cal is referred following a routine emergency room examination. Dr Luce is not only the founder a Sexual Disorders and Gender Identity Clinic but also the author of a column for *Playboy* magazine, headed 'The Oracular Vulva', in which the said organ is ventriloquised to respond to readers' enquiries and to offer some educational insights into erotic cultural history. Cal's case history is destined to become incorporated within the medical archive on which Luce founds his fame; Cal later identifies his anonymised body in one of Luce's publications: 'That's me on page 578, standing naked beside a height chart with a black box covering my eyes.'[23] However, Luce also invites the teenage Cal to write her own life history as an aid to his diagnosis. It is here that Cal's entanglements with the discourses of the normative – and his later struggle to become the author of his own life – become most tense. The autobiographical authority of Cal's teenage life history implicitly competes with the medical authority of Luce's case notes; however, it becomes evident that both authors falsify reality in order to preserve a culturally constructed 'truth' of sex.

Unaware of the hypotheses which Luce is testing, but rightly fearing the kinds of interventions which the 'wrong' response might prompt,

Cal fakes her life. This faking is not without precedent; Cal is already adept at a ruse deployed to evade unwanted parental and professional scrutiny:

> That summer – while the President's lies were also getting more elaborate – I started faking my period. With Nixonian cunning, Calliope unwrapped and flushed away a flotilla of unused Tampax. I feigned symptoms from headache to fatigue. I did cramps the way Meryl Streep did accents.[24]

Cal's anxieties about the onset of menstruation, her dread of visiting a gynaecologist and exposing herself to his invasive examination, and her self-consciousness in the presence of her more developed peers are recognisable features of 'normal' pubescent girlhood, especially given that the onset of puberty is effectively a prelude to a lifetime of gendered scrutiny. However, in her self-authored life, Cal endeavours to convince Luce of the normality of her gendered identity by concealing the truth of her emotional life as a teenage girl; principally, she conceals her attraction to other girls and her sexual experiences with her female best friend. In this fictionalised autobiography, the adult Cal remembers her first foray into life-writing as derivative and inauthentic but also, crucially, as performative in that it serves to produce an identity contingent on the needs of a specific moment:

> Half the time I wrote like bad George Eliot, the other half like bad Salinger ... But on that Smith Corona I quickly discovered that telling the truth wasn't nearly as much fun as making things up. I also knew that I was writing for an audience – Dr. Luce – and that if I seemed normal enough, he might send me back home.[25]

This ploy is effective in that Luce is convinced of Cal's successful socialisation as a girl. Luce studiously avoids gendered pronouns in his first interviews with Cal's parents, but now pronounces Cal their 'daughter' and delivers his diagnosis; concealing the reality of Cal's intersexed body, he prescribes 'corrective' surgery in order to align Cal's genitals with her gender.

Simultaneous to Luce's disclosure to Cal's parents, however, is Cal's discovery of Luce's case notes, which record the identification of undescended testes and a hypospadic penis, mistaken to date for a generous clitoris. The normative impulse at work in Luce's decision, and its potentially devastating effects for Cal as a sexual being, are made clear in the notes which Cal surreptitiously reads:

> 'Though it is possible that the surgery may result in partial or total loss of erotosexual sensation, sexual pleasure is only one factor in a happy life. The

ability to marry and pass as a normal woman in society are also important goals.'[26]

Cal's subterfuge – her attempt to pass as normal in a heteronormative culture – inadvertently licenses radical surgical intervention in the name of restoring normalcy, or rather its appearance. As Cal herself puts it:

> I had miscalculated with Luce. I thought that after talking to me he would decide that I was normal and leave me alone. But I was beginning to understand something about normality. Normality wasn't normal. It couldn't be. If normality were normal, everybody could leave it alone. They could sit back and let normality manifest itself.[27]

It is at this point that Cal takes flight, leaving the clinic, his parents and his home to protect his bodily integrity. This is without doubt an act of defiance against the medical establishment and its management of intersexed bodies. But on another level Cal remains hostage to its discourses.

It is Luce's case notes and their record of genitals palpated and examined which forms the origin of Cal's newly sexed identity rather than his own corporeal experience. Moreover, it is this medical history which inaugurates the retrospective logic which dominates the text we read. The adult Cal lays claim to an unequivocal maleness decreed by his hormonal constitution; in the earlier stages of the narrative, and in anticipation of events yet to unfold, he asserts: 'To the extent that fetal hormones affect brain chemistry and histology, I've got a male brain. But I was raised a girl.'[28] Retelling his life for his imagined avid reader, Cal rewrites his past desires as anticipating the male heterosexual destinations with which he later identifies. For example, remembering her locker room self-consciousness in the presence of a schoolgirl elite at her single-sex prep school, Cal reflects: 'I look back now (as Dr. Luce urged me to do) to see exactly what twelve-year old Calliope was feeling, watching the Charm Bracelets undress in steamy light. Was there a shiver of arousal in her?'[29] However, Cal's desires are placed firmly within a heterosexual matrix. Cal attributes her sexual attraction to girls to his belatedly discovered maleness in such a way as to infer a direct, causal link between sex and sexuality, one which seems to preclude, or at least refuse to acknowledge, the possibility of same sex desire. And yet whereas this matrix posits sex as the origin of gender and sexuality, in Cal's narrative sex becomes the rhetorical *effect* of sexuality; *her* teenage sexual attraction to girls is retrospectively explained and legitimised by the discovery of *his* 'true biological nature'.[30] Hence, the retrospective narration recuperates the same-sex desire which Cal feels as a teenage girl as a signifier of an incipient heterosexuality, which is then mobilised to authorise a sexed identity which *follows* rather than *precedes* his desires.

The middle part: adolescence and indeterminacy

The retrospective narrative strategies employed by Eugenides in *Middlesex* make it impossible for the reader to access Cal's experience as a teenage girl other than through the adult male Cal's self-consciously knowing hindsight; Cal's female adolescence is mediated by the adult Cal's conviction in his genetically sexed identity as male. This is not the first time that Eugenides has explored female adolescence through a male perspective; in his 1993 novel *The Virgin Suicides*, also set in Grosse Pointe, Michigan in the 1970s, the narrative voice represents the collective experience of a group of boys brought together by their shared obsession with a family of teenage girls and their deaths by suicide. In *The Virgin Suicides* female adolescence is mediated by male voyeurism but remains ultimately enigmatic and unknowable, the elusiveness of female subjectivity forever preserved, and indeed fetishised, by the facts of the Lisbon sisters' premature deaths. In *Middlesex*, Eugenides devises a narrative strategy which enables the author both to occupy the body and mind of a teenage girl and to speculate on teenage girlhood as an adult male. By revisiting Cal's adolescence as experienced by her as a girl I aim to recover the discontinuities of sex, gender and sexuality which the narrative seeks subsequently to contain.

Kenneth Millard has noted the ways in which contemporary fictions of adolescence situate formative experiences

> in relation to historical contexts or points of origin by which individuals come to understand themselves as having been conditioned. The individual novel often reveals a temporal structure in which the contemporary coming-of-age is contextualised gradually by a consciousness of historical events that are antecedent to it and deeply inform it.[31]

In this way, adolescence is figured as subjectively experienced but historically determined; hence narratives of adolescence can become narratives of historical, and perhaps especially national, development. *Middlesex* could be read as exemplifying this trope, especially where sexed hybridity is interpreted as a metaphor for cultural hybridity and Cal's inbetweenness as a cipher for the immigrant experience. However, the emphasis on 'points of origin' by which individuals '*come to understand* themselves as having been conditioned [emphasis added]'[32] reveals a retrospective logic by which adolescent experience is subordinated to the adult identity which supplants it. In the context of an analysis of representations of adolescence and same-sex desire, Angus Gordon suggests that 'the idea that a particular period of life is fundamentally structured by its transitionality and indeterminacy is ... a narrative construction.'[33] Expressions of sexuality and desire which depart from heterosexual norms are normalised so long as the transition to adult heterosexuality is completed and the apparent 'indeterminacy' resolved:

> The meaning of adolescence is always understood to become apparent only in hindsight; it is structured throughout by a foreshadowed denouement, which is the subject's arrival at adulthood ... the discourse of adolescence typically recuperates [same-sex desire or experience] as detours (even, at times, as *necessary* detours) on the path to an eventual heterosexual consummation [emphasis in original].[34]

In her 1996 book on sexuality and narrative *Come As You Are*, Judith Roof suggests that the middle part of the narrative is the structural location where lesbian identity is permitted to become visible, but only as a detour, a digression, a prelude to what follows: in her words, as 'the pretext for the heteronarrative's spectacular return'.[35] In a similar way I would suggest that *Middlesex* has a kind of middle part – dedicated to teenage girlhood – in which discontinuities of sex, gender and sexuality are given expression but that, ironically, their possibilities are closed down rather than opened up at the point at which Cal becomes conscious of her intersexed identity. I aim to explore tensions between normative narrative tendencies and queer textual moments, by which I mean moments in which the binary logic of the heterosexual matrix begins to fold in on itself.

Cal's emergent sexuality is overshadowed by heteronormative imperatives, namely the pressure to conform to normative heterosexual scripts and the fear of becoming, or being identified as, a lesbian. In this way, Cal's adolescence is entirely 'normal' and as such is revealing of some of the tensions and contradictions inevitably at work within normative prescriptions. The possibility of identifying as a lesbian, whether as a teenage girl or as a transgendered adult, is foreclosed by the narrative which simultaneously universalises and marginalises lesbian existence. Cal's passion for her best friend at her exclusive girls' school, is normalised through the familiar depiction of teenage female homoeroticism as a rehearsal for the main event: heterosexuality. Hence Cal notes that 'It was perfectly acceptable at Baker & Inglis to get a crush on a fellow classmate. At a girls school a certain amount of emotional energy, normally expended on boys, gets redirected into friendships.'[36]

However, the possibility of her or one of her peers identifying as lesbian is precluded by reference to the 'militantly heterosexual'[37] ethos of the school: 'Any girl suspected of being attracted to girls was gossiped about, victimized, and shunned. I was aware of all this. It scared me.'[38] Paradoxically, lesbianism is depicted as a ubiquitous sexual fashion while at the same time apparently precluded as a narrative possibility for its girl protagonist: 'Why should I have thought I was anything other than a girl? Because I was attracted to a girl? That happened all the time. It was happening more than ever in 1974. It was becoming a national pastime.'[39] The fate of Sourmelina, Desdemona and Lefty's naturalised cousin, is illustrative of the fate of lesbian representability in this novel.[40] Lina is a welcoming host to her newly arrived cousins and also their only confidante as incestuously married siblings; however, her discretion is somewhat coerced given that it is secured in return for a reciprocal silence on the matter of her sexuality:

> My grandparents had every reason to believe that Sourmelina would keep their secret. She'd come to America with a secret of her own, a secret that would be guarded by our family until Sourmelina died in 1979, whereupon, like everyone's secrets, it was posthumously declassified, so that people began to speak of 'Sourmelina's girlfriends.'[41]

The family's solution to Lina's problematic sexuality in her home country is to place her in an arranged marriage which requires her migration to the United States. The pragmatic Lina seems to suffer no personal disquiet about her sexuality – despite its implicit equation, within the narrative, with the shame of incestuous sexuality – and following her husband's disappearance sets up home with a female companion. However, at this point in the novel Lina is dispatched to another state only returning, both to the neighbourhood and the narrative, following the death of her partner. Hence she is absent and unavailable at the very point in the narrative where her example might suggest other models of identity to the adolescent Cal.

Exactly what occurs between Cal and her teenage female lover remains obscure in *Middlesex*; just as the object of Cal's passion strategically feigns unconsciousness at what her body is experiencing, so Eugenides draws a discreet narrative veil over the nature of her pleasure. While the desires which inspire these encounters raise questions for Cal about her sexuality, the acts which they prompt do not appear to raise questions about her sex. The elaborately euphemistic terms with which Cal describes her own sexual sensations are almost paradoxically evocative of the naturalising metaphors by which female sexuality and feminine sensibility have traditionally been denoted: 'For that spring, while the crocuses bloomed, while the headmistress checked on the daffodil bulbs in the flower beds, Calliope too, felt something budding ... A kind of crocus itself, just before flowering.'[42] The association between sexuality and fertility, the reference to enfolded organic forms, and the allusion to 'blooming' and 'flowering' conspire to suggest that female sexual arousal is integral to natural cycles of fertility, a process by which the female is made receptive to a reproductive destiny. However, this metaphor also allows for a significant indeterminacy with regard to its sexed referent:

> A pink stem pushing up through dark new moss. But a strange kind of flower indeed, because it seemed to go through a number of seasons in a single day. It had its dormant winter when it slept underground. Five minutes later, it stirred in a private springtime. Sitting in class with a book in my lap, or riding home in car pool, I'd feel a thaw between my legs, the soil growing moist, a rich, peaty aroma arising, and then – while I pretended to memorize Latin verbs – the sudden, squirming life in the warm earth beneath my skirt. To the touch, the crocus sometimes felt soft and slippery, like the flesh of a worm. At other times it was as hard as a root.[43]

While the 'pushing' and 'stirring' of Cal's 'pink stem' could be placed within the lexicon of euphemisms for male sexual sensation, the crocus which can be both 'soft and slippery' and 'hard as a root' has qualities of both male and female genitals. Indeed, Cal admits that 'I knew from personal experience that the Object had a crocus of her own. It swelled, too, when touched';[44] the crocus is here implicitly identified as, or at least with, the clitoris. The only difference relates to its size: 'Mine was just bigger, more effusive in its feelings. My crocus wore its heart on its sleeve'[45] and elsewhere 'I worried at times that my crocus was too elaborate a bloom, not a common perennial but a hothouse flower, a hybrid named by its originator like a rose.'[46] Such an effusive bloom would seem to offer considerable potential in terms of sexual pleasure but Cal's adolescent sexual desires are principally played out in service to the pleasure of another; as Cal laconically concedes: 'It was never my turn with the Object.'[47] Cal's teenage lover is retrospectively named after Luis Buñuel's 1977 film *That Obscure Object of Desire*; this ruse is ostensibly to protect her identity but also evokes the way in which her own identity is obscured and objectified by Cal's obsession. Cal refers to her 'crocus' as 'an obscure object all her own'[48] and indeed the elusive and enigmatic object of her affections comes to stand for the indeterminacy of her genitals. However, an indeterminacy of agency and object is a recurring motif of Eugenides' depiction of teenage sexuality.

An unspoken pact develops between Cal and her friend, whereby the Obscure Object feigns unconsciousness as Cal acts out her desires when they share a companionable bed: 'Sometimes when I climbed on top of the Object she would almost wake up. She would move to accommodate me, spreading her legs or throwing an arm around my back. She swam to the surface of consciousness before diving again.'[49] The Obscure Object's passivity, assuming that is a form of unspoken consent, can be understood as a way of enjoying Cal's attentions while disavowing the implications of their intimacy, principally the lesbian identity which it might seem to disclose. In terms of characterisation, and from Cal's perspective, it also seems an extension of a narcissistic sense of entitlement integral to the Object's privileged class and racial identity as a wealthy, white girl. In other ways, however, it could also be placed within the spectrum of normative female heterosexuality and indeed it is a role which Cal herself reluctantly plays when she finds herself cast in the sexual script pursued by the Obscure Object's brother Jerome and his friend Rex. Jerome strategically supports Rex's amorous ambitions with the Obscure Object, by engaging and disarming Cal as a companion whose presence might otherwise become an obstacle. Here Cal adopts a passivity which resembles that of the Object, but where the Object's passivity enables her to enjoy a sexual experience at odds with her nominally heterosexual identity, Cal's passivity enables her to endure a sexual experience compelled by the pressures of heteronormativity: 'I didn't stop him. I remained completely still while he did his thing ... Behind my impassive face my soul curled up into a ball, waiting until the unpleasantness was over.'[50] Cal's behaviour is within the spectrum of normative female heterosexuality so long as female sexuality is assumed to be innately passive and male sexuality innately active: hence, heterosexuality becomes something which men 'do' to women. Equally, while Jerome is not forceful and certainly not violent, the distinction between consensual and coercive sex is uneasily blurred in this scene.

However, while reluctantly going through the motions of making out with her best friend's brother, Cal fantasises about inhabiting the body of the Obscure Object's boyfriend Rex; here the boundaries between same-sex and heterosexual roles become blurred: 'And then, because I suddenly knew that I could, I slipped into the body of Rex Reese. I entered him like a god so that it was me, and not Rex, who kissed her.'[51] By assuming the fantasised agency of a heterosexual boy, Cal is able to legitimise her own desires for the Object: to make them meaningful and authentic in heteronormative terms. As Cal writes: 'I saw [her breasts]; I touched them; and since it wasn't me who did this but Rex Reese I didn't have to feel guilty, didn't have to ask myself if I was having unnatural desires.'[52] Just as the Obscure Object acts out a feminine sexual passivity as a way of normalising her same-sex desires, here Cal acts out a masculine heterosexual activity in order to normalise her desires. It is at the moment at which Cal deduces that Jerome is '*inside me* [emphasis in original]'[53] – signified by 'pain like a knife, pain like fire'[54] – that Cal experiences a revelation:

> We gaped at each other and I knew he knew. Jerome knew what I was, as suddenly I did, too, for the first time clearly understood that I wasn't a girl but something in between. I knew this from how natural it felt to enter Rex Reese's body, *how right it felt*, and I knew this from the shocked expression on Jerome's face [emphasis in original].[55]

From the retrospective vantage point of the adult Cal, this remembered fantasy is enlisted to support his recuperative narrative, whereby a male sexed identity is discovered as the cause of a sexuality which is retroactively understood as heterosexual. Nevertheless, this is a rather queer textual moment. It is not so much the 'entry' into her friend's body that is emphasised as the object of this exercise as Cal's entry into the body of a boy. Moreover, Jerome's response, apparently so pivotal to her own revelation, is quickly revealed to be entirely her own projection: 'Reader, believe this if you can: he hadn't noticed a thing.'[56] Jerome's unknowingness might be attributed to his youthful inexperience or to a self-absorbed indifference to his partner's body; however, it is also suggestive of an indeterminate sexuality reminiscent, perhaps, of Cal's earliest erotic sensations playing in the swimming pool with her childhood friend Clementine:

> I fall between her legs, I fall on top of her, we sink ... and then we're twirling, spinning in the water, me on top, then her, then me ... I'm not sure which hands are mine, which legs.[57]

Hands and legs become interchangeable and agency blissfully blurred. Similarly, in Cal's encounters with the Object, 'What pressed on our attention was that it was happening, sex was happening. That was the great fact. How it happened exactly, what went where was secondary.'[58] What has *not* happened in any of these scenes is phallic penetration, an act assumed integral to normative definitions of heterosexuality; what these scenes imagine is a sexuality whose bodily encounters defy binary categorisation and forms of sexual pleasure unencumbered by presumptions about 'what goes where'. I would suggest that the adult Cal's much lamented failure to establish enduring heterosexual relationships is attributable less to the fact of his intersexed body than to his own renunciation of the kinds of sexual indeterminacy which characterise the teenage Cal's desires.

If the adult Cal seeks to disavow the sex and putative sexuality of his teenage girl self, there nevertheless remains a continuity which inadvertently subverts the causal chain of the heterosexual matrix: this continuity relates to her masculinity. When the adult Cal detects a seductive masculinity in his remembered teenage self he is in one sense overwriting same-sex eroticism; however, his recollection may also obscure the ways in which it is precisely *as a girl* that Cal's masculinity attracts her peers:

> My body might have released pheromones that affected my schoolmates. How else to explain the way my friends tugged on me, leaned on me? ... in seventh grade, when my hair was glossy instead of frizzy, my cheeks still smooth, my muscles undeveloped, and yet, invisibly but unmistakeably, I began to exude some kind of masculinity, in the way I tossed up and caught my eraser, for instance, or in the way I dive-bombed people's desserts with my spoon, in the intensity of my knit brow or my eagerness to debate anyone on anything in class; when I was a changeling, before I changed, I was quite popular at my new school.[59]

The adult Cal lays claim to an unequivocal maleness decreed by his hormonal constitution; indeed, he employs the medical authority of his diagnosis to deny any ambiguity of sex or gender:

> Something that you should understand: I'm not androgynous in the least. 5-alpha-reductase deficiency syndrome allows for normal biosynthesis and peripheral action of testosterone, in utero, neonatally, and at puberty. In other words, I operate in society as a man. I use the men's room. Never the urinals, always the stalls ... I've lived more than half my life as a male, and by now everything comes naturally.[60]

The journey on which Cal embarks when he flees Dr Luce's surgery becomes a lifetime vocation; here Cal describes the contents of a travelling suitcase:

> Inside were all the clothes I'd chosen myself: the crew neck sweaters in primary colours, the Lacoste shirts, the wide-wale corduroys. My coat was from Papagallo, lime green with horn-shaped buttons made from bone.[61]

However, this is a wardrobe selected, with some panache, not by the adult male Cal after his diagnosis but by the teenage girl Cal just prior to her encounter with Luce. Her taste in clothes is complexly coded in terms not only of gender but also of class and ethnicity; her 'preppy' style is in part a sartorial homage to the upper class, WASPish girls with whom she schools, but is at odds with prevailing modes of femininity within her family culture. When reading this text we should not forget Judith Halberstam's reminder that 'masculinity does not belong to men, has not been produced only by men, and does not properly express male heterosexuality';[62] masculinity is a mode of gendered being available to the teenage girl and adult man alike, regardless of their sexuality. Despite his adult insistence on the unequivocal nature of his maleness, Cal nevertheless relies heavily on the props of masculine masquerade: 'The cigars, the double-breasted suits – they're a little too much. I'm well aware of that. But I need them. They make me feel better. After what I've been through, some overcompensation is to be expected.'[63] 'Passing' becomes a vocation to which Cal has a lifelong, dandyish dedication. Moreover, when he reflects on his 'old-school, gentlemanly routine'[64] it becomes clear that he is performing specific class and ethnic modes of masculinity:

> Since it was the weekend, I tried to dress down. It isn't easy for me. I wore a camel-hair turtleneck, tweed blazer, and jeans. And a pair of handmade cordovans by Edward Green ... The Dundee is a shoe designed for touring the landed estates, for tromping through mud while wearing a tie, with your spaniels trailing behind ... On the shoebox it says: 'Edward Green: Master Shoemakers to the Few.' That's me exactly. The few.[65]

Cal notes that 'In America, England is where you go to wash yourself of ethnicity';[66] millennial Europe seems to fulfil the same function for Cal, his passing masculinity encompassing complex identifications.

The last stop

The generational family narrative has acted as a productive fictional holding frame within which to explore the cultural hybridity of histories and identities; while the family provides a model of historical inheritance and collective memory, its discontinuities – often acted out in motifs of infidelity, illegitimacy and estrangement – simultaneously subvert any aspirations towards a familial form of 'grand narrative'. However, while a fictional genealogy may allow a space within which to foreground the historical and cultural contingencies of identity, in *Middlesex* it is arguably complicit with a heteronormative matrix within which queer contingencies of identity are contained. The heterosexual transgression which is posited as the cause of Cal's condition is normalised by structures of family and marriage but Cal's body remains an anomalous 'last stop'[67] in the Stephanides' family journey rather than the prelude to a differently conceived way of living.[68]

Despite his claim to an unequivocal maleness – 'I operate in society as a man'[69] – the adult Cal lives what he calls a 'closeted'[70] life, leaving the country of his birth and undertaking an itinerant career as a member of the Foreign Service as a means of escaping his body and its implications: 'After college, I took a trip around the world. I tried to forget my body by keeping it in motion.'[71] The narrative location of this retrospective life history is post-unification Berlin, where Cal works for the Foreign Service and lives among a Turkish *Gastarbeiter* community. If the parallel between sexed and cultural hybridity were to be pursued, this might seem a promising location from which to explore a post-sexed identity: 'This once-divided city reminds me of myself. My struggle for unification, for *Einheit*. Coming from a city still cut in half by racial hatred, I feel hopeful here in Berlin [emphasis in original].'[72] Indeed, Cal's reference to 'another birth'[73] in the opening of the novel might raise such an expectation. However, the indeterminacy of sexed, gendered and sexual identity suggested by the intersexed body – and played out in the 'middle' part of the narrative – has been foreclosed by a persistent investment in binary categories of identity. The possibility of living a life beyond not only national but also sexed borders remains unimagined at the end of the novel, which proves unable to fulfil its own reproductive promise.

Notes

1. Alice Domurat Dreger, *Hermaphrodites and the Medical Invention of Sex* (Cambridge, MA and London: Harvard University Press, 1998), p. 8. Christina Matta writes that 'the medical history of hermaphroditisim and the medical history of homosexuality are parallel stories.' 'Ambiguous Bodies and Deviant Sexualities: Hermaphrodites, Homosexuality, and Surgery in the United States, 1850–1904', *Perspectives in Biology and Medicine*, 48: 1 (Winter 2005), p. 75.
2. Judith Butler, *Gender Trouble: Feminism and the Subversion of Identity* (New York and London: Routledge, 1999), p. 23.
3. Dreger, op. cit., p. 60.
4. My use of gendered pronouns reflects Cal's sexed identifications at different stages in his/her life.
5. Jeffrey Eugenides, *Middlesex* (London: Bloomsbury, 2002), p. 4.
6. Ibid., p. 443.
7. Judith Halberstam, *Female Masculinity* (Durham, NC and London: Duke University Press, 1998), p. 165.
8. Ibid., p. 71.
9. 5-alpha-reductase deficiency, the condition with which Cal is diagnosed, is thought to 'have a strong genetic component' given its higher frequency in populations characterised by isolation and intermarriage. Dreger, op. cit., p. 40.
10. Ibid., p. 4.

11. Ibid., p. 361.
12. Ibid.
13. Ibid., p. 3.
14. Iain Morland, '"The Glans Opens Like a Book": Writing and Reading the Intersexed Body', *Continuum: Journal of Media and Culture Studies*, 19: 3 (2005), p. 335.
15. See Butler, op. cit.
16. Anne Fausto-Sterling, *Sexing the Body: Gender Politics and the Construction of Sexuality* (New York: Basic, 2000), p. 45. Suzanne J. Kessler also notes that 'although variant genitals rarely pose a threat to the child's life, the post-delivery situation is referred to as a "neonatal psychosexual emergency," seeming to require life-saving intervention.' *Lessons from the Intersexed* (New Brunswick, NJ and London: Rutgers University Press, 1998), p. 34.
17. Cheryl Chase, 'Hermaphrodites with Attitude: Mapping the Emergence of Intersex Political Activism', *GLQ: Journal of Lesbian and Gay Studies*, 4: 2 (1998), p. 189. J. David Hester writes: 'The obligation to have a sex is so deeply entrenched that when one is faced with a body that does not conform to the self-evidentiary ground upon which gender performance is said to take place, a sex will be surgically inscribed upon it, manufactured for it.' 'Intersexes and the End of Gender: Corporeal Ethics and Postgender Bodies', *Journal of Gender Studies*, 13: 3 (2004), p. 222.
18. For a reading of Middlesex as 'purport[ing] to transcend ... overdetermined theories of gender and sexuality' see Zachary Sifuentes, 'Strange Anatomy, Strange Sexuality: The Queer Body in Jeffrey Eugenides' *Middlesex*', in Richard Fantina (ed.), *Straight Writ Queer: Non-Normative Expressions of Heterosexuality in Literature* (Jefferson, NC and London: McFarland, 2006), p. 146.
19. See, for example, Cheryl Chase's account of her discovery that she 'had been my parents' son for a year and a half'. Chase, op. cit., p. 194.
20. Eugenides, op. cit., p. 3.
21. Morland, op. cit., p. 342.
22. Eugenides, op. cit., p. 19.
23. Ibid., p. 3.
24. Ibid., p. 361.
25. Ibid., p. 418.
26. Ibid., p. 437.
27. Ibid., p. 446.
28. Ibid., p. 19.
29. Ibid., p. 297.
30. Ibid., p. 327.
31. Kenneth Millard, *Coming of Age in Contemporary Fiction* (Edinburgh: Edinburgh University Press, 2007), p. 10.
32. Ibid.
33. Angus Gordon, 'The Retrospective Closet: Adolescence and Queer Prehistory', *Australian Historical Studies*, 36 (2005), p. 321.
34. Angus Gordon, 'Turning Back: Adolescence, Narrative and Queer Theory', *GLQ: Journal of Lesbian and Gay Studies*, 5 (1991), p. 3.
35. Judith Roof, *Come as You Are: Sexuality and Narrative* (New York: Columbia University Press, 1996), p. xxxiv.

36. Eugenides, op. cit., p. 327.
37. Ibid.
38. Ibid.
39. Ibid., p. 388.
40. For discussions of lesbian representability see Terry Castle, *The Apparitional Lesbian: Female Homosexuality and Modern Culture* (New York: Columbia University Press, 1993), Annamarie Jagose, *Inconsequence: Lesbian Representation and the Logic of Sexual Sequence* (Ithaca, NY and London: Cornell University Press, 2002) and Patricia White, *Uninvited: Classical Hollywood Cinema and Lesbian Representability* (Bloomington and Indianapolis, IN: Indiana University Press, 1999).
41. Eugenides, op. cit., p. 86.
42. Ibid., p. 329.
43. Ibid., pp. 329–30.
44. Ibid., p. 388.
45. Ibid.
46. Ibid., p. 330. Judith Halberstam writes that in the nineteenth century the 'female hermaphrodite was considered a freak of nature with an enlarged clitoris who desired to penetrate other women who might be drawn to her ambiguity.' Halberstam, op. cit., p. 55.
47. Eugenides, op. cit., p. 348.
48. Ibid., p. 329.
49. Ibid., p. 386.
50. Ibid., p. 373.
51. Ibid., p. 374.
52. Ibid., p. 375.
53. Ibid.
54. Ibid.
55. Ibid.
56. Ibid., p. 376.
57. Ibid., p. 266.
58. Ibid., p. 386.
59. Ibid., p. 304.
60. Ibid., p. 41.
61. Ibid., p. 404.
62. Halberstam, op. cit., p. 241.
63. Eugenides, op. cit., p. 41.
64. Ibid., p. 232.
65. Ibid.
66. Ibid., p. 337.
67. Ibid., p. 184.
68. Cal's tentative courtship of Julie Kikuchi, an expatriate Californian living in Berlin, fails to deliver a solution to his single state. Julie's wariness of romantic entanglements is attributed to a series of ill-fated relationships with closeted gay men; her reflections reveal the problematic nature of the conflation of sexed and racialised borders: '"Asian chicks are the last stop. If a guy's in the closet, he goes for an Asian because their bodies are more like boys".' Ibid.
69. Ibid., p. 41.

70. Ibid., p. 107.
71. Ibid., p. 320.
72. Ibid., p. 106.
73. Ibid., p. 3.

Chapter 6

Imitations of life: cloning, heterosexuality and the human in Kazuo Ishiguro's *Never Let Me Go*

There is something rather 'queer' about the protagonists of Kazuo Ishiguro's 2005 novel *Never Let Me Go*. Living outside of conventional family and kinship structures, they affirm a collective identity defined against those they term the 'normals'.[1] Taught from childhood to understand their difference as categorical and as residing in their inability to reproduce, they are subject to the irrational prejudices of others; even those dedicated to their care struggle to conceal their revulsion, as a former guardian confesses: '"Is she afraid of you? We're *all* afraid of you. I myself had to fight back my dread of you almost every day [emphasis in original]."'[2] In the face of such stigma, Ishiguro's protagonists are compelled to 'pass' in the world of 'normals'. However, strategies of assimilation cannot enable them to escape a fundamental condition of their existence: the denial of their right to agency and self-determination on the grounds of their status as less than human. If the protagonists of *Never Let Me Go* are perceived by others to be strange or suspect – in other words 'queer' in the commonplace sense – this can be attributed to their unconventional relationship to reproductive origin as human clones. However, I would argue that it is not the human status of the clone which is in question in this novel so much as the normative discourses which conspire to contest it. This chapter seeks to articulate one reader's intuition concerning the 'queer' plight of Ishiguro's protagonists: namely, that the discursive construction of the human clone as 'unnatural' and 'inhuman' is implicated in the imperatives of heteronormativity. In other words, I wish to suggest that their queerness is not merely 'commonplace' but that it also pertains to their non-normative heterosexuality; in this way, it is possible to consider Ishiguro's clones under the extended rubric of 'queer' in its theorised sense.

Recent evaluations of queer theory have, following Judith Butler in 'Critically Queer', sought to 'affirm the contingency'[3] of the term 'queer', arguing that 'if identity is a necessary error, then the assertion of "queer" will be necessary in terms of affiliation, but it will not fully describe those it purports to represent.'[4] In 'What's Queer About Queer Studies Now?', David L. Eng, Judith Halberstam and José Esteban Muñoz suggest that the ongoing interrogation of the terms by which queer defines itself exemplifies queer theory's commitment to the unsettling of identity categories; they suggest that 'what might be called the "subjectless" critique of queer studies disallows any posting of a proper subject *of* or object *for* the field by insisting that queer has no fixed political referent' [emphasis in original].'[5] Elsewhere, in 'Queer Theory for Everyone', Sharon Marcus acknowledges tensions between 'inclusive' theorisations of the term (as exemplified in the 'subjectless' critique above) and a tendency to deploy 'queer' as a 'compact alternative to *lesbian-gay-bisexual-transgender* [emphasis in original]'.[6] Moreover, she notes that 'while queerness is supposed to signify the instability of *all* sexual identities . . . there is little extant work on the queerness of those conventionally considered heterosexual [emphasis added].'[7] While the protagonists of *Never Let Me Go* – the narrator Kathy and her childhood friends Ruth and Tommy – are nominally heterosexual they are nevertheless at odds with heterosexual norms; more specifically, as the product of technologies of assisted reproduction but genetically engineered to be unable to reproduce, their relationship to reproductive sexuality is paradoxical. I would argue that Ishiguro's clones can be interpreted as embodying a heterosexual identity which is disempowered and marginalised by heteronormativity; as such they reveal the tensions and contradictions at work within and between heterosexuality as an institution and an identity. Cathy J. Cohen defines heteronormativity as consisting of 'both those localized practices and those centralized institutions which legitimize and privilege heterosexuality and heterosexual relationships as fundamental and "natural" within society.'[8] However, she goes on to question 'the unchallenged assumption of a uniform heteronormativity from which all heterosexuals benefit'.[9] This chapter does not intend to suggest an equivalence between the non-normative heterosexual and the homosexual; while an inclusive definition of the term 'queer' could encompass both, it would become problematic if it obscured the different ways in which they are subject to heteronormative institutions, practices and discourses. What this chapter seeks to do – in speculative and tentative fashion – is to investigate the possibility that Ishiguro's exploration of the contingency of human identity in *Never Let Me Go* has a significant, if oblique, relationship to heteronormative constructions of heterosexuality and the human. Textual motifs of 'passing' are central to my analysis of Ishiguro's novel. Linda Schlossberg, in her introduction to *Passing: Identity and Interpretation in Sexuality, Race, and Religion*, writes that 'heterosexual culture continually passes itself off as being merely natural, the undisputed and unmarked norm.'[10] I wish to suggest that in its exploration of the 'imitation of life' *Never Let Me Go* prompts important questions about the discursive reproduction of the human as a contested category of identity.

Remembering to be human: childhood as institution

In her extensive survey of fictional representations of human cloning, *I Am The Other: Literary Negotiations of Human Cloning*, Maria Aline Salgueiro Seabra Ferreia has described the fantasy of human cloning as 'focusing in a consummate way the widespread millennial anxieties that permeate contemporary literature, popular culture, science, and medicine'.[11] Indeed, millennial motifs of futurity, catastrophe and apocalypse have traditionally characterised fictions of human cloning. Ferreira's study was published prior to the birth of Dolly, the genetically cloned sheep, at the Roslin Institute in Edinburgh, Scotland in 1996. Dolly provoked extensive scientific, political and ethical debate and renewed public unease about the implications of the new genetics and the now foreseeable prospect of human cloning. In this context, with its tremendous potential for the imaginative investigation of issues of genetic engineering, gestational origin and industrial application, it is all the more striking that Ishiguro's novel eschews the more sensational motifs of science fiction fantasy for a deeply disquieting rendering of normality.

Never Let Me Go – published in 2005 but located in 'the late 1990s'[12] – imagines the near past as speculative future. It depicts a recognisable and far from futuristic British cultural landscape but one in which the mass production of human clones in the service of therapeutic medical technology has become normalised. In an analysis of contemporary debates about the technologies of human cloning and their ethical implications, Finn Bowring has contextualised the emergence of a distinction between 'therapeutic' and 'reproductive' cloning:

> It is because treatments derived from embryonic stem cells are likely to require the production of human embryos by cloning, that scientists and politicians have popularised the distinction between 'therapeutic' and 'reproductive' cloning, and made strong moral and legal cases for prohibiting the latter (defined as implanting a cloned embryo in a woman's womb).[13]

This semantic distinction acts to discursively construct technologies of human cloning; to the degree that such a distinction serves political as well as ethical ends it is necessarily expedient and fraught with contradiction. The categorical distinction between 'therapeutic' and 'reproductive' cloning seeks to address anxieties about the use of human embryos in medical research but cannot conceal the fact that an element of reproduction is integral to all forms of cloning. 'Reproductive' cloning is defined in order to be outlawed but this term inadvertently reminds us of the position of human cloning within a spectrum of technologies of assisted reproduction, most of which are routinely 'naturalised' as serving the 'right to a child'. The problematic nature of the use of therapeutic ends to justify medical means is already apparent, in contemporary culture, in the controversial use of technologies of assisted reproduction to produce a child whose body will act as a resource for an ailing sibling.[14] *Never Let Me Go* imagines a world in which genetically cloned embryos are not merely conceived but brought to term and lived existence. Moreover, it is a world in which the distinction between therapeutic and reproductive cloning has collapsed; the cloning depicted in the novel is both therapeutic and reproductive, in that fully developed cloned bodies are being produced in the service of medical science. As Miss Emily puts it in the dramatic denouement of the novel: '"However uncomfortable people were about your existence, their overwhelming concern was that their *own* children, their spouses, their parents, their friends, did not die from cancer, motor neurone disease, heart disease [emphasis added]."'[15] Ishiguro's novel is not concerned with speculation about the forms which this technology will take; the absence of engagement with currently contentious scientific developments only serves to reinforce the impression that this development is neither novel nor new. Indeed, it is a practice sufficiently entrenched to have generated its own counter-discourse which takes the form of a social reform movement advocating the humane treatment of cloned subjects: '"we demonstrated to the world that if students were reared in humane, cultivated environments, it was possible for them to grow to be as sensitive and intelligent as any ordinary human being."'[16] However, this complex temporal context, in which a contemporary medical and ethical controversy is depicted as a past reality, is one which the reader must deduce from the narrative which relies not on controversial public histories but on subjective memories.

The first-person narrative of Kathy H. is dominated by memories of an institutionalised childhood at Hailsham, a residential school resembling a paternalistic orphanage; the pupil population at Hailsham is only gradually revealed to the reader as consisting of human clones.[17] Kathy's memories reveal the indirect and insidious way in which she and her peers learn the truth about their origins and their fate; they are '"told and not told"'[18] through a process of gradual and partial disclosure: 'Certainly it feels like I *always* knew . . . in some vague way . . . nothing came as a complete surprise. It *was* like we'd heard everything somewhere before [emphasis in original].'[19] The reader is arguably placed in a similarly oblique position in relation to narrative knowledge: both '"told and not told,"'[20] she must resort to the same speculative and deductive strategies as Kathy. The novel further insinuates the reader into its narrator's perspective by evoking narrative tropes of childhood experience which are recognisable and familiar; Never Let Me Go can be placed within a tradition of boarding-school narratives in which the closed world of the school stands for the institution of childhood. In this way, the novel could be understood as a normalising narrative of human cloning. Indeed, the narrative evokes the peculiar idioms of childhood and young adulthood and their function in defining group and individual identities; here the identification of 'normals'[21] and later of '*possible*[s] [emphasis in original]'.[22] The struggle over prescribed and sequestered spaces – the sports pavilion, the pond, the lunch queue and all the 'hiding places, indoors and out: cupboards, nooks, bushes, hedges'[23] – recalls the ways in which child and teen identities are mapped out through peripheral social territories. The 'Exchanges' and 'Sales'[24] which punctuate the Hailsham calendar and the shared dedication to the accumulation of personal 'collections'[25] are also recognisable as practices by which a subculture circulates its meanings.

However, the rituals of child and adolescent cultures are implicated in this novel in what is essentially an institution of biotechnological slavery.[26] 'Normals' are the non-cloned humans to whom the Hailsham students are destined to donate their vital organs and 'possible' is the term given to the imagined human original from which the students have been generated. The quest for privacy evident in the struggle for personalised space is countered by the pedagogic and medical surveillance to which the students are subject to ensure their fitness for purpose. Finally, the 'Sales' and 'Exchanges' of used possessions by which the students are encouraged to construct their own identities only underline the commodified status of their condition. The clones are, to use Judith Butler's phrase, 'foreclosed from possibility'[27] by a genetic origin which determines that their human agency will be forfeited: 'If we are not recognizable, if there are no norms of recognition by which we are recognizable, then it is not possible to persist in one's own being, and we are not possible beings; we have been foreclosed from possibility.'[28] The dramatic revelation with which the narrative culminates is not so much the identification of Kathy and her classmates as clones, however, but rather the disclosure of Hailsham's identity as a social experiment established to 'prove' the humanity of clones; the mystery of the fabled gallery in which students' art work is exhibited is revealed: '"We took away your art because we thought it would reveal your souls. Or to put it more finely, we did it to *prove you had souls at all* [emphasis in original]."'[29] In other words, Kathy's first-person narrative culminates with a discovery that her very status as human is contested and that the childhood in which her sense of self is rooted was itself designed to conceal her contested status from her: '"We sheltered you during those years, and we gave you your childhoods."'[30]

Never Let Me Go generates an apprehension of what it is to discover that one's humanity has been called into question: what it is to find that one's memories, desires and aspirations are perceived to be suspect, inauthentic or illegitimate. Contemporary debate and speculation about the prospect of reproductive cloning reveals the way in which such beings, as 'copies' of human originals, challenge notions of the human, especially in relation to issues of individuality, authenticity and origin. In this context, Judith Butler's reflections, in her 2004 book *Undoing Gender*, are pertinent:

> It is the inhuman, the beyond the human, the less than human, the border that secures the human in its ostensible reality. To be called a copy, to be called unreal, is one way in which one can be oppressed, but consider that it is more fundamental than that. To be oppressed means that you already exist as a subject of some kind, you are there as the visible and oppressed other for the master subject, as a possible or potential subject, but to be unreal is something else again. To be oppressed you must first become intelligible. To find that you are fundamentally unintelligible (indeed, that the laws of culture and of language find you to be an impossibility) is to find that you have not yet achieved access to the human, to find yourself speaking only and always *as if you were human* . . . [emphasis added].[31]

Butler is exploring the implications of the heteronormative denial of the reality of homosexual existence and identity: the way in which this refusal to grant legitimacy or concede intelligibility reduces a category of beings to less than human status. What this passage begins to reveal, I would suggest, is the implication of presumptive heterosexuality in definitions of the human – and in the discourses of rights to which humans have a claim. Ishiguro's cloned protagonists are unintelligible both to themselves and to others. I wish to propose that the affective power of *Never Let Me Go* resides in its unsettling of the familiar intelligibility of heteronormative identities. The controversies prompted by the potential prospect of reproductive human cloning can be attributed in part to the ways in which it challenges the heterosexual prerogative to reproduction; in order to trace how a fiction of human cloning might give rise to questions of heteronormativity, I will foreground issues of reproduction and their relationship to normative constructions of heterosexuality.

Imitations of life: cloning and the reproduction of heterosexuality

When considered as a technology of assisted reproduction, cloning can be approached within the context of the extensive body of feminist scholarship on reproductive technologies. Feminist theorists have investigated these technologies, and their supporting discourses, in relation to gendered issues of power, agency and embodiment.[32] Central to this work is a recognition of the paradoxes of power to which these technologies give rise. On the one hand, reproductive technologies can be understood as extending and consolidating the subjection of the female and maternal body to the patriarchal power of medical science. On the other, such technologies have the potential to empower women to exercise greater agency and control over their bodies and reproductive capacities. However, while these technologies reveal the extent to which conception, gestation and birth are not merely culturally mediated but increasingly culturally constructed, these interventions have been discursively enlisted to reinforce essentialist assumptions about women's relationship to maternity, most notably through the paradoxical renewal of naturalising discourses. As Dion Farquhar has written:

> The ontology of 'natural' biogenetic married heterosexual reproduction depended on its binary other of 'unnatural' sterility (homosexuals, unmarried people, and so on.) Now, a new 'other' to 'natural' reproduction has been introduced by biotechnology – 'artificial' donor-assisted asexual reproduction – and it must quickly work to erase its otherness ... by claiming its alliance with the 'natural' – helping would-be parents have their 'own' biogenetic child ... .[33]

The converse construction of infertility and childlessness as what Deborah Lynn Steinberg has called a 'pathological medical category'[34] only reinforces the normative effect of new reproductive technologies, extending the medicalisation of female bodies. Extending feminist frameworks of analysis to media representations of human cloning, Joan Haran, Jenny Kitzinger, Maureen McNeil and Kate O'Riordan have further explored the ways in which women's bodies are both visibly employed as 'normative signs' and rendered invisible as a material resource for cloning as 'a disembodied practice'.[35]

Feminist work on reproductive technologies has focused on their implications for women's agency and experience of embodiment. However, it is not only the 'naturalness' of gendered reproductive identity which is in question, I would argue, but also, if implicitly, the 'universality' of heterosexuality as the origin of reproduction. While the 'right to reproduce' is constructed in universalising terms, in practice it is reserved for those who conform to heterosexual norms; as Steinberg has demonstrated, with reference to access to in vitro fertilisation (IVF) screening, it is not heterosexuality per se which is privileged but more specifically its normative manifestations: 'Heterosexuality is policed not only against the prospect of lesbian parenting, but indeed what are quite explicitly constructed as deviant familial heterosexualities (families without fathers).'[36] It could be argued that human cloning exponentially extends the challenge posed to heterosexuality as an institution by assisted reproduction; as Alan Petersen makes explicit in his analysis of news media coverage of the breakthroughs at the Roslin Institute: 'What seemed "unnatural" and "disturbing" to many people was the prospect of reproduction outside normative heterosexual arrangements.'[37] I would suggest that the heterosexual 'arrangements' that are at stake are not simply the sexual acts from which conception may result, and the relationships in which they take place, but also the social and cultural structures within which heterosexuality is implicated. Heterosexuality is a normative identity formation whose power is implicated in its capacity to pass unexamined. The 'impetus to render heterosexuality visible to critical scrutiny'[38] which characterises current work on heterosexuality could then be placed within a wider context of critical and theoretical frameworks, such as critical whiteness studies and masculinity studies, which seek to interrogate the 'unmarked' or 'invisible' nature of normative identities and their relationship to dominant modes of power. Lauren Berlant and Michael Warner evoke the ubiquitous and pervasive force of normative heterosexuality:

> Heteronormativity is more than ideology, or prejudice, or phobia against gays and lesbians; it is produced in almost every aspect of the forms and arrangements of social life: nationality, the state, and the law; commerce; medicine; and education; as well as in the conventions and affects of narrativity, romance, and other protected spaces of culture.[39]

The specific 'arrangements of social life' which I wish to consider in *Never Let Me Go* are those concerning heteronormative structures of family and kinship.

The relationship between genetics, eugenics and kinship, and its implications for a critique of heteronormativity, is one which Deborah Lynn Steinberg has begun to examine. Steinberg suggests that eugenics can be seen as 'expressive, indeed productive, of a dominant discourse of family, that discourse of "legitimate" kinship in which class, gendered and racialised inequalities are normalised and in which heterosexuality is assumed and (re)inscribed.'[40] Elsewhere, in a very suggestive formulation, Kaja Finkler argues that kinship organises human attachments through the production of 'significant same' groupings who 'share instrumental, moral, and affective codes that embrace feelings of obligations and responsibilities, which may be limited to one or more several generations of the living and the deceased.'[41] In one sense, Ishiguro's clones constitute an alternative form of kinship; they are 'significantly same' to each other due to their shared memories and experiences. Hence Kathy admits her preference for other students from Hailsham: 'When you get a chance to choose, of course, you choose *your own kind*. That's natural [emphasis added].'[42] However, their kinship is of a fragile constitution, rooted in memories of a place whose future is in jeopardy and motivated by the defensive vulnerability of those 'fearful of the world around us, and – no matter how much we despised ourselves for it – unable quite to let each other go.'[43] Moreover, their kinship lacks the legitimacy of a 'historical relation to futurity ... to generational narrative and reproduction'[44] which heteronormativity privileges. As *Never Let Me Go* suggests, human cloning does not simply bypass conventional modes of human reproduction but produces a new category of being whose identity is not imbricated in heterosexuality as an institution. Nominally heterosexual, Kathy and her peers are nevertheless denied the privileges with which normative heterosexuality is rewarded.[45] This can be attributed to the fact of their double alienation from reproductive norms, not only in terms of their origins outside of conventional structures of family and kinship but also in terms of their genetically engineered inability to sexually reproduce. Michael Warner alludes to this conflation of heterosexuality and reproduction in his discussion of 'reprosexuality' as

> the interweaving of heterosexuality, biological reproduction, cultural reproduction, and personal identity ... Reprosexuality involves more than reproducing, more even than compulsory heterosexuality: it involves a relation to self that finds its proper temporality and fulfillment in generational transmission.[46]

Outside of the generational narrative – without legitimate origin or reproductive legacy – the clone is expendable.

Unclaimed by their genetic kin and unable to generate their own kind, the clones are precluded from the networks of obligation and responsibility which define the 'significant same' according to Finkler; they suffer what Sarah Franklin has described as a 'genealogical shame'.[47] Franklin attributes the anxiety with which 'illicit clones' are met directly to their relationship to genealogy:

> The dangerous illicit clone, its negativity doubled by both its figurative and historical associations, is generically and traditionally an abject embodiment of a particular kind of *genealogical shame*. Suspected of being a fake, a derivative, a copy, or a mere replicant, the clone is diminished by a lack of proper genealogy – and thus identity, substance, or origin [emphasis added].[48]

And yet in other ways they uncannily mimic the 'sameness' which kinship privileges; genetically identical to their 'models',[49] they hold a mirror to the reproductive determinism of heteronormative kinship. Moreover, Kathy and her peers have been unknowingly schooled in assimilation; they are taught to 'pass' as normals within a culture which exploits them. I would suggest that this imitative motif serves less to reveal the inauthenticity of the cloned subjects than to demonstrate the performative and reiterative nature of normative heterosexuality.

Schooled to pass: performing and proving

The location of a fiction of human cloning within the narrative context of an institutionalised childhood is significant in a number of ways.[50] A residential school setting can signify either economic privilege or social marginalisation; belonging to the latter category, Hailsham's legacy in terms of childhood memory is comparable to that of other casualties of reproductive and familial norms: the abandoned, the illegitimate and the disabled child. Hailsham confirms the clones' location outside of the familial culture of reproductive sexuality and the world of what Kathy refers to as the 'ordinary family'.[51] Furthermore, it provides an apt setting for a depiction of the totalising effect of heteronormative imperatives.

The trusting docility of Hailsham's pupils is suggestive of the successful internalisation of its regime; both within and beyond the school their lives are policed by 'unspoken'[52] and 'unwritten'[53] rules and agreements, many concerning what cannot be openly acknowledged. Of the gallery, Kathy recalls 'there was an unspoken rule that we should never even raise the subject in [the guardians] presence'[54] and yet she reflects that it 'it seems to me this was a rule we imposed on ourselves, as much as anything the guardians had decided.'[55] Significantly, Hailsham's residents remain 'students' long after graduation, readily assuming the role of pupil later in life: 'We gathered round to listen, the way we might have done at Hailsham when a guardian started to speak.'[56] Moreover, in the disciplinary context of the classroom, the students are instructed in the inferiority of their identities. They are informed unambiguously that sex is more meaningful where it can result in conception and birth, something that none of them will experience; hence their sexuality and desires are constructed as poor imitations of those of the 'normals':

> Then suddenly ... [Miss Emily] began telling us how we had to be careful about *who* we had sex with. Not just because of the diseases, but because, she said, 'sex affects emotions in ways you'd never expect.' We had to be extremely careful about having sex in the outside world, especially with people who weren't students, because out there sex meant all sorts of things. Out there people were even fighting and killing each other over who had sex with whom. And the reason it meant so much – so much more than, say, dancing or table tennis – was because the people out there were different from us students: they could have babies from sex [emphasis in original].[57]

Sexuality becomes less an expression of desire, attachment or pleasure than another social discourse which must be learnt and emulated for the purposes of integration. Hence Kathy's adolescent curiosity about sexuality seems not so much expressive of her emerging sexual identity as indicative of a struggle to understand a sexuality which is given no value: 'I also spent a lot of time re-reading passages from books where people had sex, going over the lines again and again, *trying to tease out clues* [emphasis added].'[58] Her confessed interest in a discovered collection of pornographic magazines seems more studious than sexual; she discloses that she is searching for the face of her 'possible' having heard the rumour that the genetic models for clones are drawn from the socially marginalised and disempowered. As Ruth puts it: '"We're modelled from trash. Junkies, prostitutes, winos, tramps. Convicts maybe, just so long as they aren't psychos."'[59] Kathy speculates that her sexual desires, unaccountable to herself in the context of a dominant reproductive matrix, must originate in the deviance of her genetic source:

> 'It's just that sometimes, every now and again, I get these really strong feelings when I want to have sex ... I don't know what it is, and afterwards, when it's passed over, it's just scary. That's why I started thinking, well, it has to come from somewhere. It must be to do with the way I am.'[60]

Kathy's explanation for her interest in pornographic images offers another instance where an apparent imitation of conventional heterosexual behaviour reveals, instead, its contradictions. Indeed, performative motifs recur throughout the novel, with Kathy repeatedly finding herself an unwitting spectator or actor, positioned 'as if I was in the front row of the audience when she [Ruth] was performing on stage'[61] or becoming like 'people in a play she [Ruth] was watching'.[62] In one of a number of uncanny moments which consist in the discovery of being watched or in the unwitting watching of others, Kathy finds herself under the tearful surveillance of Madame, the school's enigmatic visiting patron. She is acting out the lyrics to a favourite pop song – '"Baby, baby, never let me go"'[63] – by hugging an imaginary baby to her chest; in doing so, she appears to misunderstand the heterosexual vernacular of pop in assuming the 'baby' is an infant and not a lover. Madame's reaction, unfathomable at the time, would retrospectively seem to be a response to the futility of the fantasy, both in terms of motherhood and heterosexual identity. And yet Kathy's actions seem to be symptomatic of the imitative schooling which she and her peers receive, in which they are encouraged to mimic the behaviour of 'normals': a schooling which is itself symptomatic of a wider culture which obsessively rehearses heterosexual subject positions.

In this context, it is worth noting the particular significance with which the figure of the couple is invested in *Never Let Me Go*. One might expect the vagaries of romantic and sexual partnership to play a significant role in a narrative which dwells on adolescent group identities. However, coupledom is understood less as an elective expression of a romantic or sexual affinity than as a necessary assumption of a culturally coded set of practices, that is as an index of successful assimilation into the world of the 'normals'. While staying at the Cottages, a transitional residence between Hailsham and the outside world, Kathy detects that some of the gestures and phrases by which older couples signify their status have been 'copied from the television',[64] including an American sitcom depiction of marital conflict: 'the way they gestured to each other, sat together on sofas, even the way they argued and stormed out of rooms'.[65] Kathy recalls how her assiduously conformist friend Ruth is quick to act on these cues but also Ruth's impatience with her less socially apt partner, Tommy:

> Anyway, my point is, it wasn't long before Ruth realised the way she'd been carrying on with Tommy was all wrong for the Cottages, and she set about changing how they did things in front of people ... Mind you, at first, Tommy didn't have a clue what was going on, and would turn abruptly to Ruth and go: 'What?', so that she'd have to glare furiously at him, *like they were in a play and he'd forgotten his lines*. I suppose she eventually had a word with him, because after a week or so they were managing to do it right, more or less exactly like veteran couples [emphasis added].[66]

The myth of 'deferral', which dominates the closing stages of the narrative, becomes all the more poignant given that desires and attachments between students are credible only so far as they emulate those of 'normals'. Rumours circulate among students who have begun their work as donors and carers that a couple can be permitted to postpone donations, and hence defer 'completion' – the euphemism for premature death resulting from the loss of vital organs – if they can 'prove' they are in love. This belief is symptomatic both of the students' suggestibility and of the ruthless logic of heteronormativity. Kathy and Tommy are disabused of the myth of deferral – and of the myth of Hailsham – when they locate and confront its former patron, Madame, or Marie-Claude, in what they believe to be her home. Motifs of 'performativity' and 'proof' converge to powerful effect in this scene.[67]

Kathy's attempts to orientate herself within the unfamiliar environment of a domestic interior are confounded by the sounds of unidentified movements and voices in other parts of the house. The very structure of the room in which she and Tommy wait seems to be in flux: 'Then the wall at the back of the room began to move. I saw almost immediately it wasn't really a wall, but a pair of sliding doors which you could use to section off the front half of what was otherwise one long room.'[68] The awkwardness of Madame's movements and the rather charged tone of her address, combined with the sense of shifting spatial boundaries, create the impression of a staged encounter:

> When we turned to sit down, she was over by the windows, in front of the heavy velvet curtains, holding us in a glare, like we were in class and she was a teacher ... Tommy, afterwards, said he thought she was about to burst into song, and that those curtains behind her would open, and instead of the street and the flat grassy expanse leading to the seafront, there'd be this big stage set.[69]

Moreover, Kathy discovers that she is not so much the spectator in this scene as an unwitting actor in a performance for an undisclosed audience: 'I realised, with a little chill, that these questions had never been for me, or for Tommy, but for someone else – someone listening behind us in the darkened half of the room.'[70] The revelation that Madame's rhetorical questions – '"Do I go too far?"'[71] – are addressed not to Kathy but to the former Hailsham guardian Miss Emily, dramatically anticipates the subsequent revelation that Kathy's childhood was itself effectively 'staged' for another audience. As pupils at Hailsham, the students are encouraged to compete to produce art work for selection in Madame's gallery, unaware that their efforts are being exhibited as 'proof' of their humanity. As adults, Kathy and Tommy hope to 'prove' their love to Madame and Miss Emily in order to secure what is effectively a stay of execution; however, nothing that they are able to 'produce' can reverse the conditions of their identity. The students can no more enlist the *reproductive* logic of heterosexuality to 'prove' their love than can Hailsham 'prove' their humanity when heteronormative constructions of the human define them as inauthentic in advance. Hence the spurious logic of deferral reveals a more fundamental truth: that the exclusion of clones from the human right to self-determination is expressed through the deep implication of presumptions of heterosexuality in concepts of the human.

Passing as normal

In conclusion, Ferreira has noted the 'feelings of uncanniness' which often accompany fictional representations of human clones, referring to the 'reservoir of disquiet that many of these clone characters attempt to dispel by trying to build a life predicated, as much as possible, on normality.'[72] However, the first-person narrative of *Never Let Me Go* mitigates the construction of the clone as 'other' to the reader; moreover, it is the implicitly normative status of *the reader* – which such 'othering' might serve to sanction – which is rendered uncanny by the narrative mode of address. In a recurring and poignant refrain, the narrator addresses the reader and wonders 'how it was where you were'.[73] This direct address seems to interpellate the reader as a peer, a fellow graduate of an institutionalised childhood. While this might be read as further evidence of the discomforting naivety of the adult narrator it can equally be read as being suggestive of the way in which we are *all* schooled to 'pass' as normals. In an essay assessing current work in heterosexuality studies, Annette Schlichter has argued that 'it is crucial that we develop an understanding of heterosexual subjection as an overdetermined process of "becoming straight" under the conditions of heteronormativity.'[74] The peculiarity of the Hailsham regime reveals, in metaphorical fashion, the paradoxes and perversity of heteronormativity. The imitative schooling by which the clones are taught to pass as 'normals' reveals the performative nature of heteronormativity; nominally heterosexual in terms of their sexuality, the protagonists of Ishiguro's novel nevertheless suffer the penalties endured by those constructed as 'other' to the reproductive norm. Evidently, *Never Let Me Go* is not *about* heterosexuality in any explicit or exclusive way; indeed, readers of the novel may feel that, like Madame, I '"go too far"'.[75] But such is the normative nature of heterosexuality and its 'unmarked' or 'invisible' status that few cultural narratives could announce themselves in such a way. By reading *Never Let Me Go* as a narrative of passing within a heteronormative world, I have attempted to cast into relief the contradictions inherent in the conflation of reproductive sexuality and heterosexuality by heteronormativity, that is to suggest that one effect of Ishiguro's uncanny fiction is to reveal the way in which heterosexuality as an institution both produces *and* penalises non-normative heterosexual identities.

Notes

1. Kazuo Ishiguro, *Never Let Me Go* (London: Faber & Faber, 2005), p. 94.
2. Ibid., p. 264.
3. Judith Butler, 'Critically Queer', *Bodies That Matter: On the Discursive Limits of 'Sex'* (New York and London: Routledge, 1993), p. 230.
4. Ibid.
5. David L. Eng, Judith Halberstam and José Muñoz, 'Introduction: What's Queer About Queer Studies Now?', *Social Text*, 23: 3–4, 84–5 (2005), p. 3.
6. Sharon Marcus, 'Queer Theory for Everyone: A Review Essay', *Signs*, 31: 1 (2005), p. 196.
7. Ibid.
8. Cathy J. Cohen, 'Punks, Bulldaggers, and Welfare Queens: The Radical Potential of Queer Politics?', *GLQ: Journal of Lesbian and Gay Studies*, 3 (1997), p. 440.
9. Ibid., p. 452.
10. Linda Schlossberg, 'Introduction', in María Carla Sánchez and Linda Schlossberg (eds), *Passing: Identity and Interpretation in Sexuality, Race and Religion* (New York: New York University Press, 2001), p. 5.
11. Maria Aline Salgueiro Seabra Ferreira, *I Am The Other: Literary Negotiations of Human Cloning* (Westport, CT and London: Praeger, 1995), p. 3.
12. Ishiguro, op. cit., n.p.
13. Finn Bowring, 'Therapeutic and Reproductive Cloning: A Critique', *Social Science and Medicine*, 58 (2004), p. 403.
14. I am referring here to the use of pre-implantation genetic diagnosis (PGD) or tissue typing in IVF to produce a child whose umbilical cord, blood or bone marrow can be employed in the treatment of an existing sibling; such children have come to be known as 'saviour siblings'. I would suggest that Bowring's concerns about the fate of a genetically cloned child are arguably already applicable to the genetically engineered child: 'The respect, love and recognition ideally expressed by adults towards the child will be subverted by their *expectation* that they have ordered a predetermined product, and this expectation will in turn promote the misrecognition or repression of the child's attempts to assert its autonomy and uniqueness [emphasis in original]'. Ibid., p. 405.
15. Ishiguro, op. cit., p. 258.
16. Ibid., p. 256.
17. In the context of a fictional memoir, the use of initials to abbreviate a character's surname may seem an act of narrative discretion; however, in *Never*

Let Me Go it also indicates the absence of a patronym and of the family identity to which it refers.
18. Ibid., p. 79.
19. Ibid., p. 81.
20. Ibid., p. 79.
21. Ibid., p. 94.
22. Ibid., p. 136.
23. Ibid., p. 43.
24. Ibid., p. 16.
25. Ibid., p. 38.
26. Margaret Everett makes an analogy with slavery in her discussion of the contemporary commodification of the gene: 'The commodification of the body is not a new phenomenon; slavery, prostitution and the sale of corpses, for example, attest to this fact.' Margaret Everett, 'The Social Life of Genes: Privacy, Property and the New Genetics', *Social Science and Medicine*, 56 (2003), p. 58.
27. Judith Butler, *Undoing Gender* (New York: Routledge, 2004), p. 31.
28. Ibid., p. 31.
29. Ishiguro, op. cit., p. 255.
30. Ibid., p. 263.
31. Butler, *Undoing Gender*, op. cit., p. 30.
32. See, for example, Sarah Franklin, *Embodied Progress: A Cultural Account of Assisted Conception* (London: Routledge, 1987), E. Ann Kaplan and Susan Squier (eds), *Playing Dolly: Technocultural Formations, Fantasies, and Fictions of Assisted Reproduction* (New Brunswick, NJ and London: Rutgers University Press, 1999) and Michelle Stanworth (ed.), *Reproductive Technologies: Gender, Motherhood and Medicine* (Cambridge: Polity, 1997).
33. Dion Farquhar, 'Gamete Traffic/Pedestrian Crossings', in E. Ann Kaplan and Susan Squier (eds), *Playing Dolly: Technocultural Formations, Fantasies, and Fictions of Assisted Reproduction* (New Brunswick, NJ and London: Rutgers University Press, 1999), p. 21.
34. Deborah Lynn Steinberg, *Bodies in Glass: Genetics, Eugenics, Embryo Ethics* (Manchester: Manchester University Press, 1997), p. 41.
35. Joan Haran, Jenny Kitzinger, Maureen McNeil and Kate O'Riordan, *Human Cloning in the Media: From Science Fiction to Science Practice* (London and New York: Routledge, 2008), p. 119.
36. Steinberg, op. cit., p. 83.
37. Alan Petersen, 'Replicating our Bodies, Losing Our Selves: News Media Portrayals of Human Cloning in the Wake of Dolly', *Body and Society*, 8: 4 (2002), p. 81. Moreover, in *Dolly Mixtures: The Remaking of Genealogy* (Durham, NC and London: Duke University Press, 2007), p. 46, Franklin describes as 'queer' Dolly the sheep's 'connections to sex and modes of reproduction'.
38. Richard Johnson, 'Contested Borders, Contingent Lives: An Introduction', in Deborah Lynn Steinberg, Debbie Epstein and Richard Johnson (eds), *Border Patrols: Policing the Boundaries of Heterosexuality* (London: Cassell, 1997), p. 5.
39. Lauren Berlant and Michael Warner, 'Sex in Public', *Critical Inquiry*, 24: 2 (1998), pp. 554–5.

40. Steinberg, op. cit., pp. 75–6.
41. Kaja Finkler, *Experiencing the New Genetics: Family and Kinship on the Medical Frontier* (University Park, PA: Pennsylvania State University Press, 2000), p. 15.
42. Ishiguro, op. cit., p. 4.
43. Ibid., p. 118.
44. Berlant and Warner, op. cit., p. 554.
45. Ruth and Tommy are former lovers and the more abiding bond between Kathy and Tommy finds expression when they become partners later in life. The Hailsham pupils are sufficiently entrenched in heteronormativity to have generated their own idiom for the insinuation of homosexuality: 'Gay sex, incidentally, was something we were even more confused about. For some reason, we called it "umbrella sex" ... I don't know how it was where you were, but at Hailsham we definitely weren't at all kind towards any sign of gay stuff.' Ishiguro, op. cit., p. 94.
46. Michael Warner, 'Introduction: Fear of a Planet', *Social Text*, 29 (1991), p. 9.
47. Franklin, *Playing Dolly*, op. cit., p. 26.
48. Ibid.
49. Ishiguro, op. cit., p. 137.
50. Keith McDonald suggests that 'novels which depict schooling provide a fruitful forum by which the narrator's agency in a complex power structure can be framed, questioned, and understood.' 'Days of Past Futures: Kazuo Ishiguro's *Never Let Me Go* as "Speculative Memoir"', *Biography*, 30: 1 (2007), p. 77.
51. Ishiguro, op. cit., pp. 157, 171 and 214.
52. Ibid., pp. 31 and 121.
53. Ibid., p. 40.
54. Ibid., p. 31.
55. Ibid., p. 32.
56. Ibid., p. 161.
57. Ibid., p. 82. The implications of the fact that these 'people' are women are never explored by the female narrator, whose inability to conceive seems to have no impact on her sense of gendered identity despite the close relation between motherhood and constructions of femininity.
58. Ibid., p. 97.
59. Ibid., p. 164.
60. Ibid., p. 179.
61. Ibid., p. 128.
62. Ibid., p. 216.
63. Ibid., p. 70.
64. Ibid., p. 118.
65. Ibid., p. 119.
66. Ibid.
67. The house to which Kathy and Tommy follow Marie-Claude appears also to be the home of Miss Emily; Marie-Claude is a former colleague of, and seemingly a present carer for, Miss Emily, who attributes her use of a wheelchair to recent ill health. The possibility that the two women are a couple is one which does not seem to occur to Kathy.

68. Ibid., p. 245.
69. Ibid., p. 246.
70. Ibid., p. 249.
71. Ibid., pp. 248 and 249.
72. Ferreira, op. cit., p. 35.
73. Ishiguro, op. cit., pp. 13, 67 and 94.
74. Annette Schlichter, 'Queer at Last? Straight Intellectuals and the Desire for Transgression', *GLQ: Journal of Lesbian and Gay Studies*, 10: 4 (2004), p. 559.
75. Ishiguro, op. cit., pp. 248 and 249.

Bibliography

Adler, Amy, 'The Perverse Law of Child Pornography', *Columbia Law Review*, 101: 2 (2001), pp. 209–73.
Alcoff, Linda Martín, 'Dangerous Pleasures: Foucault and the Politics of Pedophilia', in Susan J. Hekman (ed.), *Feminist Interpretations of Foucault* (University Park, PA: Pennsylvania State University Press, 1996), pp. 99–135.
An Education, film, dir. Lone Scherfig (UK/USA: BBC Films, 2009).
Angelides, Steven, 'Feminism, Child Sexual Abuse, and the Erasure of Child Sexuality', *GLQ: Journal of Lesbian and Gay Studies*, 10: 2 (2004), pp. 141–77.
Angelides, Steven, 'Historicizing Affect, Psychoanalyzing History: Pedophilia and the Discourse of Child Sexuality', *Journal of Homosexuality*, 46: 1–2 (2003), pp. 79–109.
Angelides, Steven, 'The Emergence of the Paedophile in the Late Twentieth Century', *Australian Historical Studies*, 36: 126 (2005), pp. 272–95.
Armitt, Lucie and Sarah Gamble, 'The Haunted Geometries of Sarah Waters's *Affinity*', *Textual Practice*, 20: 1 (2006), pp. 141–59.
Bataille, Georges, *Story of The Eye* [1928] (Harmondsworth: Penguin, 2001).
Bayma, Todd and Gary Alan Fine, 'Fictional Figures and Imaginary Relations: The Transformation of Lolita from Victim to Vixen', *Studies in Symbolic Imagination*, 20 (1996), pp. 165–78.
Bell, Vikki, 'The Vigilant(e) Parent and the Paedophile: The *News of the World* Campaign 2000 and the Contemporary Governmentality of Child Sexual Abuse', *Feminist Theory*, 3: 1 (2002), pp. 83–102.
Bell, Vikki, *Interrogating Incest: Feminism, Foucault and the Law* (London: Routledge, 1993).
Berlant, Lauren and Michael Warner, 'Sex in Public', *Critical Inquiry*, 24: 2 (1998), pp. 547–67.
Boddy, Kasia, 'Regular Lolitas: The Afterlives of an American Adolescent', in Jay Prosser (ed.), *American Fiction in the 1990's: Reflections of History and Culture* (London and New York: Routledge, 2008), pp. 164–76.
Bowring, Finn, 'Therapeutic and Reproductive Cloning: A Critique', *Social Science and Medicine*, 58 (2004), pp. 401–9.
Bray, Abigail, 'Governing the Gaze: Child Sexual Abuse Moral Panics and the Post-Feminist Blindspot', *Feminist Media Studies*, 9: 2 (2009), pp. 173–91.
Bray, Abigail, 'The Question of Intolerance: "Corporate Paedophilia" and

Child Sexual Abuse Moral Panics', *Australian Feminist Studies*, 23: 57 (2008), pp. 323–42.
Brontë, Charlotte, *Jane Eyre* [1847] (Harmondsworth: Penguin, 2006).
Brontë, Charlotte, *Villette* [1853] (Harmondsworth: Penguin, 2004).
Bruhm, Steven and Natasha Hurley, 'Curiouser: On the Queerness of Children', in Steven Bruhm and Natasha Hurley (eds), *Curiouser: On the Queerness of Children* (Minneapolis, MN and London: University of Minnesota Press, 2004), pp. ix–xxxviii.
Burgess, Anthony, *A Clockwork Orange* [1962] (Harmondsworth: Penguin, 2000).
Butler, Judith, 'Against Proper Objects', in Elizabeth Weed and Naomi Schor (eds), *Feminism Meets Queer Theory* (Bloomington: Indiana University Press, 1997), pp. 1–30.
Butler, Judith, 'Critically Queer', in Judith Butler, *Bodies That Matter: On the Discursive Limits of 'Sex'* (New York and London: Routledge, 1993), pp. 223–42.
Butler, Judith, *Gender Trouble: Feminism and the Subversion of Identity* [1990] (New York and London: Routledge, 1999).
Butler, Judith, *Undoing Gender* (New York: Routledge, 2004).
Camus, Albert, *The Outsider* [1942], trans. Joseph Laredo (Harmondsworth: Penguin, 1983).
Carroll, Lewis, *Alice's Adventures in Wonderland* [1865] and *Through the Looking-Glass* [1872] (Harmondsworth: Penguin, 2003).
Carroll, Rachel, '"Violent Operations": Revisiting the Transgendered Body in Angela Carter's *The Passion of New Eve*', *Women: A Cultural Review*, 22: 2/3 (September 2011), pp. 241–55.
Carroll, Rachel, 'Queer Beauty: Illness, Illegitimacy and Visibility in Dickens's *Bleak House* and Its 2005 BBC Adaptation', *Journal of Adaptation in Film and Performance*, 2: 11 (2009), pp. 5–18.
Carroll, Rachel, 'Rethinking Generational History: Queer Histories of Sexuality in neo-Victorian Feminist Fiction', *Studies in the Literary Imagination*, 39: 2 (Fall 2006), pp. 135–47.
Castle, Terry, *The Apparitional Lesbian: Female Homosexuality and Modern Culture* (New York: Columbia University Press, 1993).
Caughie, John, '*Morvern Callar*, Art Cinema and the "Monstrous Archive"', *Scottish Studies Review*, 8: 1 (2007), pp. 101–15.
Chase, Cheryl, 'Hermaphrodites with Attitude: Mapping the Emergence of Intersex Political Activism', *GLQ: Journal of Lesbian and Gay Studies*, 4: 2 (1998), pp. 189–211.
Cohen, Cathy J., 'Punks, Bulldaggers, and Welfare Queens: The Radical Potential of Queer Politics?', *GLQ: Journal of Lesbian and Gay Studies*, 3 (1997), pp. 437–65.
Croft, Jo, 'Writing the adolescent body', in Jan Campbell and Janet Harbord (eds), *Psycho-Politics and Cultural Desires* (London: UCL Press, 1998), pp. 190–202.
Dreger, Alice Domurat, *Hermaphrodites and the Medical Invention of Sex* (Cambridge, MA and London: Harvard University Press, 1998).
Duggan, Lisa, 'The New Homonormativity: The Sexual Politics of Neoliberalism', in Dana D. Nelson (ed.), *Materializing Democracy: Toward a Revitalized*

Cultural Politics (Durham, NC and London: Duke University Press, 2002), pp. 175–94.

Dworkin, Andrea, *Intercourse* (London: Secker & Warburg, 1987).

Eng, David L., Judith Halberstam and José Esteban Muñoz, 'Introduction: What's Queer About Queer Studies Now?', *Social Text*, 23: 3–4, 84–5 (2005), pp. 1–17.

Erhart, Julia, "She Could Hardly Invent Them!" From Epistemological Uncertainty to Discursive Production: Lesbianism in *The Children's Hour*', *Camera Obscura*, 35 (1995), pp. 87–105.

Eugenides, Jeffrey, *Middlesex* (London: Bloomsbury, 2002).

Eugenides, Jeffrey, *The Virgin Suicides* (London: Bloomsbury, 1993).

Everett, Margaret, 'The Social Life of Genes: Privacy, Property and the New Genetics', *Social Science and Medicine*, 56 (2003), pp. 53–65.

Faderman, Lillian, *Surpassing the Love of Men: Romantic Friendship and Love between Women from the Renaissance to the Present* (London: Women's Press, 1981).

Farquhar, Dion, 'Gamete Traffic/Pedestrian Crossings', in E. Ann Kaplan and Susan Squier (eds), *Playing Dolly: Technocultural Formations, Fantasies, and Fictions of Assisted Reproduction* (New Brunswick, NJ and London: Rutgers University Press, 1999), pp. 17–36.

Fausto-Sterling, Anne, *Sexing the Body: Gender Politics and the Construction of Sexuality* (New York: Basic, 2000).

Ferreira, Maria Aline Salgueiro Seabra, *I Am The Other: Literary Negotiations of Human Cloning* (Westport, CT and London: Praeger, 1995).

Fielding, Helen, *Bridget Jones's Diary* (London: Picador, 1996).

Fink, Janet and Katherine Holden, 'Pictures from the Margins of Marriage: Representations of Spinsters and Single Mothers in the mid-Victorian Novel, Inter-War Hollywood Melodrama and the British Film of the 1950s and 1960s', *Gender and History*, 11: 2 (1999), pp. 233–55.

Finkler, Kaja, *Experiencing the New Genetics: Family and Kinship on the Medical Frontier* (University Park, PA: Pennsylvania State University Press, 2000.

Foucault, Michel, *Discipline and Punish: The Birth of the Prison* [1975], trans. Alan Sheridan (Harmondsworth: Penguin, 1977).

Foucault, Michel, *Madness and Civilisation: A History of Insanity in the Age of Reason* [1961], trans. Richard Howard (London: Random House, 1965).

Foucault, Michel, *The Will to Knowledge: The History of Sexuality: Volume One* [1976], trans. Robert Hurley (London: Penguin, 1978).

Frank, Arthur W., *The Wounded Storyteller: Body, Illness and Ethics* (Chicago: University of Chicago Press, 1995).

Franklin, Sarah, *Dolly Mixtures: The Remaking of Genealogy* (Durham, NC and London: Duke University Press, 2007).

Franklin, Sarah, *Embodied Progress: A Cultural Account of Assisted Conception* (London: Routledge, 1987).

Gill, Rosalind, 'Empowerment/Sexism: Figuring Female Sexual Agency in Contemporary Advertising', *Feminism and Psychology*, 18: 1 (2008), pp. 35–60.

Goldman, Eric, '"Knowing" Lolita: Sexual Deviance and Normality in Nabokov's *Lolita*', *Nabokov Studies*, 8 (2004), pp. 87–104.

Gordon, Angus, 'The Retrospective Closet: Adolescence and Queer Prehistory', *Australian Historical Studies*, 36 (2005), pp. 315–31.

Gordon, Angus, 'Turning Back: Adolescence, Narrative and Queer Theory', *GLQ: Journal of Lesbian and Gay Studies*, 5 (1991), pp. 1–24.

Gullette, Margaret Morganroth, 'The Exile of Adulthood: Pedophilia in the Midlife Novel', *NOVEL: A Forum on Fiction*, 17: 3 (1984), pp. 215–32.

Halberstam, Judith, *Female Masculinity* (Durham, NC and London: Duke University Press, 1998).

Hanson, Clare, 'Save the Mothers? Representations of Pregnancy in the 1930s', *Literature and History*, 12: 2 (2003), pp. 57–61.

Hanson, Ellis, 'Screwing with Children in Henry James', *GLQ: Journal of Lesbian and Gay Studies*, 9: 3 (2003), pp. 367–91.

Haran, Joan, Jenny Kitzinger, Maureen McNeil and Kate O'Riordan, *Human Cloning in the Media: From Science Fiction to Science Practice* (London and New York: Routledge, 2008).

Haug, Frigga, 'Sexual Deregulation or, the Child Abuser in Neoliberalism', *Feminist Theory*, 2 (2001), pp. 55–78.

Heller, Zoë, *Notes on a Scandal* (London: Penguin, 2003).

Hellman, Lilian, *The Children's Hour* [1934] (New York: Kessinger, 2010).

Henke, Suzette A., 'The Ideology of Female (Re)Production: The Spinster in Twentieth-Century Literature', *Works and Days: Essays in the Socio-Historical Dimensions of Literature and the Arts*, 6: 1–2 (1988), pp. 167–83.

Hester, J. David, 'Intersexes and the End of Gender: Corporeal Ethics and Postgender Bodies', *Journal of Gender Studies*, 13: 3 (2004), pp. 215–25.

Hodgkins, Hope Howell, 'Stylish Spinsters: Spark, Pym, and the Postwar Comedy of the Object', *Modern Fiction Studies*, 54: 3 (2008), pp. 523–43.

Homes, A. M., *The End of Alice* (London: Granta, 1995).

Ishiguro, Kazuo, *Never Let Me Go* (London: Faber & Faber, 2005).

Jackson, Stevi, 'Gender and Heterosexuality: A Materialist Feminist Analysis', in *Heterosexuality in Question* (London: Sage, 1991), pp. 123–34.

Jackson, Stevi, 'Heterosexuality, Heteronormativity and Gender Hierarchy', in *Heterosexuality in Question* (London: Sage, 1991), pp. 159–85.

Jagose, Annamarie, 'Remembering Miss Wade: *Little Dorrit* and the Historicizing of Female Perversity', *GLQ: Journal of Gay and Lesbian Studies*, 4: 3 (1998), pp. 423–51.

Jagose, Annamarie, *Inconsequence: Lesbian Representation and the Logic of Sexual Sequence* (Ithaca, NY and London: Cornell University Press, 2002).

James, Henry, *The Turn of the Screw* [1898] (Harmondsworth: Penguin, 2003).

Jeffreys, Sheila, *Anticlimax: A Feminist Perspective on the Sexual Revolution* (London: Women's Press, 1989).

Jeffreys, Sheila, 'Heterosexuality and the desire for gender', in Diane Richardson (ed.), *Theorising Heterosexuality: Telling It Straight* (Buckingham and Philadelphia: Open University Press, 1996), pp. 75–90.

Jeffreys, Sheila, *The Spinster and Her Enemies: Feminism and Sexuality, 1880–1930* [1985] (Melbourne: Spinifex, 1997).

Johnson, Richard, 'Contested Borders, Contingent Lives: An Introduction', in Deborah Lynn Steinberg, Debbie Epstein and Richard Johnson (eds), *Border Patrols: Policing the Boundaries of Heterosexuality* (London: Cassell, 1997), pp. 1–31.

Jones, Carole, 'The "Becoming Woman": Femininity and the Rave Generation in Alan Warner's *Morvern Callar*', *Scottish Studies Review*, 5: 2 (2004), pp. 56–68.
Jones, Carole, *Disappearing Men: Gender Disorientation in Scottish Fiction 1979–1999* (Amsterdam and New York: Rodopi, 2009).
Julien, Heather, 'School Novels, Women's Work, and Maternal Vocationalism', *NWSA Journal*, 19: 2 (2007), pp. 118–37.
Kaplan, E. Ann and Susan Squier (eds), *Playing Dolly: Technocultural Formations, Fantasies, and Fictions of Assisted Reproduction* (New Brunswick, NJ and London: Rutgers University Press, 1999).
Kauffman, Linda, 'Framing Lolita: Is There a Woman in this Text?', in *Special Delivery: Epistolary Modes in Modern Fiction* (Chicago and London: University of Chicago Press, 1992), pp. 53–80.
Kessler, Suzanne J., *Lessons from the Intersexed* (New Brunswick, NJ and London: Rutgers University Press, 1998).
Kutulus, Judy, '"Do I Look Like a Chick?" Men, Women, and Babies on Sitcom Maternity Stories', *American Studies*, 39: 2 (1998), pp. 13–22.
LeBlanc, John, 'Return of the Goddess: Contemporary Music and Celtic Mythology in Alan Warner's *Morvern Callar*', *Revista Canaria de Estudios Ingleses*, 41 (2000), pp. 145–53.
McDonald, Keith, 'Days of Past Futures: Kazuo Ishiguro's *Never Let Me Go* as "Speculative Memoir"', *Biography*, 30: 1 (2007), pp. 74–83.
McGarry, Molly, 'Spectral Sexualities: Nineteenth Century Spiritualism, Moral Panics, and the Making of U.S. Obscenity Law', *Journal of Women's History*, 12: 2 (2000), pp. 8–29.
McIntosh, Mary, 'Social Anxieties About Lone Motherhood and Ideologies of the Family: Two Sides of the Same Coin', in Elizabeth Bortolaia Silva (ed.), *Good Enough Mothering? Feminist Perspectives on Lone Motherhood* (London and New York: Routledge, 1996), pp. 148–56.
Mann, Kirk and Sasha Roseneil, '"Some Mothers Do 'Ave 'Em": Backlash and the Gender Politics of the Underclass Debate', *Journal of Gender Studies*, 3: 3 (1994), pp. 317–31.
Mann, Thomas, *Death in Venice and Other Stories* [1898], trans. David Luke (London: Vintage, 1998).
Marcus, Sharon, 'Queer Theory for Everyone: A Review Essay', *Signs*, 31: 1 (2005), pp. 191–218.
Marsh, Cristie L., *Rewriting Scotland: Welsh, McLean, Warner, Banks, Galloway and Kennedy* (Manchester and New York: Manchester University Press, 2002).
Matta, Christina, 'Ambiguous Bodies and Deviant Sexualities: Hermaphrodites, Homosexuality, and Surgery in the United States, 1850–1904', *Perspectives in Biology and Medicine*, 48: 1 (2005), pp. 74–83.
Merck, Mandy, Naomi Segal and Elizabeth Wright (eds), *Coming Out of Feminism?* (London: Blackwell, 1998).
Mezei, Kathy, 'Spinsters, Surveillance, and Speech: The Case of Miss Marple, Miss Mole, and Miss Jekyll', *Journal of Modern Literature*, 30: 2 (2007), pp. 103–20.
Millard, Kenneth, *Coming of Age in Contemporary Fiction* (Edinburgh: Edinburgh University Press, 2007).

Moody, Roger, 'Man/Boy Love and the Left', in Daniel Tsang (ed.), *The Age Taboo: Gay Male Sexuality, Power and Consent* (Boston and London: Alyson Publications/Gay Men's Press, 1982), pp. 147–55.

Morland, Iain, '"The Glans Opens Like a Book:" Writing and Reading the Intersexed Body', *Continuum: Journal of Media and Culture Studies*, 19: 3 (2005), pp. 335–48.

Nabokov, Vladimir, *Lolita* [1955] (London Penguin, 1995).

Nabokov, Vladimir, *Pale Fire* [1962] (London: Penguin, 1973).

Negra, Diane, 'Quality Postfeminism? *Sex and the Single Girl* on HBO', *Genders*, 39 (2004), n.p.

Oram, Alison, 'Repressed and Thwarted, or Bearer of the New World? The Spinster in Inter-War Feminist Discourses', *Women's History Review*, 1: 3 (1992), pp. 413–34.

Owen, Alex, *The Darkened Room: Women, Power, and Spiritualism in Late Victorian England* (London: Virago, 1989).

Patnoe, Elizabeth, 'Lolita Misrepresented, Lolita Reclaimed: Disclosing the Doubles', *College Literature*, 22: 2 (1995), pp. 81–104.

Petersen, Alan, 'Replicating our Bodies, Losing Our Selves: News Media Portrayals of Human Cloning in the Wake of Dolly', *Body and Society*, 8: 4 (2002), pp. 71–90.

Petrie, Duncan, *Contemporary Scottish Fictions: Film, Television and the Novel* (Edinburgh: Edinburgh University Press, 2004).

Phoenix, Ann, 'Social Constructions of Lone Motherhood: A Case of Competing Discourses', in Elizabeth Bortolaia Silva (ed.), *Good Enough Mothering? Feminist Perspectives on Lone Motherhood* (London and New York: Routledge, 1996), pp. 175–90.

Prins, Yopie, 'Greek Maenads, Victorian Spinsters', in Richard Dellamora (ed.), *Victorian Sexual Dissidence* (Chicago: University of Chicago Press, 1999), pp. 43–82.

Rich, Adrienne, 'Compulsory Heterosexuality and Lesbian Existence', *Signs*, 5 (1980), pp. 631–60.

Roiphe, Katie, *Still She Haunts Me* (New York: Delta, 2001).

Roof, Judith, *A Lure of Knowledge: Lesbian Sexuality and Theory* (New York: Columbia University Press, 1991).

Roof, Judith, *Come as You Are: Sexuality and Narrative* (New York: Columbia University Press, 1996).

Rose, Mark, 'Mother and Authors: Johnson V. Calvert and the New Children of Our Imaginations', in Paula A. Treichler, Lisa Cartwright and Constance Penley (eds), *The Visible Woman: Imaging Technologies, Gender and Science* (New York and London: New York University Press, 1998), pp. 217–39.

Roseneil, Sasha and Kirk Mann, 'Unpalatable Choices and Inadequate Families: Lone Mothers and the Underclass Debate', in Elizabeth Bortolaia Silva (ed.), *Good Enough Mothering? Feminist Perspectives on Lone Motherhood* (London and New York: Routledge, 1996), pp. 191–210.

Schlichter, Annette, 'Queer at Last? Straight Intellectuals and the Desire for Transgression', *GLQ: Journal of Lesbian and Gay Studies*, 10: 4 (2004), pp. 543–64.

Schlossberg, Linda, 'Introduction: Rites of Passing', in María Carla Sánchez and Linda Schlossberg (eds), *Passing: Identity and Interpretation in Sexuality,*

Race and Religion (New York: New York University Press, 2001), pp. 1–12.

Scott, Sara, 'Surviving Selves: Feminism and Contemporary Discourses of Child Sexual Abuse', *Feminist Theory*, 2: 3 (2001), pp. 349–61.

Sedgwick, Eve Kosofsky, *Epistemology of the Closet* (Berkeley and Los Angeles: University of California Press, 1990).

Seymour, Anne, 'Aetiology of the Sexual Abuse of Children: An Extended Feminist Perspective', *Women's Studies International Forum*, 21: 4 (1998), pp. 415–27.

Sifuentes, Zachary, 'Strange Anatomy, Strange Sexuality: The Queer Body in Jeffrey Eugenides' *Middlesex*', in Richard Fantina (ed.), *Straight Writ Queer: Non-Normative Expressions of Heterosexuality in Literature* (Jefferson, NC and London: McFarland, 2006), pp. 145–57.

Skeggs, Beverly, *Class, Self, Culture* (London: Routledge, 2004).

Smart, Carol, 'A History of Ambivalence and Conflict in the Discursive Construction of the "Child Victim" of Sexual Abuse', *Social and Legal Studies*, 8: 3 (1999), pp. 391–409.

Smart, Carol, 'Collusion, Collaboration and Confession: On Moving Beyond the Heterosexuality Debate', in Diane Richardson (ed.), *Theorising Heterosexuality: Telling It Straight* (Buckingham and Philadelphia: Open University Press, 1996), pp. 161–77.

Smart, Carol, 'Deconstructing Motherhood', in Elizabeth Bortolaia Silva (ed.), *Good Enough Mothering? Feminist Perspectives on Lone Motherhood* (London and New York: Routledge, 1996), pp. 37–57.

Stabile, Carol, 'Shooting the Mother: Fetal Photography and the Politics of Disappearance', in Paula A. Treichler, Lisa Cartwright and Constance Penley (ed.), *The Visible Woman: Imaging Technologies, Gender and Science* (New York and London: New York University Press, 1998), pp. 171–97.

Stanworth, Michelle, 'Reproductive Technologies and the Deconstruction of Motherhood,' in Michelle Stanworth (ed.), *Reproductive Technologies: Gender, Motherhood and Medicine* (Cambridge: Polity, 1997), pp. 10–35.

Stanworth, Michelle (ed.), *Reproductive Technologies: Gender, Motherhood and Medicine* (Cambridge: Polity, 1997).

Steinberg, Deborah Lynn, *Bodies in Glass: Genetics, Eugenics, Embryo Ethics* (Manchester: Manchester University Press, 1997).

Stockton, Kathryn Bond, *The Queer Child, or Growing Sideways in the Twentieth Century* (Durham, NC and London: Duke University Press, 2009).

Stokes, Mason, 'White Heterosexuality: A Romance of the Straight Man's Burden', in Chrys Ingraham (ed.), *Thinking Straight: The Power, the Promise and the Paradox of Heterosexuality* (New York and London: Routledge, 2005), pp. 131–50.

Taylor, Jenny Bourne, 'Nobody's Secret: Illegitimate Inheritance and the Uncertainties of Memory', *Nineteenth-Century Contexts*, 21 (2000), pp. 565–92.

Taylor, Jenny Bourne, 'Representing Illegitimacy in Victorian Culture', in Ruth Robbins and Julian Wolfreys (eds), *Victorian Identities: Social and Cultural Formations in Nineteenth Century Literature* (London: Routledge, 1996), pp. 119–42.

Teichman, Jenny, *Illegitimacy: A Philosophical Examination* (Oxford: Basil Blackwell, 1982).
That Obscure Object of Desire, film, dir. Luis Buñuel (France/Spain: Greenwich Film Productions, 1977).
Tincknell, Estella, 'Jane or Prudence? Barbara Pym's Single Women, Female Fulfilment and Career Choices in the "Age of Marriages"', *Critical Survey*, 18: 2 (2006), pp. 31–44.
Tromp, Marlene, 'Spirited Sexuality: Sex, Marriage, and Victorian Spiritualism', *Victorian Literature and Culture* (2003), pp. 67–81.
Tropp, Laura, '"Faking a Sonogram": Representations of Motherhood on *Sex and the City*', *Journal of Popular Culture*, 39: 5 (2006), pp. 861–77.
Tsang, Daniel, 'Introduction', in Daniel Tsang (ed.), *The Age Taboo: Gay Male Sexuality, Power and Consent* (Boston and London: Alyson Publications/Gay Men's Press, 1982), pp. 7–13.
Tyler, Imogen, 'Chav Mum Chav Scum', *Feminist Media Studies*, 8: 1 (2008), pp. 17–34.
Vance, Carole, 'Pleasure and Danger: Toward a Politics of Sexuality', in Sandra Kemp and Judith Squires (eds), *Feminisms* (Oxford: Oxford University Press, 1997), pp. 327–34.
Vicinus, Martha, *Independent Women: Work and Community for Single Women: 1850–1920* (London: Virago, 1985).
Warner, Alan, *Morvern Callar* (London: Vintage, 1995).
Warner, Alan, *These Demented Lands* (London: Jonathan Cape, 1997).
Warner, Michael, 'Introduction: Fear of a Queer Planet', *Social Text*, 29 (1991), pp. 3–17.
Waters, Sarah, *Affinity* (London: Virago, 1999).
Watson, Roderick, *The Literature of Scotland: The 20th Century* (London: Macmillan, 2007).
Whelehan, Imelda, *The Feminist Bestseller: From* Sex and the Single Girl *to* Sex and the City (New York and Basingstoke: Palgrave Macmillan, 2005).
White, Patricia, *Uninvited: Classical Hollywood Cinema and Lesbian Representability* (Bloomington and Indianapolis, IN: Indiana University Press, 1999).
Wilkinson, Sue and Celia Kitzinger (eds), *Heterosexuality: A Feminism and Psychology Reader* (London: Sage, 1993).
Wittig, Monique, 'One Is Not Born a Woman', in *The Straight Mind and Other Essays* (Boston: Beacon Press, 1992), pp. 9–20.

Index

Adler, Amy, 77–8
Adolescence
   in Jeffrey Eugenides, *Middlesex*, 18, 117, 119–25
   in Zoë Heller, *Notes on a Scandal*, 58
   in A. M. Homes, *The End of Alice*, 67, 75
Affinity see Sarah Waters
Alcoff, Linda, 55, 76, 78–9, 82
An Education, dir. Lone Scherfig (UK/USA: BBC Films, 2009), 53
Angelides, Steven, 61, 79, 83–5

Barber, Lynn, 53
Bataille, Georges, *Story of the Eye*, 67
Bayma, Todd, 70
Bell, Vicki, 16, 56, 72, 77–9, 83
Berlant, Lauren, 7–8, 138
Bloom, Allan, 61
Boddy, Kasia, 72
Bowring, Finn, 133
Bray, Abigail, 70, 78, 83–5
Brontë, Charlotte
   Jane Eyre, 49
   Villette, 49
Bruhm, Steven, 68–9, 76–7, 82–5
Buñuel, Luis, *That Obscure Object of Desire*, 122
Burgess, Anthony, *A Clockwork Orange*, 67
Butler, Judith
   on the contingency of queer, 131–2
   on the discursive construction of sex, 115
   on feminism and queer theory, 9
   on the feminist category of women, 11
   on gender identity and intelligibility, 6, 8, 13, 39, 41, 111, 135–6
   on the heterosexual matrix, 8, 11, 39, 118, 120, 125
   on normative violence, 41n

Camus, Albert, *The Stranger*, 93–4
Carroll, Lewis
   Alice's Adventures in Wonderland and *Through the Looking Glass*, 16, 69, 85
   and child pornography, 76, 78
   and Alice Liddell, 76
   queer appropriations of, 76–7
Castle, Terry, 37–9
Caughie, John, 93
Celebrity
   and criminality, 86
   and deviance, 56
   and intersex, 111, 116
Chase, Cheryl, 20–1n, 115
Chick lit, 48; *see also* Helen Fielding
Child sexual abuse
   in Zoë Heller, *Notes on a Scandal*, 12, 15, 55–9, 60–1
   in A. M. Homes, *The End of Alice*, 12, 16, 67–87
Child sexuality
   in Zoë Heller, *Notes on a Scandal*, 55–7, 60–1
   in A. M. Homes, *The End of Alice*, 16, 67–87
Class
   and heteronormativity, 20n
   in Jeffrey Eugenides, *Middlesex*, 123, 125, 126
   in Zoë Heller, *Notes on a Scandal*, 46, 49, 50, 53–4, 57, 58
   in A. M. Homes, *The End of Alice*, 74
   in Alan Warner, *Morvern Callar*, 17, 91–2, 95–100, 101–5
   in Sarah Waters, *Affinity*, 12, 25, 26, 31, 33
Cloning, human, 18–19, 131–45
Cohen, Cathy J., 7, 8, 105, 132
Compulsory heterosexuality (Adrienne Rich), 2–3, 26, 37
Criminality, discourses of, 26, 30–3, 38
Critical whiteness studies, 158
Croft, Jo, 75
Cross-generational sexuality *see* intergenerational sexuality

Dickens, Charles, *Little Dorrit*, 36
Dickinson, Emily, 74
Dodgson, Charles *see* Lewis Carroll
Dreger, Alice Domurat, 111, 116
Dworkin, Andrea, 4–5, 82

Education *see* schooling
Eliot, George, 117
Eng, David L., 21n, 132
Erhart, Julia, 49
Eugenides, Jeffrey
  Middlesex, 14, 17–18, 111–27
  The Virgin Suicides, 119

Faderman, Lilian, 37
Farquhar, Dion, 137
Feminism
  and the category of women, 3–4, 11–13
  and child sexual abuse, 56–7, 68–9, 70–80, 83–5
  and child sexuality, 81–2, 83–5
  and class, 101–3
  and Michel Foucault, 78–9, 84–5
  and heteronormativity, 9–11
  and heterosexuality, 2–5, 8–12
  and human cloning, 137–8
  and illegitimacy, 92, 104
  and intergenerational sexuality, 55–61, 45, 68–9, 76
  and motherhood, 92, 100–5, 137–8
  and pregnancy, 100–5
  and queer theory, 2, 8–11, 12–13, 16, 83–5
  and rape, 77
  and reproductive sexuality, 100–5
  and reproductive technology, 101, 137–8
  see also lesbian feminism; postfeminism; Second Wave feminism
Ferreira, Maria Aline Salgueiro Seabra, 133, 144
Fielding, Helen, *Bridget Jones's Diary*, 14, 48, 50
Fine, Gary Allen, 70
Fink, Janet, 17, 27, 47
Finkler, Kaja, 139
Firestone, Shulamith, 82
Foucault, Michel
  and child sexual abuse, 57, 76, 77–9
  and feminism, 78–9, 84–5
  on homosexuality, 5, 11, 38
  and intergenerational sexuality, 57, 83
  on power, 33, 77
  and queer theory, 5–8
Frank, Arthur, 116
Franklin, Sarah, 139–40
Freud, Sigmund, 84, 92

Genetics
  in Jeffrey Eugenides, *Middlesex*, 113–14
  in Kazuo Ishiguro, *Never Let Me Go*, 12, 138–9
Gill, Rosalind, 15, 60
Goldman, Eric, 70
Gordon, Angus, 120
Greg, W. R., 46–7
Gullette, Margaret Morganroth, 58–9

Halberstam, Judith, 21n, 113, 132
Hanson, Clare, 102
Haran, Joan, 137
Haug, Frigga, 77
Heller, Zoë, *Notes on a Scandal*, 12, 13, 15, 45–61
Hellman, Lillian, *The Children's Hour*, 49
Henke, Suzette A., 50
Heteronormativity, definitions of, 7–8, 10–11, 132
Heterosexuality
  feminist perspectives on, 2–5, 8–12
  and invisibility, 17, 14–15
  lesbian feminist perspectives on, 2–5
  queer perspectives on, 2, 5–12
  and sexuality, 4–5, 7–8, 15–17, 56, 123–5
Holden, Katherine, 17, 27, 47
Homes, A. M., *The End of Alice*, 12, 13, 16, 61, 67–87
Homophobia
  and the age of consent, 83
  and female homosexuality, 15, 46
  and heternormativity, 138
  and male homosexuality, 81
  and paedophilia, 79, 81
  and reproductive sexuality, 92
  and the spinster, 53
  and the women's movement, 4
Homosexuality
  Judith Butler, on, 6, 41
  Michel Foucault, on, 5–6, 11, 14, 38
  and intergenerational sexuality, 69, 80, 82–3, 85
  male homosexuality, 11, 80–1
  and paedophilia, 79
  representations of homosexuality on film, 49
  and reproductive sexuality, 91
  see also lesbian identity
Hurley, Natasha, 68–9, 76–7, 82–5
Hybridity, cultural, 113, 119, 126–7

Illegitimacy, 17, 91–2, 94–5, 104–5
Imprisonment
  in A. M. Homes, *End of Alice*, 12, 67, 74, 80–1, 86
  in Sarah Waters, *Affinity*, 25, 28–9, 30–5
Intergenerational sexuality
  in Zoë Heller, *Notes on a Scandal*, 15, 16, 45–6, 53–61
  in A. M. Homes, *The End of Alice*, 68–9, 73, 75–6, 79–85

Intersex, 12, 17–18, 20–1n, 111–27
Invisibility
  and heterosexuality, 1, 7, 14–15
  and lesbian identity, 14–15, 36–41
Ishiguro, Kazuo, *Never Let Me Go*, 12, 14, 17, 18–19, 131–45

Jackson, Stevi, 9–11
Jagose, Annamarie, 7, 36
James, Henry, *The Turn of the Screw*, 49, 90n
Jeffreys, Sheila, 4–5, 37, 47–8, 53
Johnson, Richard, 1
Jones, Carole, 21n, 93–4, 98–9, 100, 103–4
Julien, Heather, 49

Kauffman, Linda, 75
Kitzinger, Celia, 5
Kitzinger, Jenny, 137
Kutulus, Judy, 103

LeBlanc, John, 100
Lesbian continuum (Adrienne Rich), 3
Lesbian feminism, 2–5, 8, 10, 14–15
Lesbian identity
  in Jeffrey Eugenides, *Middlesex*, 12, 120–3
  in Zoë Heller, *Notes on a Scandal*, 47, 52–3
  and invisibility, 14–16, 36–41
  and lesbian feminism, 2–4
  in Sarah Waters, *Affinity*, 14–15, 25–41
Liddell, Alice, 76

Mann, Kirk, 103
Mann, Thomas, *Death in Venice*, 59
Marcus, Sharon, 9, 132
Marsh, Cristie, 100, 103–4
Masculinity
  female, 18, 125–6
  male, 58–60, 79, 94, 97–8
Masculinity studies, 138
McNeil, Maureen, 137
Medical discourses
  in Jeffrey Eugenides, *Middlesex*, 18, 111–12, 113–19, 125
  in Kazuo Ishiguro, *Never Let Me Go*, 133–4, 137–40
  in Sarah Waters, *Affinity*, 26, 29, 31–3, 38
Middlesex see Jeffrey Eugenides
Millard, Kenneth, 119–20
Millett, Kate, 82
Moody, Roger, 81–2
Morland, Iain, 114, 116
Morvern Callar see Alan Warner
Motherhood
  as ideological construction, 3, 27, 47, 49, 50, 100–3, 104, 137–8
  lone motherhood, 17, 91–2, 103–5
  see also reproductive technology
Mothers

  in Zoë Heller, *Notes on a Scandal*, 45–6, 50
  in A. M. Homes, *The End of Alice*, 70, 75
  in Sarah Waters, *Affinity*, 28, 32, 34
Muñoz, José Esteban, 21n, 132
Murray, Charles, 103

Nabokov, Vladimir
  Lolita, 16, 59, 69–76, 85
  Pale Fire, 52
Narration, first person, 12
  in Jeffrey Eugenides, *Middlesex*, 112
  in Zoë Heller, *Notes on a Scandal*, 45–6, 51–2
  in A. M. Homes, *The End of Alice*, 69, 85–7
  in Alan Warner, *Morvern Callar*, 93–4
  in Sarah Waters, *Affinity*, 33–4
Narrative, retrospective
  in Jeffrey Eugenides, *Middlesex*, 17–18, 111–12, 113–20, 124, 127
  in A. M. Homes, *The End of Alice*, 69
Negra, Diana, 102
Neo-Victorian, 12, 14, 25–41
Never Let Me Go see Kazuo Ishiguro
Notes on a Scandal see Zoë Heller

O'Riordan, Kate, 137
Oram, Alison, 47

Paedophilia
  in Zoë Heller, *Notes on a Scandal*, 58–9, 61
  in A. M. Homes, *The End of Alice*, 78–85
  see also child sexual abuse
Passing
  in Jeffrey Eugenides, *Middlesex*, 126
  in Kazuo Ishiguro, *Never Let Me Go*, 131–3, 140–5
Patnoe, Elizabeth, 71
Pederasty, 60–1, 83
Petersen, Alan, 138
Petrie, Duncan, 93, 97
Plath, Sylvia, 74
Pornography, 57, 77–8, 141
Postfeminism
  and masculinity, 58–60
  and retreatism (Diana Negra), 102–3
  and Second Wave feminism, 48
  and sexual agency, 15, 55–6
  and the singleton (Helen Fielding), 14, 48
  and the spinster, 14, 50
Pregnancy, 17, 91–2, 94–5, 100–5
Prins, Yopie, 26

Queer theory
  and adolescence, 120
  and Lewis Carroll's Alice, 76–7
  and child sexuality, 60–1, 76–7, 81–5
  and feminism, 2, 8–11, 12–13, 16, 83–5

Queer theory (*cont.*)
  and heteronormativity, 7–8, 10–11, 132
  and heterosexuality, 2, 5–12
  and intergenerational sexuality, 60–1, 68–9, 81–5
  and intersex, 111, 114–15
  and paedophilia, 79
  and reproductive sexuality, 39, 139
  see also Judith Butler; Michel Foucault; Eve Kosofsky Sedgwick

Race
  in Jeffrey Eugenides, *Middlesex*, 17, 111, 113, 123
  and heteronormativity, 20n
  and whiteness, 113, 123
  see also critical whiteness studies
Rape, 4, 77, 81, 86
Reproductive sexuality
  in Jeffrey Eugenides, *Middlesex*, 122
  in Zoë Heller, *Notes on a Scandal*, 47
  and heterosexuality, 3, 11, 12–13, 16–18, 139
  in A. M. Homes, *The End of Alice*, 80
  in Kazuo Ishiguro, *Never Let Me Go*, 18–19, 131–3, 137–40, 144–5
  in Alan Warner, *Morvern Callar*, 16–17, 91–2, 100–5
  in Sarah Waters, *Affinity*, 27, 30, 39–40
Reproductive technology, 12–13, 17–18, 101, 137–8
Reprosexuality (Michael Warner), 139
Retreatism (Diana Negra), 102
Rich, Adrienne, 2–4, 8, 10
Roof, Judith, 39–41, 91–2, 120
Rose, Mark, 104
Roseneil, Sasha, 103
Roslin Institute, 133, 138

Salinger, J. D., 117
Same-sex desire
  in Jeffrey Eugenides, *Middlesex*, 18, 120–5, 118–19
  in A. M. Homes, *The End of Alice*, 86
  in Sarah Waters, *Affinity*, 14–15, 25–41
  see also homosexuality; lesbian identity
Same-sex, parenting, 13, 138
Schlichter, Annette, 144
Schlossberg, Linda, 1, 132–3
Schooling
  in Jeffrey Eugenides, *Middlesex*, 113, 118, 120–1
  in Zoë Heller, *Notes on a Scandal*, 15, 45, 49–50, 53–5

  in Kazuo Ishiguro, *Never Let Me Go*, 134–6, 140, 142
  in Alan Warner, *Morvern Callar*, 99
Scott, Sara, 71, 75, 78–9
Second Wave feminism
  and child sexual abuse 71
  and heterosexuality, 2, 10
  and identity politics, 8, 58
  and postfeminism, 48
  and sexuality, 46, 48, 60, 82
  and women's writing, 12
Sedgwick, Eve Kosofsky, 6–7, 38–9, 60–1, 83
Seymour, Anne, 71–2
Singleton (Helen Fielding), 14, 46, 48
Skeggs, Beverly, 99
Smart, Carol, 5, 71, 78–9, 100–1, 103
Spinster
  in Zoë Heller, *Notes on a Scandal*, 45–53
  and unmarried mother, 17
  in Sarah Waters, *Affinity*, 12, 14–15, 17, 25–41
Spiritualism, 25–6, 33, 35–6
Stabile, Carole, 101
Steinberg, Deborah Lynn, 137–9
Stockton, Kathryn Bond, 82
Suicide
  in Jeffrey Eugenides, *The Virgin Suicides*, 119
  in Alan Warner, *Morvern Callar*, 91, 93–6, 98–9
  in Sarah Waters, *Affinity*, 25, 26, 30–3, 36

Taylor, Jenny Bourne, 104
Teichman, Jenny, 104
Transgender, 20–1n, 120, 132
Transsexuality, 113
Trilling, Lionel, 70–1
Tropp, Laura, 103
Tsang, Daniel, 82
Tyler, Imogen, 102

Vance, Carole, 16, 73, 87
Vicinus, Martha, 48, 53
Virgin Suicides see Jeffrey Eugenides

Warner, Alan, *Morvern Callar*, 1, 13, 16–17, 91–105
Warner, Michael, 7–8, 138, 139
Waters, Sarah, *Affinity*, 13, 14–15, 25–41
Watson, Roderick, 93–4, 100
Whiteness *see* critical whiteness studies; race
Wilkinson, Sue, 5
Wittig, Monique, 3–4, 8, 10, 27, 39
Women, feminist category of, 3–4, 11–13